# THE FALL OF THE PRIESTS AND THE RISE OF THE LAWYERS

This fast-paced, inspiring and original work proposes that, if religions fade, then secular law provides a much more comprehensive moral regime to govern our lives. Backed by potent and haunting images, it argues that the rule of law is the one universal framework that everyone believes in and that the law is now the most important ideology we have for our survival.

The author explores the decline of religions and the huge growth of law and makes predictions for the future of law and lawyers. The book maintains that even though societies may decide they can do without religions, they cannot do without law.

The book helpfully summarises both the teachings of all the main religions and the central tenets of the law—governing everything from human relationships to money, banks and corporations. It shows that, without these legal constructs, some of them arcane, our societies would grind to a halt. These innovative summaries make complex ideas seem simple and provide the keys to understanding both the law and religion globally. The book will appeal to both lawyers and the general reader.

The book concludes with the author's personal code for a modern way of living to promote the survival of humankind into the future.

Vividly written by one of the most important lawyers of our generation, this magisterial and exciting work offers a powerful vision of the role of law in the 21st century and its impact on how we live.

# The Fall of the Priests and the Rise of the Lawyers

Philip R Wood

·HART·
PUBLISHING
OXFORD AND PORTLAND, OREGON
2016

Published in the United Kingdom by Hart Publishing Ltd
16C Worcester Place, Oxford, OX1 2JW
Telephone: +44 (0)1865 517530
Fax: +44 (0)1865 510710
E-mail: mail@hartpub.co.uk
Website: http://www.hartpub.co.uk

Published in North America (US and Canada) by
Hart Publishing
c/o International Specialized Book Services
920 NE 58th Avenue, Suite 300
Portland, OR 97213-3786
USA
Tel: +1 503 287 3093 or toll-free: (1) 800 944 6190
Fax: +1 503 280 8832
E-mail: orders@isbs.com
Website: http://www.isbs.com

© Philip R Wood 2016

Hart Publishing is an imprint of Bloomsbury Publishing plc.

British Library Cataloguing in Publication Data
Data Available

**Library of Congress Cataloging-in-Publication Data**

Names: Wood, Philip (Philip R.), 1942– author.

Title: The fall of the priests and the rise of the lawyers / Philip R Wood.

Description: Oxford ; Portland, Oregon : Hart Publishing Ltd, 2016.  |
Includes bibliographical references.  |  Description based on print version
record and CIP data provided by publisher; resource not viewed.

Identifiers: LCCN 2015049636 (print)  |  LCCN 2015049493 (ebook)  |
ISBN 9781509905560 (Epub)  |  ISBN 9781509905546 (hardback : alk. paper)

Subjects: LCSH: Law—Philosophy.  |  Religion and law.  |  Rule of law.  |  Law—History.

Classification: LCC K240 (print)  |  LCC K240.W66 2016 (ebook)  |  DDC 340/.1—dc23

LC record available at http://lccn.loc.gov/2015049636

ISBN: 978-1-50990-554-6

Typeset by Compuscript Ltd, Shannon
Printed and bound in Great Britain by
TJ International Ltd, Padstow, Cornwall

To my family

# *Preface*

I had been thinking about this book for many years, probably more than a decade, but it took two brief encounters with doom to spur me into action. Destiny is a great reminder not to procrastinate.

It is not just a book about religions and law. It is about our duties to the future, to those who come after us. It is about our search for survival, about the purpose of our existence.

Philip Wood
Knowle Grange Gardens
Shere
Surrey

Summer 2015

# *Acknowledgements*

Some of the maps in this book are based on maps which were first published in my work *Maps of World Financial Law* (Sweet & Maxwell, 2008). A number of passages about the law, especially chapter 8 about the families of law, were based on or inspired by passages in my books in the series *The Law and Practice of International Finance* in five volumes published by Sweet & Maxwell in 1995 and subsequently in the nine volumes published by Sweet & Maxwell in 2007–08. Quite a few of the concepts were developed and refined in various articles in legal journals subsequently, including in *Butterworths Journal of International Banking and Financial Law*. Chapter 15 'Who rules the world?' is based on an article I wrote appearing in *Business Law International*, the leading journal of the International Bar Association, May 2010.

I am most grateful to the above for enabling me to include the items concerned in this work.

My warmest thanks to the following who read all or part of the book in draft and made numerous very helpful comments: Vanessa Cordery, the Reverend Sarah Hutton, Matt Jenkinson, Humphrey Keenlyside and John O'Conor.

I am grateful to Melissa Hunt for carrying out research into specific issues and for managing the production of the book during the drafting stage. I am also grateful to the numerous people who were involved in document production and the preparation of the maps and charts.

My thanks are due to Sinead Maloney and her team at Hart Publishing for their excellent professional and expert work in the publication process. Robert McKay very kindly introduced me to the publishers and discussed the book with me at that stage.

I owe a great debt to the members of my family for their forbearance and tolerance and for the very robust discussions we had about the contents of this book.

My wife Marie-Elisabeth read the book critically and made many valuable suggestions as to how I should orient it. She encouraged me to complete the work with love and loyalty and to her I owe my special gratitude.

None of the above are of course responsible for what is in this book which is my responsibility alone.

# The Author

Philip Wood was for many years a partner in a major international law firm based in the City of London. He is a Visiting Professor in International Financial Law at the University of Oxford, Yorke Distinguished Visiting Fellow at the University of Cambridge and Visiting Professor at Queen Mary College, University of London. He has lectured at nearly 60 universities worldwide. He has written 18 books on international financial law and practice and is a leading world expert on comparative law.

He was born in Livingstone, Northern Rhodesia, now Zambia. He has a BA from the University of Cape Town, an MA from Oxford University in English literature and an honorary LLD from Lund University in Sweden. In 2010 he was appointed honorary Queen's Counsel and in 2015 he was made a Commander of the British Empire in the Queen's New Year Honours List for services to English law and financial law.

He is married with four children and lives in the English countryside, near London.

# Contents

# 1

# *The Questions*

At first sight, things are not looking too good for us.

At one time we thought we were at the centre of the universe which did not stretch very far. The stars were like a ceiling. Then Galileo finally showed that we were orbiting the sun, one of many planets doing the same. By the time we got to Hubble's telescope in the 1920s it turned out that the universe was much, much bigger than we thought. And it was expanding at a fearsome rate so that our loneliness was becoming even greater. All we could see out there were terrible fires, huge furnaces of superheated gases roaring in this silence with nothing in between except strange forces of light, magnetism, gravity and yet other energies or forces or dark matter which we do not understand.

We now know that we are a long, long way from anywhere else. The nearest star is 25,000 billion miles away (40,000 billion kilometres). We are lonely, out here on this tiny planet travelling round a middling star, in our tiny suburb of our galaxy, one of billions. Our planet is infinitesimally minute in relation to the size of the universe. It is not even a speck, a grain of sand. The universe and all the other universes or whatever they are, stretching beyond, do not communicate with us. Whatever the forces are, the energies, the shapes, the ghosts out there, we are almost non-beings, a void, we are hardly even a shiver or a shimmer or a momentary vibration in the dark nullity, we have virtually no light or substance, we are almost nothing.

And yet we are here. A miracle has happened. Something amazing happened on this nothing planet. Some collision or spark or combination set off a process of replication. This occurrence was unique, completely unexpected and might have occurred only once in the universe. After huge periods of blind but logical evolution, a creature emerged which could think, which had consciousness, which knew in advance about death. We may be the only intelligence in the universe. It was only over the incredibly short period of the last four hundred years or so that we have seriously begun to work out what makes the universe tick. Newton discovered a fundamental equation published in 1687. Einstein published another in the early 1900s. Now we have our hands on the lever of ourselves through genetics. So if we can stay alive long enough and can keep going at this astonishing rate, we may be able to beat the universe. If the universe has no plan for us, then we have to have a plan for ourselves. If the universe has no god, we will make ourselves god.

The great religions provided an explanation of the universe and the meaning of life. They provided certainty as to the creation of the universe and certainty as to the purpose of our lives. The supernatural religions provided the answers for almost everyone and everything. They answered the question of creation, of how the world and the universe came into being, a cosmological explanation which most people could follow with unquestioning conviction and certainty. The religions provided a solution to what was the purpose of our lives, whether the purpose is to worship god, or is how to conduct ourselves so as to attain everlasting life. They provided the rationale for morality. They furnished codes as to how we should control our emotions so that we should live in peace with ourselves and with others. Every aspect of our lives in simpler times was covered off—from our public duties to our parents, our families, our communities and the wider world through to our most private and intimate thoughts which we would fear to divulge to anyone else, however close. But now the old certainties are being challenged.

If the religions are wrong, then we are faced with a vast pitiless universe which cares nothing for our planet or the people on it, which has no plans for us at all, which is not concerned one way or the other whether we survive for a few centuries more or whether we die out a hundred years from now or after only a few more years on this beautiful planet.

We have always had wars, genocides and violence. But never before have the means to wreak violence been so lethal.

This book charts the growth and slow decline of religions over centuries and the fantastic and sudden growth of law. It explores why these things happened and how they affect our view of life. It is about how we survive. In particular, it is about whether the law could fill the gaps left by religion and whether a philosophy of life and of the meaning of life can be formulated without religion.

The purpose of ensuring our survival is for humans to live long enough to unlock the secrets of the universe so that we can master it and continue to survive. So that we, as a species, can be immortal. The main task for us is how to remain in existence to enable us to find out how we survive. If we are alone in this universe, we have a unique responsibility to stay alive. That is the purpose of our existence.

It does not follow that the alternative is the cataclysmic destruction of ourselves and our children, either deliberately with our own hand or by some external catastrophe we could not foresee or stop—a terrible disease, a meteorite smashing into us, some fantastic galactic outburst of radiation. But these things could happen.

We can only survive for the necessary time by maintaining a moral order. We have a duty to be moral in order to survive.

All the great religions have been in place for at least nearly 1500 years and some for possibly 4000 years. They are not going to disappear in a puff of smoke tomorrow. Yet their supernatural doctrines are under threat and they have retreated from the government of most of our societies. In many countries, particularly advanced economies, the number of practising adherents has been shrinking and belief is often only nominal. The moral role of religion is weakening. If religions fail to provide the rules and the justification for them, what do we put in their place?

The law is the one universal secular religion which practically everybody believes in. The question is whether the law can step into the gap left by fading religions and whether the law can carry forward the flame. The law is a highly sophisticated moral system. It is true that the law does not cover private thoughts and petty unkindnesses which most religions do regulate, but that kind of intrusion would not be acceptable. Otherwise the law has immense scope and modern relevance.

The comparison therefore is between the religions and the law, expressed allegorically through their symbolic representatives—the priests and the lawyers.

The legal territory of religions has been reduced in most of the world to matters of private morality. Even codes governing, for example, family law, sex, inheritance and basic crimes—murder, theft—are now outside the territory of religion in most countries. Secular authorities have in most countries over time excluded the clerics from law-making power with the result that it is these secular authorities which frame the fundamental aspects of our laws.

Some of the modern realms of law are of enormous contemporary importance. Examples are the law relating to political democracies, the rule of law and the law between states. Such matters as money, corporations, banks, insurance companies, central banking and taxation are at the centre of our affairs. That applies also to the bankruptcy of corporations and sovereign states, to equity and capital markets and to the massive regulatory regimes which dominate our legal systems. Religions had little to say on these subjects, and, where they did, the religious codes did not approach the specificity and modern relevance of the law. It was left to secular law to deal with the development of even basic topics like contract and liability to others. When the law took off during industrialisation, the religions were taken by surprise and were left with ancient and narrow codes of morality in their scriptures settled during times of simple agricultural and pastoral cultures.

Most people, in developed countries at least, work in businesses, often owned by corporations. The amounts involved are very large. In developed countries, agriculture is typically around only 2 per cent of total production. Our economies are completely different from the agricultural and pastoral economies typical of the periods when the main religions were developed.

The modern domains of law, if badly framed or badly executed, can have devastating consequences on people's lives and can cripple whole societies. The scope of the law and the things it has to do go far beyond the basic crimes and sexual morality, these well-trodden paths which everybody knows about, more or less.

This book will survey wider arenas of law than the basic subjects and seek to explain why the large modern areas of law are central to our societies and their future, why they directly affect the lives of most people, why they ought to be governed by a moral regime and not be left to purely functional rationales which omit the ethical dimension, why, in other words, they should be governed by the moral law. Everything in the law from rule of law principles to bankruptcy through to taxation expresses the degree of the sense of justice of the jurisdiction concerned.

When the great religions were first announced, they were sensational in the salvation they offered and the hope that they gave. They were inspirational and visionary. Yet the last great universal religion—Islam—is already nearly fifteen centuries old, formed in a completely different world.

We live in a society which is suffused with law and morality. Unlike religions, the law has no burdensome rituals. You do not have to perform sacrifices. You do not have to prostrate yourself before it or utter words of devotion and worship or sing hymns or go on pilgrimages. In ideal conditions, it derives its content from consensus and the will of the people. It is willing to change when change is necessary. It faces scientific and other challenges with equanimity and coolness. It is the foundation of our civilisation, our societies and our survival.

The rule of law does not offer the consolations of religion. But the rule of law empowers and liberates us and makes it possible for us to do things in peace which otherwise we would not be able to do. It enables us to pursue happiness. It gives us the order and freedom to pursue a greater goal. We control it. The law is our servant not our master. The law at its best is the most important ideology we have.

As I write I see the second hand on my watch hasten round the dial in ferocious frenzy, an insistent remorseless madness. Surely we don't have to be reminded of mischievous time quite so constantly as we plod along, hoping for the best, searching for some meaning in all this. Yet it is to the future that we look—not just ten years or a hundred years or even a thousand years, or even a million years, but longer, much longer.

This is not a melodramatic book intended to torment us about the apocalypse. Yet at our back we always hear some terrible chariot hurrying near, pulled by foaming horses coming out of the forests of the night whipped by the blind charioteer, a charioteer who cares nothing about this tiny insignificant planet, who cares nothing about morality or law or religion, who is intent on some shocking and pitiless purpose, who is relentless, ruthless, who has always been there.

This image of the terrible chariot is one of the three key images which are bass notes which resonate throughout this book, even though I mention these images quite sparsely. Who is this charioteer who horrifies us? What is the meaning of this image?

The second image which we will meet soon and at other crucial points in this book is that of the raft or the small boat out in a stormy sea far from anywhere with virtually zero hope of survival.

The third image is a cluster of concepts about time—clocks, God as a watchmaker, history, the future, mortality. Time is a quality which we anxiously measure but don't understand. Together these images represent deep things which haunt us.

# 2

# *The Purpose of Morality and Law*

## Introduction

This chapter elaborates on the reason for morality and law, why we have these institutions, and does so by a parable or allegory of two highly symbolic paintings and a mining disaster.

The first painting is the allegorical painting by Delacroix, *Liberty Leading the People*, painted in 1830 and hanging in the Louvre in Paris. The whole of society is represented in this picture—the merchant class, the academics, the military, the peasants and youth. All of the people in this tumultuous scene are astir and infused with some burning ideal. They are well armed. The youth has two pistols. The representative of the merchant class, with the big black hat, holds a formidable barrelled gun. Liberty herself clutches in her left hand a long rifle with the bayonet out. These people intend to get their way for their cause, whatever it is.

*Liberty Leading the People*

In the original, the lady is holding the French tricolour flag. In our version, she is holding the flags of many nations because the issue is not just limited to France in 1830. The boldness of her ideal is symbolised by the fact that she does not care one way or the other whether she does up her buttons. The revolution always happens when you are in the shower. The gentleman lying on his back in the bottom left-hand corner did not even have time to put on his trousers. He has got only one sock on.

In Delacroix's mind, the liberty she was fighting for consisted of basic political freedoms of democracy, freedom of speech and the like, freedom from despotism and autocracy. You could also say that what she allegorises is freedom from restriction, a universal symbol of hope and our aspirations.

Some of the biggest restrictions in our lives are the restrictions imposed by moral and religious codes, legal systems, customary law and statutory law. Indeed you could conclude that morality and the law are systems of restriction, manacling, fettering and tying us down.

The answer to the question of why all this is considered necessary is debated in the next painting.

*The Raft of the Medusa*

This is *The Raft of the Medusa* painted by Géricault between 1818 and 1819. It also hangs in the Louvre in Paris, a stupendously huge canvas, in the same hall and on the same side and on the same wall as Delacroix's picture. This is one of the most iconic and powerful pictures ever painted. It really gets to the point—the point of where we are and what we are.

The French frigate the *Medusa* hit a sandbank about 60 miles (90 kilometres) off the west coast of Africa, then Senegal but now Mauritania, on 2 July 1816 at 3.00 pm. The terrified passengers and crew built a raft out of parts of the ship. The idea was that the crew would tow the raft with six rowing boats to the nearest coast. Hence nothing was left on the raft to navigate, no oars, no compass, no rudder.

The crew, including the captain, had other ideas. They cut the tow ropes and disappeared over the horizon. Most of them died on the 300 kilometre walk along the desert coast to St Louis in Senegal. The raft was left to float around helplessly in the scorching mid-summer Saharan sun.

Altogether 147 people got on the raft. There was one woman who was subsequently thrown overboard because she was screaming. When the 147 first got on, they were up to their waists in the sea. So they threw away some of the barrels of biscuits and brandy to lighten the load.

They rolled around in the sea for the next 12 days, before they were rescued by the brig *Argus*. Only 15 out of the 147 survived. In fact Géricault has 20 survivors in his picture for the sake of the composition. In particular he painted in three Africans, including the man waving his shirt at the distant rescuing ship, in order to celebrate his views about the anti-slavery movement, freedom and liberty.

The man pointing excitedly is Corréard who subsequently wrote an electrifying and accusatory bestseller about what happened on the raft. This set him on a collision course with the authorities. The figure with black hair lying on his face with his hand over the beam is Delacroix, the same Delacroix who painted *Liberty Leading the People*. He was a friend of Géricault, who used Delacroix as a model. When he first saw this painting, it was reported that he ran down the Place de Vendôme in Paris screaming from terror and ecstasy.

The picture portrays the immensity of human nobility, of suffering and courage in the face of adversity. The figures are heroic, yet the reality was very different. When the rescuing ship arrived, the raft stank. The survivors were crazed. There were bits of human flesh hanging on the makeshift mast to cook in the sun.

Most of those who died on the raft did not die from famine or thirst. They were killed in the fighting for the remaining brandy and biscuits.

A schooner discovered the hull of the *Medusa* 52 days after the shipwreck. Three people were still on the ship. If everybody had not panicked and had stayed on board, they would probably all have survived. That is how you make simple mistakes when fear and unreason take over.

So the main question which this picture poses is whether Delacroix's lady with the flags continues to be right in her ideology when we are on the raft. Can we survive with liberty and freedom from law when we are in dire straits? If our livelihoods are threatened, don't we need iron rules for that situation—to try and avert the disaster and then deal with it toughly when it happens? Does not liberty deserve to be snuffed out when survival is at stake?

My third picture is of the Chilean mine disaster in 2010.

**Chilean miners**
*Photo from the* Observer, *17 July 2011*

On 5 August 2010, 33 miners were deep down in the San José mine. They had stopped working for lunch in a tiny safety shelter which was 688 metres underground—more than half a kilometre or nearly half a mile. Ten minutes later there was a huge crack and rumbling, a thunderous sound reverberating through the mine.

A massive slab of rock the size of a skyscraper had shed off the mountain, trapping the men below tons of collapsed rocks.

They were down in the mine for 69 days. There were 33 of them. All of them survived.

Yet in the comparable case of the *Medusa*, only a fraction survived. So what was the difference, apart from the obvious difference of circumstances?

One of the key differences was that the miners, faced with their terrible predicament, made rules. They elected a leader, a captain of the ship. They measured their available food and water and agreed on the rations for each person for each day. They were not university-educated learned types, but they all had an instinct about what had to be done.

So they passed laws, they constituted a makeshift legal system to govern their conduct. There was a captain who was to be in charge and whom they would obey. In other words, they had a legal constitution and a lawful government. They promulgated laws parcelling out the food on an equal basis since, in the face of death, we are all equal. They fettered themselves by rules so that they could liberate themselves, be free.

# The Answer to Why We Need Law

So that is the answer as to why we have law. We have law in order to survive. We have a duty to survive in order to discover if there is ultimate meaning, to answer the questions, to ensure our permanent survival if we can. We have made great advances in understanding but we are still nowhere near understanding, for example, what is beyond the universe, what came before the universe or how we got here or get there, or even understanding ourselves or whether our minds are developed enough to understand if we can understand. Our science is in its infancy.

This duty is an obligation which we on earth here now owe to future generations who come after us, the future unborn. We owe it to our children, to our children's children and to their children. And their children into forward times unknown to us in a world undreamt of by us, when all the towers of the mind we have built up to now become in comparison an airy nothingness.

As the astronomer Carl Sagan observed, we owe this duty also to all who came before us, all living things, stretching back to the miracle creatures of ancient times which led to us.

This duty is born of how we are made: the most natural instinct for us is to preserve ourselves and to preserve our issue. Yet the duty has a more profound basis. If we are unique, we can't just turn our backs, walk away and heedlessly let go of something miraculous, let it slip away. We have this duty because we are a miracle. And the duty is now a positive one. If evolution was at one time blind, now it must be with open eyes, all-seeing, deliberate. The preservation of humankind must be our chosen path, not just carelessly left to destiny or mechanical cause and effect or the freakishness of fate, but specifically willed by us. We must do everything we can to enhance our chances of survival and do nothing to endanger our chances of survival. The history of the species has granted us the gift of free will, the ability to choose, to decide if we will end up as nothing, squashed, incinerated, sand and ashes, scattered in the winds of the cosmos, just particles returned to particles. Or to elect if we will be the elect.

We have this duty too because we could be on the raft or in the deep mine without knowing it.

You do not need to read scholarly tomes on the philosophy of law or jurisprudence to know the basic purpose of law.

Many other theories are advanced as to why we need law. Some say that the purpose of law is the general good or the reconciliation of the will of one with the liberty of all others, or that the aim is to have an existence which is peaceful and orderly as opposed to nasty, brutish and short. Others say we need law to promote equality, or to impose a redistribution from the rich to the poor, or to satisfy the desire for retribution, or to fulfil our feelings to see that justice is done, or to protect our property or protect ourselves from injury, or to improve the chances of prosperity, or to ensure the greatest happiness of the greatest number. All these theories have force and truth in the particular case, but they all have as their base and foundation the need to survive.

I mean survival in its widest sense, not just our brute survival, but also the survival of our civilisation, our learning, our freedom to pursue our lives, everything which advances us.

It goes without saying that much law is not directly concerned with survival, for example, restrictions on where you can park your car. Vast swathes of law are of minor import or technical. But even in these areas, the orderliness in minutiae, in tiny detail, has a greater overall purpose. You can imagine the confusion if we had no parking laws, no rules about which side of the road to drive on, no rules about traffic lights or roundabouts or stop signs. You can arrange laws in a hierarchy of needs.

We do not need to enquire exactly what law is, for example, whether it is a divinely ordained set of natural and immutable rules handed down by a supreme deity up there in the sky, or a tradition of ancient wisdom transmitted by saintly elders, or whether it is a social contract or crystallisation of customary co-operation, or whether it is a set of commands by some sovereign, or whether it is a body of rules imposed by the ruling class on the suffering people, or whether it is a set of principles discovered by experience or experiment or founded upon philosophical speculation. All of these questions, much debated by the philosophic jurists, come down to the same issue—survival. And law is a characteristic of all societies which have progressed beyond barbarism.

The rules which promote survival are not some savage rules about the survival of the fittest. They rely on deep principles of the rule of law, morality, justice, whatever you like to call it.

There is no question that the creation of law is the most fundamental and important creation of civilisation. It is the foundation of society. Hume correctly said in his *Treatise of Human Nature* 'Human nature cannot by any means subsist without the association of individuals: and that association never could take place were no regard paid to the laws of equity and justice': *Treatise of Human Nature*, m ii 'Of Justice and Injustice'.

# A World Without Law

Without law, there would be no democracy or safety from tyrants, no security from violence or theft, no protection of women from sexual attack, no property. Anybody could occupy your home or take your food or money. There would be no power or freedom to govern your life by contract or to give away your property by will, no contracts to govern trade, no compensation for negligent injuries done to you, no redress for lies or misrepresentations, no remedy for physical injury, no money as a means of exchange, no banks to put it in, no corporations to conduct business and indeed no business at all. Gangs would rampage through the cities smashing what they liked and taking what they liked. The biggest gang of brigands and thugs would take over, terrorise the people, expropriate their property, arrest and execute anybody they liked according to their whim or some arbitrary emotion or fanatical creed. The world would be savage and barbaric. In the end, somebody would say 'why don't we have laws to stop this behaviour?' Exactly what has happened on countless occasions from ancient times to the failed societies of the present and exactly what should have happened on the raft of the *Medusa*.

When I say the fundamental purpose of law is survival, I do not mean just survival of oneself. All of us want to survive personally and have a very strong instinct of self-preservation. I include that in the concept of survival but I really mean that the ultimate purpose of the law is the survival of humans.

Some people think that humans are basically good and that, if left alone, the obvious rational case for forbearance would be enough, that all is needed are customary understandings which are not subject to coercion or police sanctions, which are not subject to forcible compensation if violated. They think that social pressures, hostile reactions, contempt and in serious cases ostracism, would be enough to sanction wrongful conduct inimical to the orderly conduct of society and that the desire for moral reputation would be stronger than a system of law based on coercion. Some think that shame and guilt are enough.

This view is unduly optimistic as pointed out by the jurisprudential lawyer HLA Hart in *The Concept of Law* (Oxford University Press 3rd edition, 2012). As he says, if most people are not devils, nor are they angels. People are mostly in between these extremes. There are at one extreme a group of people who are devils. This extreme, and the fact that people tend to lose their social morality and look after only themselves at times of threat or danger, means that legal rules are necessary in order to survive. Some people are saints. Most people have an innate or acquired sense of basic morality and most people are good most of the time. But some people are not good most of the time. On occasion large parts of the population of a society can be pushed into barbarity.

There must be some protections of the people from death and injury at the hands of others and expropriation of their assets. People must be able to sell things and their services, they must have the power to contract and bequeath their property by will in a legal environment which enforces these things so that they can have guarantees and confidence in the future conduct of others. Reliance on the rationality of mutual forbearance on the grounds that it is rational to co-operate voluntarily and to renounce and give up and sacrifice some of one's freedoms of behaviour in the common interest does not seem sufficient. This is so even though there are many people who would observe this prudential calculation, as well as a few who have an altruistic interest in the welfare of others or who honour the moral system as deserving of respect in itself in the same way as they honour religious morality.

All of these things support voluntary co-operation, but there needs ultimately to be a coercive system in the background. The theory of the innate natural goodness of man—which was announced by the 18th-century French philosopher Jean-Jacques Rousseau that humans are noble savages corrupted by social institutions—is an illusion. We have not been able to live without police forces or the military or enforcing courts, even at the most minimal level.

The briefest acquaintance with history shows how savage humankind has been, how shocking the atrocities and killings.

There are other reasons why non-coercive customs, habits, traditions, and social conformity or standards or just plain common sense are insufficient. In the first place they can operate only in very small societies, such as primitive bands and villages where hostile reactions and scorn can have direct effect quickly. These social pressures cannot in practice operate universally in urbanised societies where the biggest cities have tens of millions of people and where there is no means to organise voluntary ostracism other than by a coercive legal system.

Secondly, customs tend to stagnate and are immune to the changing needs of a society whereas the law is capable of swift change if necessary, often too swift. Hence custom and tradition tend to be static and quickly become out of date, the result of inertia.

Thirdly, the scope of customs is uncertain and unpredictable so that it can be hard to determine what is allowed and what is not. In the case of the law, there is a recognised authority, in the form of a ruler or a democratic parliament, which promulgates the law and in most countries publishes the law. Indeed there is a principle of the rule of law that, especially in the criminal law, violations should be clear so that the citizen knows exactly what is prohibited. In private law, such as contract, there is also a strong emphasis on predictability, again so that the parties know exactly what they have to do and what liabilities they have. They need to be able to plan and to insure. You do not get this result from unwritten customs which tend to mean just what people think they mean on the day and which are subject to prejudice, anger, the desire for revenge and the passions of the moment. All this is well explained by Professor Hart and endorsed by human experience.

Our societies may decide that they can do without religion, but they can't do without law.

So if you ask if the law affects just about everybody's life, it certainly does.

# Conclusion

This still leaves the basic questions. What should our laws say? How much law should there be? We still have to resolve the issues of freedom against despotism, of anarchy against discipline. We are still left with the question of how much risk and restriction we create in order to control risk and improve our chances of survival, of staying alive long enough to discover that we need to discover.

There is another version of Delacroix's famous lady. This is the figure which faces you as you come into New York Harbour. She is slightly better dressed than Delacroix's version. She is holding, not a gun, but rather a torch in her uplifted right hand. In her left hand she holds a tablet invoking the law. She represents not only liberty, but also welcome to the peoples of the world: she represents the idea of one planet. And she represents the rule of law.

# 3

# *The Past and the Future*

## Introduction

This chapter synthesises the rapidity of change over the last couple of centuries, how this increases the complications and the intensity of the conflicts which potentially face us, and why this underlines the need for a moral order to ensure that we enjoy the survival benefits of our achievements.

I choose 1830 as the pivotal date. This is about the time that we estimate that the population of the world first reached a billion people (give or take a decade) and accelerated after that up to the present seven billion. The year 1830 is a symbolic date to express a wider circle of time around that date—everything did not happen just in one year and often the changes took place over many decades. Around that date there commenced a burst of scientific invention and technological progress which completely transformed our lives and which posed challenges to the traditional beliefs of religion. At the same time there was a surge in wealth expressed as gross domestic product—GDP—of the world, although very unevenly spread.

In turn the law was also transformed, as it adapted with quite some agility to take into account what was happening. The great religions had more or less settled their moral systems by around 900 CE at the latest (and often many centuries earlier) and did not participate in the legal revolution that was taking place—a revolution which involved laws dealing with corporations, banks, insurance companies, the regulation of products and services, and a host of other topics including constitutional democracies and codifications of the rule of law. This clerical withdrawal, often forced on them by secular rulers, had in addition to science the adverse effect of giving fresh impetus to secularisation and allowed secular authorities to determine the ethical orientation of the new topics of law.

In this chapter I also offer some tentative predictions for the future which have a bearing on the moral regimes which govern us and our survival. I surmise that the changes we have experienced over the last couple of centuries will be as nothing compared with what is to come. If that transpires, then the implications for human beings and the ethical regimes they construct will be profound.

In addition I touch on a subject which haunts us—time. Our lives and our future are played out against the background of time. We do not know if we are in the fresh dawn or the darkening twilight of our existence on this planet, whether it is within our grasp to master our destiny, whether our span of time is long enough or too short.

## Growth of Social Development

First we take a very long view of history to measure very broadly the rate at which humans have learnt to master their environment to the present extent over many centuries. This progress can, if you like, be called 'social development'. Most of the astonishing advance took place after around 1750 to 1830.

The figure below 'Growth of social development' shows social development in the West (coloured red) and in the East (coloured blue) since 14,000 BC. The figure is based on one by Professor Ian Morris *Why the West Rules: For Now* (Profile Books, 2010). See also Nick Bostrom, *Superintelligence* (Oxford University Press, 2014) p 3 which exhibits a similar figure.

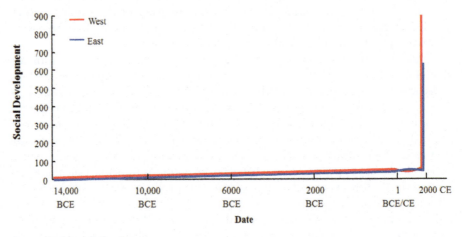

Growth of social development

Professor Morris explains that social development is roughly the state of development and technological mastery of a society. The lines on the figure are built up out of four variables which are considered indicators of human social development.

1.  The first variable or trait is the ability of societies to capture energy. Energy capture includes such things as extracting energy from plants and animals to feed ourselves, and capturing energy from wind and coal and from explosives. Energy capture is considered so fundamental to social development that in 1940 the celebrated anthropologist Leslie White proposed reducing all human history to a single equation: $E \times T \rightarrow C$. E stands for Energy, T for Technology and C for Culture. That is, if you combine energy and technology, you achieve an advanced civilisation.

    The simplest way to think about energy capture is in terms of consumption per person, measured in kilo calories per day. For example, in the year 2000 the average American burned through some 228,000 kilo calories per day.

2.  The second trait counting towards human social development is organisational ability for which Professor Morris uses a proxy, closely related to organisational capacity but easier to measure. The one chosen is urbanism because the organisation needed to keep a city going is vastly beyond anything earlier society could have managed. Running Lagos with a population of 11 million or Tokyo with a population of 35 million would have been far beyond the Roman Empire's capabilities. This is why social scientists regularly use urbanism as a rough guide to organisational capacity.

3.  The third trait included in the calculation is information processing. The term is used in its wider sense so as to include the ability to process and communicate prodigious amounts of information—the invention of writing, then printing, then computers. Information processing is critical to social development.

4.  The fourth trait is the capacity to make war, where technology has often proved to be the winner. An example is the victory of the Spaniard Francisco Pizzarro who in 1532 at Cajamarca in Peru, together with 60 horseman and 90 tired foot soldiers, overcame the army of the Inca leader Atahualpa and 90,000 warriors and thereby conquered the Inca Empire in Peru of between five and ten million people.

These traits are not the only way to measure social development but it is probably true that even if one used different traits to measure similar things, the overall pattern and the overall scores would not change much.

The graph is similar in intent to the United Nations Human Development Index which measures life expectancy, education and income, ie, whether people have the opportunity to realise their potential.

Professor Morris admits the figures are chainsaw data but it does not really matter that there may be very large inaccuracies in terms of the overall result. A chart covering 16,000 years is going to iron out occasional lumps and bumps: sometimes the West was ahead of the East (in 2000 BCE for example) and sometimes the East was ahead of the West (at the time of the Song dynasty (960–1279)). It is certainly arguable that the sudden upward turn is exaggerated, for example, that development lifted earlier on so that the near-vertical spurt in 1830 started from a higher plateau.

In any event, what the figure shows is that until about 1750 to 1830 social development in both the East and the West was extremely low. Then it suddenly shot up around about 1830. On this view, nothing much really happened in terms of social development until then.

The figure does not measure moral development since ancient times. In particular it does not take into account the launch and articulation of the great religions. It does not take into account the development of that other great ethical system, the law. These are subjects which we will be debating throughout this book. The figure does however show the pace of our intellectual feats, the bound with which we leapt up in the last two centuries—a leap which carries with it both hopes and threats.

# Understanding Time

Before we continue with the analysis, it is useful to have a long perspective on time. To understand history and to understand ourselves, we have to understand the measure of time and how very short relevant human time is when compared with the time of the universe and the earth.

Time to most of us is a continuous series of events and circumstances which seems to be perpetual and to us seems only to go forward. The universe is thought to be about 14 billion years old and the earth about 5 billion years old. Human beings were bipedal about 2.5 or 3 million years ago, maybe more. The Neanderthals appeared about 200,000 years ago but were wiped out by the new *homo sapiens* by 25,000 BCE. There were probably 40–50 ice ages between 190,000 and 90,000 BCE. The population of humans in 100,000 BCE could have been as low as 20,000.

The expansion of *homo sapiens* out of Africa took place between 150,000 and 60,000 BCE, reaching Western Europe around 35,000 BCE. In 16,000 BCE you could walk on dry land from southern England to Jakarta and then up to Alaska where you would be met by a wall of ice stretching across Canada to Europe and beyond. The great melt started from about 17,000 BCE and was halted for about a thousand years from 10,800 to 9000 BCE—called the Younger Dryas. In the interim, the sea rose perhaps 140 metres or 400 feet.

Ancient history is known to us almost exclusively through archaeology and supposition. Visible history really only began around 3100 BCE when the Nile Valley was united into the largest kingdom in the world. King Khufu's 450-foot Great Pyramid was built around 2550 BCE and was the world's tallest building until the construction of Cologne Cathedral in Germany in 1880. It remains the heaviest building in the world at a million tonnes.

Although there were early advances in terms of the use of fire, the use of stone and metal tools, the domestication of animals, the domestication of grasses, pottery, the invention of glass, the daubing of art in caves and the like, we have little evidence of the detail of what happened in history until about 3000 BCE and in practice not much before 1000 BCE in most regions of the world. What evidence there is indicates that humans were almost asleep until then. It seemed to take centuries for anything momentous to happen. So reasonably visible history occupies only about three thousand years.

A span of time of three thousand years is absolutely tiny. There have been many comparisons of how small this is by reference to fractions of a second before twelve o'clock or a fraction of a width of a hair at the end of your finger nails if you hold your arms outstretched, when compared with geological time and the age of the earth. We may take it that it is only a tiny sliver and slice of time since human beings really got going, infinitesimally small. We are so far just a fleeting flicker.

This fact underlines our minuteness in the universe and it also underlines the magnitude of our achievements and hence the urgency of our duty to ensure that we are the masters of ourselves and hence potentially the masters of what is around us.

# Measuring the Closeness of History

We who are alive now are separated from those who came before us in history by only a few steps in time. If you laid the lives of selected prominent people, each living around 70 years, end to end from now back into history, there would only be seven people between you and Nicolaus Copernicus, who (apart from an ancient Greek philosopher) first suggested that the earth was going round the sun and who died in 1543. The lives could be those of kings or prime ministers or philosophers or scientists or artists. Seven lives of 70 years each is just under 500 years.

If you took another 21 lives of 70 years, each laid end to end, this would bring you back to the time of Christ. Another seven lives would bring you back to the time of the Buddha and Confucius around 500 BCE. Yet another seven lives would bring you back to King David of the Israelites in 1000 BCE—around the beginnings of recorded history. So 42 lives in all would more or less cover the whole of 3000 years of recorded history aside from history discovered by archaeology.

The lives provide a framework for the memorisation of history. It does not really matter that there are gaps or overlaps and the lives do not have to be exactly 70 years.

To show you how this works, let's take an example for those born in 1973—long before your time, of course, but let's say it's you. The links of lives could be:

1. Pablo Picasso            1881–1973
2. Charles Darwin           1809–82
3. Franz Joseph Haydn       1732–1809
4. Isaac Newton             1642–1727
5. Galileo Galilei          1564–1642
6. Michelangelo             1475–1564

Only five lives between you and Michelangelo! You are linked back nearly 500 years, to 1475.

That puts you back not only to Michelangelo but to a number of other extraordinary people active at the time—Leonardo da Vinci, Raphael, Titian, Machiavelli, Christopher Columbus, Nicolas Copernicus, Martin Luther and John Calvin who, like Michelangelo, also died in 1564. That was the year William Shakespeare was born.

So this shows how history squeezes like an accordion if you compose a memorable tune to keep the time and organise time into bars of music. The abbreviation of time to give order to the noise has the advantage that we reach a better sense of the volatility of events. It would be out of the question for anyone to guess at the beginning of a recent century what the world would be like at the end of the century. Even if we took the decades of the 20th century, few could have guessed at the beginning of each decade what would happen during that decade. Events are very unexpected which means that our ethical regimes have to be resilient.

If the past is so close, then the future is also close. Even a thousand years is close, even ten thousand or a hundred thousand, even a million years. We can already trace ourselves back much further than that to a creature recognisably like us, and life itself is billions of years old. If we can contemplate time past, we can also contemplate time future. In contemplating time future, we should get above the preoccupations of time present.

# The Inventiveness of *homo sapiens sapiens*

An example of why the line in the graph suddenly shoots up from about 1800 is the sudden acceleration of scientific invention since then.

It may have taken humans a few thousand years to get going but once they began inventing in a big way, the advances were dramatic. Apart from breathtaking discoveries in the 17th century—Galileo's confirmation in 1632 that the sun was the centre of the solar system, Newton's announcement of gravity in 1687, and William Harvey's discovery of the circulation of the blood in 1628, for example—and apart from gathering inventiveness in the eighteenth century—such as the first steam engine (1785), the spinning machine in 1769, and Edward Jenner's inoculation against smallpox in 1796, for example—apart from all these, nearly all modern science and technology was produced in the 19th and 20th centuries. If you wrote a large tome on the history of science, the period before then would be the first paragraph. Inventions begat inventions. We moved from glimmers in the darkness to the sweet light of dawn.

It is true that writing, paper, Arabic numerals and printing were much earlier inventions—and also the basis of the later bound ahead—but it was during the last two centuries when science took off.

Medicine hardly existed before that, channelled as it was by the erroneous theories of Galen (c 130 to c 210) that the human body is dominated by four fluids—blood, yellow bile, phlegm and black bile. Cures were dangerous and irrelevant, for example, bloodletting. But then came vaccines, anaesthetics, antiseptics, pharmaceuticals of all kinds, accurate diagnosis and elegant surgery. Big killers became treatable, for example, tuberculosis. After the accidental discovery of penicillin by Alexander Fleming in 1928, penicillin was first produced in commercial quantities in 1942.

In chemistry, like Galen, Aristotle (384–322 BCE) put us on the wrong track for nearly two thousand years by his simplistic classification of elements into air, earth, fire and water. In 1789 the treatise of Antoine Lavoisier, a French tax collector and lawyer, revolutionised chemistry. He was guillotined for his financial dealings, a reminder of what a revolutionary mob thinks of science. Joseph Priestley had earlier discovered oxygen in 1774. This was the man who sold a recipe for soda water for practically nothing to Mr Schweppes. Lavoisier's work paved the way for the triumph of chemistry and the omnipresence of its products. The Russian Dmitri Mendeleev finally demolished Aristotle with his periodic table of the elements in 1869. When it was reported that Mendeleev had technically committed bigamy under Russian law (because he had not waited seven years before remarrying), the Tsar observed 'Mendeleev may have two wives, but Russia has only one Mendeleev'.

One could go on through all the sciences, adding to the accumulating pile. If one were to choose the ten most transformative inventions of the last two centuries, the following would surely be worthy of consideration:

1.  The invention of power, first the steam engine (James Watt), then electricity (largely the work of Michael Faraday (1791–1867), then the petrol engine (Gottlieb Daimler, 1882), then the aeroplane, then the jet engine (Frank Whittle, 1937) and then the rockets which put man on the moon in 1969. In 1935 the British driver Malcolm Campbell drove Bluebird at 276.8 mph at Daytona Beach, Florida. In 1936 the British female aviator, Amy Johnson, flew from England to Cape Town in three days, 6 hours and 25 minutes—in 1941 she drowned after crashing into the Thames Estuary.

2.  The announcement by Charles Darwin of the workings of evolution in his *Origin of Species by Natural Selection*, published in 1859. This work completely transformed our view of history and our view of ourselves.

3.  The invention of radio waves, mainly the work of Heinrich Hertz (1857–94). In 1901 Marconi sent the first radio signal across the Atlantic from Cornwall to Newfoundland.

4.  The special and general theories of relativity produced by Albert Einstein in 1905 and 1915. These established that only the speed of light is constant for everybody; time and space are relative.

5.  The terrifying discovery by Edwin Hubble in the 1920s that galaxies were receding from us at a velocity which increased the further away they were from us, so that we become more and more lonely.

6.  The production of the first atom bombs in the 1940s. Enrico Fermi's first atomic pile went critical in 1942 in a Chicago squash court.

7.  The production of a contraceptive tablet in 1952.

8.  The discovery in 1953 of the DNA double helix by Francis Crick and James Watson, building on the work of Rosalind Franklin. The DNA helix has a diameter of two nanometres. A human hair is about 25,000 nanometres in diameter. They discovered the notes on the piano of inheritance and genetics, leaving it to subsequent generations to learn to play them.

9.   The theoretical development of the Standard Model of particle physics in the 1960s onwards, following on from Ernest Rutherford's discovery in the 1920s that atoms have nuclei. Particle physics led to 'Big Science' and enormous cyclotrons. The first cyclotron atom-smasher was devised in 1931. One awaits practical results from these conjectures in order to qualify them for the top ten. So far we are advised that there are vast numbers of neutrinos, although we have not found any, and that around 96 per cent of dark matter and dark energy have gone missing.

10.   The invention of the computer and the internet. The first personal computer was marketed in the United States in 1975.

Other inventions of these two centuries could easily be entered in the competition—the camera, television, the germ theory of disease, radioactivity, x-rays, the radio telescope, the electron microscope, the Doppler Effect, quasars, pulsars and black holes, carbon-dating, the machine gun, cement, reinforced concrete, continental plates, dyes, bleaches, thermometers, even nylon, frozen peas, and the humble vacuum cleaner, fridge and washing machine.

Inventions have given us a degree of mastery over ourselves and our future that we never had before. They have dramatically improved our potential for survival and mastery of the ultimate destiny of human beings. The promotion of science is a priority for us.

The sprint of science over the past two centuries is matched by quickening velocity in other fields—the novel, the film, styles of painting, architecture, music. Until the late-18th century, the novel was a novelty. Artists at that time never contemplated impressionism.

One consequence of the acceleration of science and technology is greater prosperity but also greater risk. Never before have we had weaponry of such destructive capability. Hence the need for an international legal order, for what it is worth, to endeavour to mitigate the dangers. Another consequence is that the rational spirit of enquiry at the heart of science and the inventions of science sometimes cast doubt in the minds of some people on the assertions of their religion.

A third consequence is that, if we rightly admire the magnitude of our achievements to date, they are not enough, nowhere near enough. Too much is unexplained. At a date not so far from now—even 50 years, let alone a few thousand, we may well regard our present state of the art as antique and archaic, quaint. If we are to give time for invention and enquiry to further our knowledge to enable us to survive, there must be a moral order which ensures that we preserve what we have done so far and what we have yet to do.

## Growth of Population, Wealth and Law

The next figure to look at is the 'Growth of population, wealth and law' which tracks population growth, the increase in GDP and the growth in law since

500 BCE. We will see that it was from around 1830 onwards that the law expanded with colossal rapidity and in the process applied ethical principles in contexts unknown until then on such a scale.

---

Growth of law: 500 BC to 2010 AD

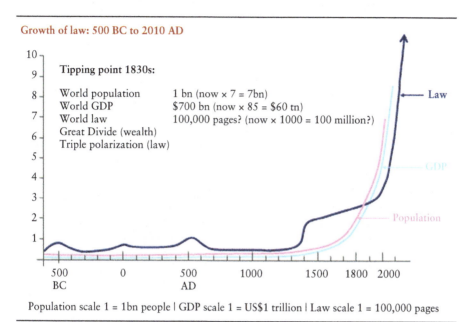

Tipping point 1830s:

| | |
|---|---|
| World population | 1 bn (now × 7 = 7bn) |
| World GDP | $700 bn (now × 85 = $60 tn) |
| World law | 100,000 pages? (now × 1000 = 100 million?) |
| Great Divide (wealth) | |
| Triple polarization (law) | |

Population scale 1 = 1bn people I GDP scale 1 = US$1 trillion I Law scale 1 = 100,000 pages

---

Growth of population, wealth and law

The figures for population and for GDP are based on Angus Maddison, *Contours of the World Economy 1–2030 AD* (Oxford University Press, 2007). The figures for the growth of law are mine and are speculative.

This figure shows that since 500 BC relatively not much happened in the growth of population, wealth or law until around 1830 when the volumes of all three took off. This result is consistent with Ian Morris's figure on human social development just discussed which showed that social development also took off around 1800.

The figure demonstrates a simple progression. It shows that as population increases, so does wealth go up at a greater speed and so does the growth of law at an even greater speed.

**Growth of population** Let us first consider population. Some estimates put world population of human beings at as little as 20,000 in 100,000 BCE. This may be too low but in any event around 8000 BCE the world population was probably around ten million, about the population of today's Paris. By 1 CE it seems to have been about 250 million, less than present-day Indonesia. In 1830 it was around one billion. It took 100 years to get to two billion (1930), but then just 30 years to reach three billion (1960), half that—17 years—to reach four billion (1977), 13 years to reach five billion (1990) and the even shorter time of ten years to reach six billion (2000). Now we are over seven billion.

So if one draws a line representing population from 1 CE, nearly all of the line represents population growth since 1830 as shown in the above figure. In other words population was pretty static in gross terms until 1830 when it really took off at a massively accelerating pace. The population line creeps around at the bottom of the chart until this point when it suddenly shoots up almost vertically. **Growth of GDP (wealth)** Around 1830 there was a similar dramatic upward shift in wealth, as measured by GDP.

By 1 CE world GDP in 1990-adjusted US dollars was around $100 billion, about the GDP of present-day Hungary or New Zealand. Around 1830 it was $700 billion, broadly equivalent to, say, Australia or South Korea in the mid-2000s. By 1975 it was $16 trillion (more than 20 times as much) and it more than doubled to over $37 trillion by 2001. In 2012 it was $60 trillion.

Again if one draws a line representing GDP growth from 1 CE, as shown in the graph, the GDP would again cling closely to the bottom of the graph until around 1830 when suddenly it lifts off and accelerates upwards.

Per capita GDP in 1 CE worldwide was about $500, less than that of present-day Burundi, Malawi or Sierra Leone, ie, less than that of the world's poorest countries today. By 1830 it was $700. By 1975 it was $4000, $6000 by 2001 and $12,000 by 2012. So virtually all the growth has been since 1830.

In 1 CE and even by 1830, most people worked on the land. Now usually more than 80 per cent of the population of advanced countries is urban, with the tiny amount of around 1 per cent or 2 per cent engaged in agriculture. Typically in these countries, the contribution of agriculture to GDP is around 1 per cent, of industry around 25 per cent and the remaining 75 per cent comprised of services—banking, insurance, retail, construction, etc.

So what happened is that the sudden spurt in population beginning around 1830 produced a spurt in science and technology as already discussed, or the technology induced a spurt in population—it does not matter which way round it happened.

**Growth of law** The law came of age in the centuries after 1830, almost exactly matching the precocious advances in science and technology. First we need to measure the growth very roughly and then to debate the reasons that this happened and what the implications are.

The figure on the growth of population, wealth and law shows a slight rise in the amount of law at the time of the Greeks and the early Romans; a rise at the time of the first great philosophers or religious leaders, such as Siddhartha Gautama (Buddhism) and Confucius, both of whom died round about 480 BCE; a further rise at the time of Justinian's codification of Roman law (533 CE); a sharper upwards movement at the time of the Renaissance a thousand years later; and then virtually a vertical line upwards from 1830 onwards. The contribution to the law by the Christian bible (about 50 to 100 CE) and by the Koran (about 650 CE) was small.

To get the growth of law into perspective, one has to keep it simple to focus on some simple arithmetical figures, the basic statistics. I do this by showing the previous graph in the form of a bar chart to bring out the huge growth in law.

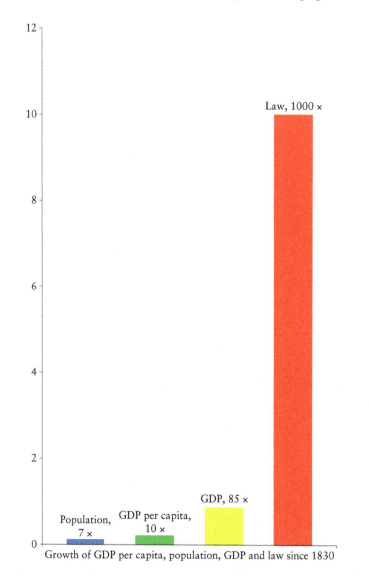

Growth of GDP per capita, population, GDP and law since 1830

The bar chart shows very roughly the comparative increase in the size of world population, GDP per capita, GDP of the world and the law, but showing law as growing at the lower estimate of 1000 times since 1830—the actual figure is probably much more.

Since 1830 world population grew seven times. That is, for every one person in 1830 standing next to you in a train or on the elevator, there are now seven people.

Over the same period GDP per capita grew by about ten times, slightly more than population. World GDP grew by 85 times.

How much has the law grown since then? This is extraordinarily difficult to measure but I suggest that the growth of written law in the books since 1830 has been between 1000 and 100,000 times. It probably does not really matter that we cannot be precise, since it is evident that there was a huge surge upwards from the early 19th century onwards.

The line representing growth of law in the bar chart is only tentative and impressionistic. It is based on the fact that back in 500 BCE, the content of law, at least written law, seemed rather small. Hammurabi's code of more than a thousand years earlier in 1772 BCE, which is contained on the 2.25 metre (7.4 feet) stele now in the Louvre in Paris, contains 282 rules of law. Hammurabi was a Babylonian king. The early Romans were reputed to have had Twelve Tables dated about 450 BCE. The laws in Leviticus, in the biblical Old Testament, amount to a few hundred articles—tiny compared with modern legislation.

We can work out the length of the codes of Justinian codifying Roman law around 533 CE and we can measure the barbarian codes of following centuries in the Dark Ages. When a collection of all current laws in Castile was printed at the king's command in 1569, it filled only two volumes, albeit there were 4000 laws. In the next hundred years or so there was a proliferation of local codes in Europe. We can also measure the size of the codes in the early codification movement, starting in France in 1803. We can measure the size of US tax law in the 19th century as against the size of US tax law now. We know that prior to the 19th century, company law hardly existed and there was no such thing as securities or financial regulation, let alone the other fields of regulation which now are monsters on the legal landscape. So it does not seem too unreasonable to estimate that the growth of law is well in excess of a thousand times larger since the early 19th century and could in fact be much, much larger.

Although one must be careful about establishing cause and effect relationships when there is only a correlation, what seems to have happened around 1830 is that, when the population of the world hit the first billion and subsequently accelerated, the increased number of people produced more wealth. Compared with a million people, a billion people think of more things, invent more things, make more things. The result of this prodigious multitude of effort by such a vast number of people produces wealth which is measured by GDP. The money went into banks and capital markets. This wealth in turn was funnelled into corporations by way of investment by share capital, bank loans and bonds. Banks made loans out of the cash deposited with them to finance new businesses. Insurance companies and banks invested in equity share capital and bonds for the new industries of the industrial revolution. Modern corporate law was invented—previously business was conducted through partnerships where the partners were each liable for all the debts of the firms, a risk which was inconceivable for investors in the new businesses who had no day to day control over the management of the business. The rapid expansion of business led to a demand for credit which in turn led to bankruptcies and losses. The reaction of lawmakers then as now was to rush in new laws to mitigate the devastation wrought by large corporate bankruptcies, including the bankruptcy of banks. Hence the advent in due course of financial and corporate regulation, corporate governance, financial statements and generally a massive increase in the amount and sophistication of law, including basic subjects such as the law of contract and the law of sale. The inventiveness of science was accompanied by the exhilarating ingenuity of the law.

Meanwhile the religious authorities in the Western industrialising countries left it to the secular authorities to mould the new legal regimes which became so important to our welfare and survival. In many cases the intervention of clerics was discouraged. The moral codes of the religions had been settled centuries earlier and the religious authorities saw no reason to change. In effect they handed the baton of moral progress in these new realms to the secular leaders. To them, God had little interest in corporations or banks.

If we were also to plot the amount of the growth of the corpus of all the scientific subjects, from medicine to physics, we would see a growth probably greater than the growth of law by a large margin.

# Predictions for the Future

Since it is to the future that we look, it is worth attempting a prediction, a forecast of what might happen over the short term and what this portends for us. By short term, I mean over the next 15 to 20 years and a little beyond, not next year.

Predictions about the future are extremely unsafe. Nobody can tell exactly what will happen in three months, in one week or even tomorrow with certainty. Economists struggle to make economic predictions beyond three months of general trends, let alone the detail. It is obvious therefore that the predictions made here are bound to be tentative and the real future could be entirely different.

Time future is perhaps contained in time present. Time past forms time present, but the arrow of time changes our perspective of the past. As we travel past a distant mountain range the shadows and the shapes change. As to the future, we live in Plato's cave and can see the future only as a shadow of a present reality.

In 2014 the World Bank predicted that by 2100, world population, now just over seven billion, will grow to between nine billion and twelve billion. The World Bank also predicted that by 2100 the population of Tanzania will be over 300 million (the population of the present-day United States) and the population of Nigeria will be over 700 million.

As to wealth, if we go back a little in the recent past and use the present to suggest a trajectory, we can posit a rough guess of world GDP in 2030. This is shown in the figure 'GDP football fields'.

GDP FOOTBALL FIELDS ($10 trillion)

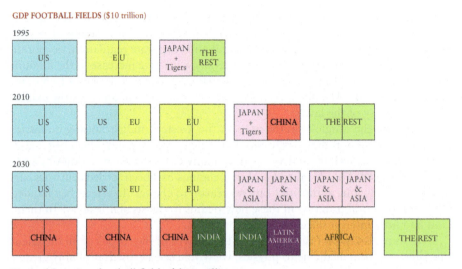

**Each oblong is a football field of $10 trillion**

In 1995, as shown in the figure, world GDP was roughly $30 trillion, ie, three football fields. This was weighted in favour of the United States and Western Europe, mainly as a result of developments in the 19th and 20th centuries for which many explanations have been attempted. From about 1830 the West pulled away from the rest in terms of technology and GDP so that, of the three football fields, by 1995, the United States was one, Europe and its offshoots was the second and the rest of the world was the third football field. Japan and the Asian Tigers occupied half of the third football field and the rest of the world the other half. Africa at that point had only about 3 per cent of world GDP.

The British Empire alone covered roughly one-quarter of the world's land surface (the French Empire about 9 per cent) and about the same proportion of population. The United States overtook Britain economically between 1870 and 1913 as the world's largest economic power. In 1860 Britain was the only thoroughly industrialised economy, producing half the world's iron and textiles. 1n 1913 11 western empires, including Russia and the United States, controlled nearly three-fifths of the territory of the world and nearly 80 per cent of the world's GDP. Even by 1990 the average American was 73 times richer than the average Chinese.

In 1500 the world's ten biggest cities had nearly all been in the East. Beijing was the biggest and was more than ten times the size of London. In 1900 the biggest cities were nearly all in the West. London was more than four times the size of Tokyo which was then Asia's largest city. In 1950 Western Europe, North America and Australasia had 20 per cent of the world's population. According to the United Nations by 2050 the figure will drop to 10 per cent.

The economic split from 1830 forward is often referred to as the Great Divide.

A further major result of European dominance from at least 1800 onwards was that European imperialism carried the European religion with it—Christianity.

So Christianity, as the religion of the settlers and the conquerors, displaced the customary religions of the indigenous people—in the whole of the Americas, in most of sub-Saharan Africa, in Australia and New Zealand. This massive implantation did not happen in places where the indigenous religion was well developed, such as Islam in North Africa and the Middle East, or Hinduism in India. It did not happen in countries which were not completely colonised such as Japan, Thailand and China, although the strong nationalisms in those countries and other factors contributed to the relative non-reception of Christianity.

At the same time there was another development, a major development in the context of world law, which is what I call the triple polarisation of the law, that is, the division of the world into three great families of law and their offshoots. The triple polarisation is discussed later, but suffice it to say here that the military and technological dominance of the West from the 19th century onwards meant that Western countries colonised almost the entire world and in the process imported their legal systems. In countries which they did not colonise or which became independent, they hugely influenced the legal systems which were copied by modernisers in those countries. The result was that out of the 320 jurisdictions in the world, probably more than 250 are based on a Western legal system.

If we went back a few hundred years, the economic situation would have been in contrast to what it was in 1995 because at one time China had 30 per cent of world GDP, a situation which may well transpire again in the future.

In any event, in around about 2010 there were five or six football fields of ten trillion each with China showing marked advances.

We are locked in the present. For us the present minute, the next few hours, the next day, the next week, the next month, these preoccupy us. The presence of the present deadens us to the future. But it is to the future which we must look. In our planning, we should be looking into a future much, much further away, not just a few decades, not just a few centuries, not just a few millennia.

By 2030, provided there is no terrible disruptive event in the meantime, economists have predicted a world GDP of around 11 or 12 football fields or even more. So things are really looking up in terms of more food, more health, more power stations, more hospitals, and so on for the peoples of the world.

Much of that increase in wealth results from the increase in population. Yet the amount of average personal wealth per person—GDP per capita—is likely to increase too so that the new wealth is spread.

Some futuristic prophesies show much faster growth from technology and science, for example, that if growth continues at the same rate as during the last 50 years, the world will be nearly five times richer by 2050 and 34 times richer by 2100. We would be doubling economic growth in our own lifespan.

In any event, all this extra GDP is not going to go under the mattress in the form of cash. It is going to go into banks, capital markets and funds and in turn be channelled through to corporations.

On the other hand, if three or five football fields can produce the mayhem of recent bank collapses and if they can produce the financial crisis of 2007/2008, surely 12 football fields or even more will produce much more money sloshing around in banks and capital markets, more competition between nation states, much more interconnectedness of countries, and this will surely produce more risk. A tempestuous future could therefore lie ahead and our ability to cope with that could be crucial.

# Conclusion

We can now pull together some of the themes discussed in this chapter. In the last two centuries there has been a very rapid growth in population, wealth, science and law and these trends look set to continue. We can hope for an increase in international prosperity but there is also a greater risk of dangerous instability and conflict which could stretch the capacities of our moral regimes, once expressed through our religions but now largely expressed through our legal systems. If the experience of the rich West is anything to go by, there may be a greater questioning of the supernatural beliefs of the great religions and hence a greater secularisation of our societies, topics to which we will return. In that event the law would be left as the main bulwark against instability and disruption threatening our societies and calling our survival into question.

We must now embark on an examination of religions and the law to see how they compare.

# 4

# *What is Religion?*

Religions have been one of the most powerful and potent ideologies the world has ever seen. They have penetrated pervasively into every society, they have driven history, they have driven wars, they have driven inspiration since the very earliest times.

## Belief in a Supernatural God and Immortality

The first question to consider is the meaning of religion which is important both for describing the role of religions and for determining the number of adherents.

A strict definition of religion is that it is an ideology which has a belief that (1) humans have a supernatural spirit which lives on after death—for example, by going to heaven or by transmigrating to another creature, and (2) there is some sort of supernatural god out there who is more than just a force of nature and who takes a personal interest in us. The god must take an interest in us because the immortality of the soul is determined by our conduct which can be measured only by the god. The mainstream features of religion are a dual belief in the supernatural—a god and the immortality of the soul. A test of seriousness as to whether you are religious is whether you perform the main rituals regularly, such as attending church, mosque, synagogue or temple once a week. These requirements are how the main religions define themselves in their scriptures.

Various philosophical schools, such as humanism, are not religions in this sense. Political philosophies, such as communism, are not religions. Confucianism is not a religion. Confucianism is a philosophy of life, a programme of living in societies. All these philosophies are ways of life and many propose a meaning of life and a moral system. They are contenders for serving the function of survival and have to be considered, but they are not religions, defined strictly. The main defects of historical philosophies of life as moral systems are that they do not have the sanctions of religion or the law, they are typically vague and they tend to cover only a sliver of what needs to be covered.

The law is not a religion. One can believe in the rule of law or the role of law in our societies without constituting the law as a religion. It is a secular belief. I sometimes in this book describe the law as a secular religion, but that is only a metaphor and not intended to connote that I regard the law as sharing the essential attributes of a religion.

Ordinary superstitions, such as believing in ghosts or in the evil eye, do not qualify as religions. Practically everybody is superstitious to some degree. Isolated irrational beliefs are also not religions, such as a belief that your destiny next week is foretold by the star signs in your horoscope or by the lines in your left palm.

I will discuss this question of the core meaning of religion later but for the moment we must recognise that people mean different things when they talk about religion, for example, what counts as a belief in God, what counts as a belief in the immortality of the soul, whether practising the rituals is necessary, whether you need all these things at all. My definition is not the only one. But we have to draw a line somewhere between believing in football and believing in a religion. When we measure things, we have to be especially careful to define what we are measuring.

The largest religions in terms of members are Christianity and Islam, then third is Hinduism and fourth is Buddhism. Other smaller religions include Taoism, Shinto (mainly Japanese), Sikhism and Judaism. In addition there are a number of very small religions in terms of adherents, such as Zoroastrianism and Jainism.

Whether you count the innumerable sects as separate religions depends on whether you are a lumper or a splitter. As with the law, there is a quite fantastic fissuring and fragmentation of religions into schismatic cults.

# Map of Religions

One of the remarkable achievements of the great religions, apart from Judaism and Hinduism, is that they transcended local boundaries and achieved a notable degree of internationalism. Set out below is a map of the families of the main religions and their distribution around the world. This map shows which religion has the most number of adherents in each country. This is not necessarily a majority of the population. Thus if Christians are 30 per cent of the population and all the other religions are smaller, then the country is classed in the map as Christian. The countries are identified on the map found at page 124.

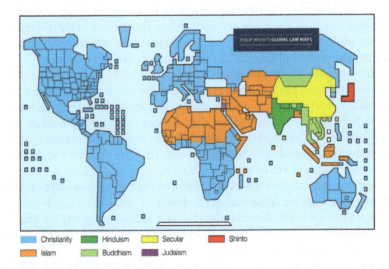

| | Christianity | | Hinduism | | Secular | | Shinto |
| | Islam | | Buddhism | | Judaism | | |

**Largest religion per country**

Christianity is coloured blue. It is the biggest religion in terms of countries and nominal adherents. It spans the world.

Islam is coloured orange. Islam predominates in the old Islamic empires of North Africa and the Middle East, spreading eastwards through to Iran, Afghanistan, the Central Asian republics, Pakistan, Bangladesh, Malaysia and Indonesia. The religion straddles a large portion of the upper centre of the globe above the equator. In terms of numbers of nominal adherents, it is the second largest religion by a considerable margin, but on stricter tests or practice and belief it may be neck and neck with Christianity or even larger. The country with the biggest Muslim population is Indonesia.

Judaism is coloured purple and is a lonely outpost on the eastern Mediterranean surrounded by a sea of Islam.

Hinduism, coloured dark green, is almost entirely an Indian religion, with only small communities—largely Indian immigrants—elsewhere, for example, in Mauritius. Nepal is mainly Hindu. Apart from Indian immigrant communities elsewhere in the world, Hinduism never escaped the boundaries of India and never became a universal religion. Its early outbreaks into South-East Asia were, in the main, subsequently repulsed.

Buddhism, coloured pale green, is an offshoot of Hinduism and is an Asian religion with its main adherents in such places as Sri Lanka, Myanmar (Burma), Thailand, Laos, Cambodia, Vietnam and Korea. It has virtually disappeared from India.

China is the only country coloured yellow representing secularity. I suggest later that only between 6 and 9 per cent of the Chinese regularly practise and believe in a supernatural religion.

Shintoism, coloured red, is peculiarly a Japanese religion but in fact Japan is largely secular nowadays and could reasonably be coloured yellow, as with China. Indeed some former Christian countries could also now be treated as secular if we apply strict tests of religiosity.

So what you have on the map is the regions dominated by Christianity—the Americas, Europe and the west of Russia plus Western offshoots in Australia and New Zealand plus most of sub-Saharan Africa. The swathe of North Africa through the Middle East and eastwards is dominated by Islam. The triangular wedge of India is Hindu and the rest to the east is mainly Buddhist in patches and Muslim in patches.

# Decline in Religions

At one time in history not so long ago—say around the year 1600—practically everybody in Europe was pious. We cannot prove this by statistics but it seems a reasonable surmise. The Reformation was recent and religion was a topic of heat and acrimony for most people. Continental Europe was about to fight one of the most atrocious wars ever on the subject of religion—the Thirty Years War (1618–48). Religion was crucial in people's lives. Nearly everybody said their prayers every day and went to church on the Sabbath. Religion was the great driver of politics. It made and unmade kings and fomented revolutions. Universities almost wholly taught theology and were led by theologians.

The Ottoman Empire based in Istanbul was at the zenith of its power and glory. In its religious schools pupils learnt the Koran by heart. Mullahs presided over massive and beautiful mosques built by the architect Sinan to celebrate Allah and amaze the faithful. It was unthinkable not to observe the Prophet's admonitions to murmur prayers five times a day and to prostrate oneself in devotion on Fridays in one of these glorious buildings. Over in India the Mughal Empire bestrode India and the entire territory from Arabia to the Indus was Muslim. Islam was already occupying Malaya and Indonesia via its traders.

Everywhere religion was triumphant and the most important spiritual force in the world in people's everyday lives. The churches and the mosques, the temples and the synagogues were full. It appeared to nearly everyone that there was nothing to challenge the supreme power of religion. Religion was permanent because truth is permanent.

In those days, to confess that you did not believe in God was shocking. It was out of the question to admit that you were an atheist: this would often also be a criminal offence.

But soon Galileo was to announce that the earth was not at the centre of the universe. Francis Bacon (1561–1626) heralded a new spirit of scientific rationalism which was to gain momentum in the 18th century Enlightenment and to sweep all before it in the science of the 20th century. And the first erosion of a major religion had crept up in the Far East with the attacks on Buddhism. That religion was at various times previously the state religion of India, China, Korea and Japan—all the aces of the East—but by the 12th century it had almost disappeared from India. It had long before been persecuted in China and more recently it had been threatened in Korea. Later it was dethroned in Japan. The ultimate devastation of Buddhism shows what can happen to a religion. Now with maybe 350 million nominal adherents, maybe more, maybe less, Buddhism is no longer a major force and is dwarfed by the other two universal religions— Christianity and Islam. Nobody thought that one day the same might happen to these two as well.

So far the two giant religions are still great forces in terms of nominal numbers. The nominal numbers of religious people in the world is often quoted as over 80 per cent, with Christians comprising around 31 per cent of the population and Islam around 23 per cent. But if you look more closely at the numbers and only count those who believe in the basic supernatural tenets of the religions and also practise the religion regularly, a different picture emerges. For example, a former Archbishop of Canterbury said in 2014 that Britain was now a secular country since less than 15 per cent were practising adherents. In Norway, the number of practising adherents is about 4 per cent. China and Japan are secular. If you apply these statistics to the figures often cited about the size of religions, the figures are a fraction of those cited. The nominal figure often quoted for Christians in Britain is more than four times as many as the 15 per cent of practising Christians cited by the Archbishop. The number of Christians in Norway has been reported to be nearly 20 times the reported number of practising Norwegians. Another frequently quoted figure is that there are 65 million Shintoists in Japan which has a population of about 127 million. The actual figure for practising Shintoists is about four million or even less, so that the nominal figure is 16 times larger than the actual figure.

The actual number of true practising adherents who believe in the main tenets of their religion has sunk—as a proportion of the population—from the almost universal devotion of the year 1600 and continues to sink at a significant rate. My assessment is that the number of qualifying devotees who regularly practise a supernatural religion and satisfy the criteria discussed later is between a quarter and two-fifths of the world's population. I explore these numbers in more detail later.

In addition the religions which once had great sway over the policies of the realm have now been displaced by secular rulers almost everywhere. The number of true theocracies is almost zero and instead, apart from a few exceptions, most states in the world have separated religion from politics. Rulers were not content to have competition in law-making, to have another power in the land which they had to bow to. Hence they no longer allowed the clerics, rabbis, imams, ministers, monks and gurus to interfere, as they saw it, in the workings of state. The role of the religions was to endorse and legitimise the rulers, not to challenge them. The priests were subordinated.

# The Meanings of God

God has had many names—Yahweh, Brahma, Zeus, Baal, Allah, Wotan, Mithras, Vishnu, Jupiter. The concept of God differs according to the believer.

Most people will admit that at least they believe in something out there, or that there is a probability of more than zero that there is something out there. But exactly what is out there admits of wildly different views.

To some people, probably not many nowadays, God is a kindly old man in the sky with a bald head, a long white beard and sitting on a cloud surrounded by golden-haired angels with wings playing harps. The human God, the anthropomorphic God, has been portrayed in the religious books as everything from a vindictive jealous bully to an ineffably gentle and merciful magus. To many devotees, God is interested in each one of the seven billion people on earth. That is, he listens to their prayers, answers some of them, hears confessions, absolves sins and keeps records of the good and unredeemed bad deeds of each individual so that he can decide whether they should go to heaven on the final judgement day or else be smitten down to hell to burn in agony forever. This is the God of the Jews, the Christians and the Muslims.

To many people in the ancient world, God was everywhere, in every river, mountain or rock, in every tree, bush and flower, in every human or cow or ant, in every emanation of visible creation on earth. This god was either many gods or incarnations or manifestations of one spirit, one God. This multiplicity in oneness was how the Hindus explain their apparent polytheism and how the Christians explain their trinity of gods. There is only one God but he has many shapes.

To believers of this class, you could therefore have statues, idols or icons to help you worship and they did not have to be the same as those of the believers in the next village. You can worship images of Vishnu, Shiva and their consorts or any of them, it doesn't matter; they were all part of the same show. This approach was anathema to most Judaic sects and to Muslims who both object to any portrayal of God or his emanations as idol worship.

If you added the angelic hosts, boddhivistas, saints, atavars and the like, you could end up with very large numbers of godlike creatures looking after us down here on earth. There are over five thousand saints in the Roman Catholic pantheon.

To others, God is the great physicist, the great inventor, who starts off the universe with a big bang, a gigantic explosion out of nothing, out of a singularity, and then retires to let the whole thing run its course—including the establishment of time and the four great forces of nature, the formation of galaxies and stars, the creation of particles and atoms and chemical elements, and even the processes of evolution which eventually resulted in us. A few believe that God designed everything in the year 8004 BCE (completing the work on Sunday 23 October to be exact), a view still typical of more literalist American creationists. Others are happier with the theory that God's role in design was simply that of the intelligent scientist who set the machine in motion, Newton's great watchmaker. This God was never interested in all the burnt offerings roasted to propitiate him, even if of Aztec human beings, does not listen to the prayers and supplications that are daily sent to him by millions of his devotees and, although benevolent, is presumably too busy on other creations to pay attention to us. This is the God of the 18th-century deists.

To yet others, God is beyond comprehension and there is no point in trying to describe him or picture him. He has no substance, no essence, no being. He has no face, no eyes, no arms, no legs, no gender. He is imageless. He is not even a force or a motion or a glow of energy or anything which can be contemplated by the human imagination. All the great religions have had sects which adhere to this view, including sects of Hindus, Buddhists and Christians. This is the mainstream view of Muslims. The nearest the Greeks came to this concept was Plato's doctrine of ultimate forms out there. Indeed this view—that God is beyond understanding—is probably held by millions of people who secretly or openly profess themselves to be non-religious. Despite their scepticism about the God of established religion, they still believe that there must be something; it can't just be nothing when we can see so much of something.

For an excellent discussion, see Karen Armstrong, *A History of God* (Vintage, 1993). The variety of beliefs is one reason why it is hard to measure religiosity accurately. Devotees often have never explained to themselves what exactly they believe in so there is a lot of blur.

When we come to the idea of heaven, again there is a profusion of descriptions as to what awaits the faithful, ranging from a leafy garden in the skies to a virtual abode of spirits beyond our power of words and imagination.

# Consciousness and the Soul

The idea that mind and matter are separate is very ancient. This is dualism, ie, the doctrine that people have a corporeal and tangible body which is flesh and blood, muscle and bone, but they also have a mind or spirit, a consciousness which is not made of corporeal matter. Our mind is our soul.

This dualism was developed by philosophers and religious thinkers from very early times and was, for example, articulated by the 17th-century French philosopher Descartes. This approach is hardly surprising since brain science is of very recent origin—not more than a hundred years old, centuries after the first religions were invented. Our mind embodies our memories, our thoughts, our imaginations, our emotions, our fears, our guilts, our will, our drives, our fortitude, our good and our evil. Our mind feels like our real self, a spirit separate from flesh and bones. It is our individuality, our identity.

It is still hard for people to accept that our consciousness is produced by chemical reactions and electronic impulses in the brain. To a monist, mind is just a product of matter. Nobody has yet been able to identify a separate ghost or ether or gas or spirit which inhabits our body and then escapes on death with a hiss.

To many people the notion that our mind, our consciousness is spiritual is routine. The idea of reincarnation developed by Hinduism or of the immortality of the mind made sense. Even now physiologists of the mind struggle to work out what consciousness is. It is quite natural to regard us as having a spirit which is our consciousness and hence quite natural to regard this spirit as not dying with our physical body but living on to exist in some other body or to travel to some other abode.

On the question of the ultimate destiny of the soul, it is useful to group the four religions plus Judaism into two great camps, the Eastern and the Western. In the first camp we have the Eastern religions, Hinduism and its main offshoot Buddhism. This camp also incidentally includes the very small religions of Jainism and Sikhs. Hinduism and Buddhism both originated in India. Both embraced the concept of reincarnation, that is, that each human has an individual spirit or soul which, when you died, would be reincarnated within another being, depending on your conduct in this life. If you were bad, you could end up as vermin next time around. Since Hinduism was an early religion just breaking out of primitive folk religions and ancestor worship, the Hindus had lots of gods, ie, they were not monotheistic. Buddhism is more complicated on the topic of God. Sikhism is monotheistic.

The second group comprises the trilogy of Judaism, Christianity and Islam, together with the earlier religion of Zoroastrianism which has now more or less died out. They all grew out of religious ideas current in the Middle East from perhaps as early as 2000 BCE. These ideas were that there was only one God and that, if you were good, you would go to heaven, and if you were bad, you would go to hell.

These ideas were perhaps based on the teachings of Zoroaster who was a Persian and who lived somewhere between 1700 BCE and 500 BCE. Actually the three religions maintained that their ideology originated in the ideas of a patriarch from Ur in Mesopotamia (present-day Iraq) called Abraham around 2000 BCE.

The crucial connection between Eastern and Western religious ideas on the destiny of the soul was their emphasis on the good life and good conduct—morality and ethics. This was by far their greatest contribution to civilisation. If you were good, you would have everlasting bliss, but, if you were bad, then forget about having a nice time. This message carries some conviction because if we are good, we may get somewhere in discovering the secrets of the universe but if we are bad, then it is tickets for us here on planet earth.

# Origins of Religions

The history of religions has often been described as a progress of ordered sequence. Primitive humans embraced tribal animism, where everything on earth, whether river or mountain or tree or creature, contained a god and where one's ancestors hung there in the air keeping an eye on their progeny. Next came polytheism, where there were many named gods, and then finally monotheism with only one god. In other words the progress was one of simplification and reduction from a proliferation of spirits down to just one. This progression has merits, but history is, as always, more complicated.

The earliest shamans persuaded their communities that they could talk to ancestors and were the sole means of communication with the gods. They also persuaded their communities that the gods would be displeased unless there were considerable sacrifices, including human sacrifices. In the Fertile Crescent there was an obsession with ancestors. Religion began to be taken seriously there around 10,000 BCE. Burying multiple generations of the dead under house floors was common. At an ancient site in Turkey, almost every house had bodies under the floor and ancestral skulls were plastered into the surfaces of the walls. There was similar evidence of grisly ancestor burials and human sacrifices in China around 4000 BCE. So it is not only the Aztecs who carried out mass orgies of human sacrifice. The early origins of religion were indeed gruesome.

Fertility goddesses were everywhere. Fertility was sacred. The Mother Goddess was painted on cave walls or sculpted as a naked, pregnant woman. She morphed into Innana in ancient Sumeria, Ishtar in Babylon, Anat in Canaan, Isis in Egypt and Aphrodite in Greece.

The main religions were formed at intervals of about 500 years from 1000 BCE (Judaism, maybe Zoroastrianism, Hinduism), then 500 BCE (Buddhism), then zero CE (Christianity), then 500 CE (actually in the early 600s—Islam). The religions came in four bursts stretching over more than 1500 years, like a volcano of incandescent spirituality erupting every 500 years.

It is surprising that the major religious experiment stopped around mid-600 CE. Notwithstanding the astonishing advances in every other field of intellectual achievement, religion languished. Of course there were endless commentaries, endless new sects and split-offs but you could hardly say that there were major advances in the ideology. No new major religious philosophy attracting a substantial following has emerged since Islam of the 6th century. One has only to compare the way that both science and law leapt ahead with huge bounds to see the difference. For some reason, the core moral systems of religions just froze as unchangeable ancient wisdom whose work was done.

## Comparisons Between Religion and Law

It is worth comparing some of the major features of religion on the one hand and law on the other. For one thing this would tell us what we lose if religions fail and the world becomes completely secular. In those countries which are already largely secular, the fact that people are willing to forego the advantages offered by religion would indicate that these people no longer value these advantages or have so little faith that they are not prepared to invest the time and expense which are required to practise a religion.

The comparison is between law and religion. I am not comparing priests and other religious leaders with lawyers—they obviously have completely different jobs. Despite some overlaps, lawyers do not carry out the same functions as priests.

**Survival** The basic purpose of law is to enable us to survive. There is no question that the fundamental inspiration of religion is the desire to survive, the same motive which underlies law. That is why nearly all the great religions have rules about basic morality, such as the prohibition on killing and the protection of the family, principles which were seen as fundamental to the continued existence of humans or the particular tribe.

Law promotes the survival of ourselves in this life and the survival of our children and all future generations in their lives. Religion promotes immortality, the survival of ourselves and all future generations in the afterlife, forever, for eternity, since the basic premise of religion is that the souls or spirits of people are immortal. Religions defy death. Secular law does not make us individually immortal. It can however create the conditions which enable us to make the human race immortal. The law is also salvationist and redeems us.

**Belief in the supernatural** Religions in the true sense require a belief in the supernatural, a god or a soul which is immortal and which ends up in heaven or hell or which migrates from one being to another by a process of reincarnation or joining the spirits of one's ancestors. The god of religion delivered the moral laws to humans.

Law does not require a belief in the supernatural. It does not require a belief that morality has its origin in the commands of some supernatural being, that the basic laws were dictated from on high by a messenger from God. It is a secular belief.

In the past many legal philosophers debated how much law was given by God and how much by man. They debated what law was natural and what was artificial and manufactured. This was an extraordinarily sterile debate, but one which has preoccupied writers on jurisprudence for centuries.

**Protection** Religions provide a super-normal and all-powerful being who provides protection from the dangers of the world and help in adversity and who is specifically interested in the welfare of each person.

The law also provides protection but not by the same medium.

**Consolation** Religion gives consolation to the bereaved and to those suffering. It comforts us when somebody close to us dies, gives us some hope when we are in misery. It heartens those who feel mediocre or a failure, who feel redundant or superfluous, who would otherwise feel self-disgust and depression. Religions give individuals a direct personal relationship with a god whom you can talk to.

The law does not provide these consolations, or a personal relationship. But where the law promotes prosperity or where it safeguards personal safety so as to enable people peaceably to carry on their jobs unmolested, then the law enhances our potential for happiness.

**Control over destiny** Religions at one time provided the reassurance of apparent control over our future, our fate, our destiny. If we prayed to the gods, performed the right rituals and made the right sacrifices, then the gods might be persuaded to deliver rains to ripen the crops, hold back the thunderbolt and call off the pestilence.

The law does give us better control over our lives by empowering us. The rule of law liberates us. In that way we are better able to control our destiny.

**Cosmic explanations and the meaning of life** Religion affords explanations of the universe and creation. The early religions were early science. They provided a solution to how we got here. They proffered the purpose of our existence, a world view, the meaning of life.

The law does not in most states (outside fundamentalist theocratic states) lay down rules about what we are to believe about the creation of the planet, the universe and ourselves. This is left to the scientists. The law is not in the business of creation stories.

The law does not tell us what is the meaning of life. At its finest, the law backs freedom of speech, freedom of enquiry, and in that way seeks to improve our ability to provide explanations. The law promotes the conditions which give us the freedom to develop our views on the meaning of life and to communicate them.

**Guilt and forgiveness** Some religions provide a release from guilt and the fear of retribution for wickedness. Christianity specialises in these pardons.

The criminal law rarely pardons. The enforcement of the ordinary non-criminal law, such as contract law, depends on the forbearance of the offended party. But once the penalty or compensation is paid, the transgression is cured. So redemption is possible, though it is not free.

**Identity** Religion enhances our sense of identity with our group and promotes our sense of group loyalty, support and safety. The members of the group are on the same side. If group loyalty is improved by religion, then the group has a better chance of surviving. It is not usually the objective of religion to enhance identity (except perhaps in early Judaism), but that has been the effect in nearly all cases. The distinctiveness of the group is strengthened by common beliefs and rituals, clothing and hairstyle, the wearing of icons. Religions deliver an emotional fulfilment born from the overcoming of alienation and loneliness, the escape from solitude and the sweet comfort of togetherness and belonging.

The disadvantage of this reassuring identity is sectarian hatred and violence, a massively destructive defect which has resulted in some of the most shocking atrocities and wars, usually caused primarily by other competitive conflicts but legitimised by the label of a religion. The distinctions between the sects are often so minuscule and inconsequential that one wonders why one sect should regard another as being malevolent and wicked on such flimsy grounds.

**Passion** Religions inspire passion and emotional fervour—at least in some. It was this passion which inspired the music, the glorious chorales, the soaring architecture and the spiritual art associated with religions. It is ironic that many religions, via their ascetic and puritan wings, attempted to curb the love of beauty and the aesthetic. One of the great religions—Islam—takes iconoclasm (the rejection of images) to the ultimate, by banning images of the human form altogether.

Worship in some sects is ecstatic, accompanied by wild singing, dancing and clapping, dramatic exorcisms and speaking in tongues. In others a devotee may be enthralled and enraptured by love of the chosen god, in a trance. As a result of these emotions, religions are ideologies which can lead to destruction and devastation, to crusades and terrorism.

The law is not enthusiastic about enthusiasm, but don't be misled. Most parts of the law inflame deep passions and rages, for example, the law relating to sex or to capital punishment or pollution and, in despotic countries, the law governing freedom and democracies. Since a large part of the law is intended to restrict freedoms in the interests of the collective good, these restrictions may be seen by some as unjust. Few emotions provoke such mayhem as a sense of injustice. Few things divide the peoples of the world at a visceral level more than attitudes to the family and sex.

As with religions, law is ultimately an ideology and, like all ideologies,— especially moral ideologies—it excites emotions and sometimes fanaticism. The difference is that an overriding objective of the law is to tame our savage cruelties and to be rational, to promote peace. The suppression of savagery is also an objective of religion, but the passions are so strong that it has not always worked that way. If the law is cooler than hot religion, that coolness has a purpose.

Scientists often confess to a sense of awe and wonder at the cosmos and a sense of excitement about discovery. I feel these things too. To me, the law also has romance and excitement. This is because of its role in our societies, because it articulates our moral ideals and hopes.

**Evolutionary programming** Some evolutionists have suggested deeper psychological reasons for our adherence to religion which are hard-wired into our minds, some deep yearnings which are genetically programmed, something profound in our natural psyche, an inclination of the genes towards religion so that those who have these genes tend to preserve their own gene pool. The argument is that, if you have a good gene which enhances your survival prospects, then that gene will be more successful in the survival of the fittest. Or the religious instinct is a by-product of some other part of our mindset which enables us to survive: see Richard Dawkins, *The God Delusion* (Black Swan, 2007) p 238.

Whether there is a pre-disposition for law is an interesting speculation. There is no doubt that the instinct to survive and stay alive personally is wired into us at the most fundamental level and is far more powerful and universal even than the desire for sex. The sense of justice also seems to be quite primitive and innate. Experiments by psychologists have shown that notions of fairness are acquired by children at a very young age.

**Membership** Religions normally expect some indication of membership of the community. This is sometimes shown by an initiation process, such as baptism, and by other visible badges of commitment, such as dress or hairstyle.

The law is universal. You do not have to join a club. Everybody believes in the rule of law. They may differ in the scope of law and its content, but the basic idea that there should be rules of justice and rules for survival is common to all people.

Religious belief and becoming a member of a religion is voluntary—at least in most countries. In a few countries, mainly Muslim, apostasy—the abandonment of a belief—is a criminal offence.

The law is not voluntary. Generally you are subject to the law of the country where you happen to be located. You can, for example, contract under the laws of another country if you want to, but criminal, regulatory and civil liability laws are usually mandatory.

**Founders** Most of the great religions have a founding father, a dominating heroic figure who crystallises the main beliefs into a coherent theological code, who announces the creed with charisma, often with a group of disciples. One thinks of Zoroaster, Moses, Siddartha Gautama, Mahavira, Jesus Christ, Lao-Tzu and Guru Nanak, all discussed later. Only Hinduism does not have such a triumphant messenger from the gods. Ditto the various forms of animistic belief and ancestor worship.

The law has great figures but no epic heroes on this scale. The law has codifiers, such as Hammurabi of the Babylonians, Justinian's lawyers in the 7th century, the French codifiers at the turn of the 18th century led in effect by Portalis, and the German codifiers of the 19th century drafting the German codes. It has genius commentators and glossarists, inspired legislators, such as the Greek Solon of the 6th century BCE. It has judges famed for their eloquence and sense of justice, such as Judge Cardozo of the United States in the 1920s and Lord Mansfield of 18th-century England. It has authors who more or less invented whole fields of law single-handedly, such as Grotius on the law of war.

Yet none of these commendable leaders of the law commanded the intense adoration devoted to the glorious supermen of religion. After all, these triumphant messengers from the gods were announcing that the people were being looked after by an all-powerful supreme being and that they could hope for immortality, redemption, salvation for ever. The lawyers did not have an ace like that. To me, it is thrilling that the law does not rely on the supernatural: the law makes us rely on ourselves.

**Rituals** Religions typically require the carrying out of onerous rituals as a sign of commitment and as a showing to the supernatural god or whoever is responsible for reincarnation or one's ancestors that the believer is serious.

These rituals may include daily prayers, regular attendance at temples, churches, mosques or synagogues, taking communion, fasting, going on pilgrimage, singing holy music and walking in processions, feasting, wearing special clothes or sacrificing useful animals. The investment in time and effort can be enormous.

Religions are preoccupied with rituals and precise observance to the last detail. If you defaulted in the required performances, God might get angry and send down a famine or plague. Hence the importance of priests to show the people what they had to do to please the gods. But some of the most important rituals centre around rites of passage—birth, puberty, marriage, death, times of intense celebration and also of grief and mourning.

At the centre of these rituals is the worship of God or the gods. Hymns, prayers, liturgies, offerings, attendance at the temple are almost exclusively focused on the worship of the divine. This honouring of a god is an affirmation of belief. Prayers for help come second to that.

Religions also typically have sacred objects—icons, crosses, a black box, statues, beads.

The law does not require its adherents to observe any rituals to honour an ideal or principle. It is true that the opening of the courts or a parliament is often attended by a ceremonial ritual, often more a genuflection to a god than to the law. But these rituals are limited to only a few participants. Worshipping the law is not required. Since everybody is a member of a community governed by law of some sort, there is no need to engage in onerous conduct to show one's commitment to the chosen religion. Since there is no supernatural god to please, there is no need to prove one's obedience by shows and propitiating ceremonies or to worship sacred objects.

**Clerics** Religions have specialised clerics—priests, ministers, pastors, imams, rabbis, pujas, gurus, scholars learned in doctrine—to interpret the scriptures and to conduct collective rituals. Sometimes they have to be ordained, often not. Sometimes they are organised according to seniority, such as popes and archbishops.

Lawyers generally have to be qualified to practise or teach. Like some religious clerics, lawyers are arrayed in hierarchies from Supreme Court judges downwards. Like priests, they are concerned with the ultimate values which bind societies. Unlike priests, they do not teach supernatural doctrines, their practice is with earthly reality.

One may sum up so far by remarking that it is obvious that the law will not be a substitute for some of the advantages offered by religions—the promise of immortality, the consolation, the emotional support and the release from guilt. But if the population ceases to believe in the supernatural messages of religion, then these things inevitably disappear as well and we are left with what we have. It is hard to conjure up belief if it has vanished: all the comforts then become false and humanity faces a different reality.

The things which are lost can be sought by other means which the law facilitates. And our lives still have a meaning and a purpose but on a much grander and altruistic scale, that is, the survival of future generations and the discovery of the truth.

There is a big literature written by sociologists, encrusted with statistical methodologies, debating whether religion makes you happier or wealthier. Whatever the outcome of those debates, there is no question that the absence of law would make us more miserable and poorer, and that the presence of law makes happiness and prosperity real possibilities. Religion can bring happiness, but religion is not necessary for happiness; law is. People can take delight in their existence and celebrate and glory in their lives without religion.

## Religious Moral Codes and Secular Legal Codes

The most obvious similarity is that both religion and law have codes of conduct—rules, regulations, codes, that is, laws. These codes were originally aimed at ensuring survival and still are in the widest sense. The religions were right: we do need moral rules which are backed by sanctions to encourage compliance.

The original moral codes of most of the great religions were said to be handed down by the gods and were therefore immutable, cast in stone. This is true, for example, of Judaism, Christianity, Islam and Hinduism.

The religious moral codes and indeed the beliefs of the religion itself are usually contained in scriptures—ancient holy books, some of which are held to be of divine origin—dictated by a god or delivered by a god to some specially favoured messenger or prophet. These scriptures are then enlarged and commented on by spiritual leaders in books which enjoy special authenticity.

Both religions and law have sanctions for violations—hell or rebirth as a worm in religions or, in the case of the law, conviction for a crime or compensation for civil transgressions.

Many people think that morality is just about sex and serious crimes, like murder. All the rest is technical. We shall see that this is a misconception.

Religious codes typically cover primitive rules necessary for people to stay alive and reproduce—rules about sex, family, prohibitions against murder and injury of others, and against theft and a prohibition against lying (mainly to ensure justice and to keep the peace).

There were rules about unsafe or protected foods, for example, alcohol, pork, carrion, meat generally. There were rules about hygiene and washing. There were rules and expectations about charity and almsgiving—the proto welfare state. Later with the development of economies and trade, some religions developed rules about money, such as a prohibition against usury, typical of present-day Islam and also, until fairly recently, Christianity. For a bibliography of religious law, see Marylyn Johnson Raisch, *Religious Legal Systems in Comparative Law: A Guide to Introductory Research* (on the internet, (2006) with updates).

There are major differences between the scope of religious codes and secular legal codes. In particular:

— **Rewards and punishments** Both religions and the law have a system of rewards and punishments to encourage adherence. In the case of religions, the reward for virtue is heaven or moving up a caste or two next time. The punishment is hell or inhabiting a low-caste individual in the next round.

In the case of the law the reward for observing, say, the rule of law is living in a society which is peaceable and has a better chance of survival. The punishment for non-compliance is a criminal sanction, such as a fine or prison, or in the case of violation of some lesser duty such as breach of contract, the punishment is payment of compensation.

One crucial difference is that the rewards and punishments for religious transgressions depend for their efficacy on belief in the supernatural. Once that belief disappears, then the prop of the religious morality goes with it and we are left with a moral ideology that has lost its framework of reward and punishment. Only the secular framework of the rewards and punishments of the law can ultimately step into the gap.

Another crucial difference is that the punishment for religious violations is postponed to the afterlife. Religions therefore have to rely on the secular authorities to mete out punishment on this earth for crimes and compensation for other civil transgressions.

The religious God knows everything and sees all violations. The secular authorities do not have the same omniscience, but some of them are doing their best to improve their surveillance.

— **Limited scope of religious codes** Religious codes are too limited and basic to deal with the legal framework required for modern societies. For example, they have no useful codes about democracy, taxation, corporations, money, insurance, bankruptcy or intellectual property. Even their principles about the rule of law are thin by comparison. One of the reasons that the religions did not develop rules for these areas is that the leadership of states became secular and the secular leaders insisted on exercising law-making powers. Hence the religions lost control of law-making, were pushed into the corner and relegated to jurisdiction only over areas considered exclusively religious. There are other reasons too why the legal codes are vastly more comprehensive than the religious moral codes. In general, religions provide a generic framework of morality without sophisticated detail.

— **Religions cover private morality** Religious codes are intimate in the sense that they govern your innermost thoughts and how you treat other people short of actually harming them. The law does not and only comes into effect above a threshold.

— **Religious codes are ancient** Most of the religious legal codes belong to past eras. The authentic scriptures of the great religions stopped being written 1500 years ago when they reflected a system of law very different from our own now. The immutability of the original version and the authenticity of the ancient commentaries and additions had the regrettable result that religious moral codes tended to ossify, petrify, many centuries ago, long before the law really began expanding. Their codes were cut off from the future and only looked backwards to the mores of traditional agricultural societies, simple and uncluttered. The law was not similarly held back, notwithstanding frequent conservatism and reluctance to change.

# Is there a Moral Gap in Secular Law?

Religions tend to apply their principles of morality to wicked thoughts without overt expression, and to various unkindnesses and the like which are too low level for the law to interfere with. Does this mean that there is a serious moral gap in secular law which can be covered only by religion?

Thus religious codes cover internal states of mind which are never outwardly expressed, such as hatreds and envy, jealousies and rages, surges of inner xenophobia, unwarranted disgust with others, murderous desires for revenge, evil thoughts which are all hidden from others but which boil in the mind and which are the source of future violence. In one form or another, all of the major religions promote loving kindness, charity and compassionate conduct towards others. For example, the idea of loving your neighbour is central to Christianity. Good conduct is a key motif in the precepts of Buddhism, and the ethic finds expression in Islam. In Hinduism, the discipline is embedded in the concept of duty or *dharma*.

Religions claim jurisdiction over these things and indeed they would argue that the regulation of the intimacies of how people conduct their lives is essential for the survival and wellbeing of societies.

This intrusion was rejected by secular law, because it was beyond the function of law, because it was impractical and because people would not tolerate control by the thought police. Morally censurable conduct, like unreasonable anger, is too vague to be sanctioned by the law. It would not be feasible for the law to impose a general obligation to be nice to other people in your private affairs and then to impose punishment or compensation for violations. Problems of evidence put private rages out of the reach of the law. The law should not impose standards which would send most of the population to jail. Individuals are entitled to privacy. Hence generally the law only regulates conduct which harms someone else.

On the other hand, private emotions are often crucial in legal responsibility. For example, in serious crimes like murder, there has to be a deliberate intent to kill. This is what distinguishes ordinary negligence, like a motor accident, from deliberately driving a car into somebody to kill. The degree of remorse is often relevant to sentencing. The state of knowledge is critical to liability for misrepresentation, ie, whether the untruth was innocent without knowledge of the inaccuracy or was negligent (you did not check) or was knowing—which is a criminal fraud as well as a civil wrong. The savagery of an attack is again material to sentencing.

Secular law does not impose sanctions on low-level expressions of anger or hatred, such as unkindness to others, verbal insults, anger, cruelty, contempt, vindictive remarks, hurtful ostracisms and the like. All of these can be a source of misery to the victims especially if meted out by a spouse or a parent or a child. They can be a source of mass rage and hence mass violence. They can humiliate foreigners or minorities. On a mass scale, they can incite whole nations into violence. Nor does the law insist on kind thoughts.

On the whole, religions do claim jurisdiction over private conduct of this type—through general admonitions to love your neighbour, to be virtuous, to be compassionate.

People's sense of shame at their own cruelty is a control on humiliating and hurtful words and conduct, imbued in many. The law specifically restricts the most egregious breaches—provocations, threatening the peace, racialist slurs, libellous insults. But for unpleasant conduct below the legal threshold, the law leaves it to the parties to resolve their differences.

Still, there is no question that these religious principles fill some sort of gap below the threshold of law. They require private virtue. One can certainly debate whether or not these doctrines are in practice influential in policymaking and the conduct of government. One can also debate whether, when people are kind to each other, they are kind because Jesus or the Buddha said they should be kind or because it is a common sense and learnt reciprocal reality which would exist apart from religions. But there seems little doubt that for many people—one is not quite sure how many—their religion strengthens these moral principles. If that is the case and if religions fade, then the sanctions backing these moral commandments are weakened. This is one of the losses which the peoples of the world suffer if they cease to believe in the supernatural religions.

# A World Without Religion: Auguste Comte and Karl Marx

Many thinkers in the past have imagined a world without religion and what the consequences would be. Two of them—Auguste Comte and Karl Marx—showed startling differences between their philosophies but both failed to see what was wrong with their proposals, the omission staring them in the face.

The 19th-century French philosopher Auguste Comte was born shortly after the French Revolution in 1798 and died in the middle of the 19th century in 1857.

He proposed to replace fading religions with a new religion of humanity. This religion of humanity would do two things—(1) it would teach the best versions of the ethical and moral systems developed by religions, and (2) it would meet the emotional needs of its devotees. He thought it obvious that the ancient religions were improbable and absurd and he saw himself as having a historic opportunity to introduce a new religion.

He planned a huge priesthood (more than 100,000 in France alone) which would comprise both philosophers and writers who would nurture the happiness and morality of the people and give them comfort, consolation and advice on how to live. A network of secular churches would be constructed whose halls would be decorated with the busts of secular saints, such as Cicero, Pericles, Gutenberg, Shakespeare, Descartes and Goethe. Emblazoned up in the west of the church there would be a motto in gold letters—'Know yourself to improve yourself'—the archetype of modern self-help. There would be festivals, as in the religions. Each month in the year would be dedicated to a particular topic, such as marriage or art or science. Each day of that month would be devoted to an individual who had made a significant contribution to the field. Effectively he was drawing on the schedules of Catholicism which provided its worshippers with a daily calendar on what to think about. Comte later began to refer to himself as the 'Great Priest'. Critics said that his philosophy was Catholicism without the religion.

Unhappily for Comte a scheme like that required large amounts of money which were not forthcoming, despite his desperate pleas to kings and queens, bankers and industrialists. All that remained was a converted apartment on the first floor of a building in Paris looking like a chapel.

To his contemporaries, Comte's religion of humanity came across as just another secular cult of the type spawned by the atheism of the French Revolution. He died a disappointed man—the lot of many true visionaries. Comte believed that there were no institutions which could supply the backbone of morality. But he did not appreciate that there already were the vast institutions of the law.

Karl Marx (1818–83) was born in Prussia of well-to-do parents. His mother's family in due course founded the Philips electronics company. Marx was horrified by the oppressed and miserable state of the working class, especially in industrialising Britain. His two famous books were *The Communist Manifesto* (1848), which he wrote jointly with Engels, and the almost unreadable *Das Kapital* (1867–94). He developed a novel theory of history which proposed that capitalism would inevitably lead to two great classes—the bourgeoisie, who lived lazily off the profits they made out of the work of the working classes, and the proletariat. In due course the proletariat would revolt ('you have nothing to lose but your chains') and usher in a society where there would be universal suffrage (after a period of the dictatorship of the proletariat), where all property would be owned in common without any private property, where there would be no classes any more, no money and no state. The state would wither away and all there would be would be collective management by the happy people as a whole. Religion would be banned as the opiate of the masses. The communist philosophy was entirely secular. The family would also be abolished and replaced by a community of women (a proposition once put forward by none other than Plato) and there would of course be no such thing as inheritance.

The first great success was Russia which in 1917 formed the communist USSR, physically by far the largest country in the world. The next really big coup was the People's Republic of China in 1949. By 1980, one in three people lived under a communist dictatorship. Many more countries, especially in Latin America, Africa and India, adopted policies which were communist in effect, although sometimes diluted.

The whole edifice collapsed in the dust of the fall of the Berlin Wall, although nominally dictatorship continued, and still does in such countries as China.

The theory of the stateless state without property or money or government was on a par with the absurdities of the most ridiculous of ideologies. What was really happening was the imposition of a terrible tyranny which in addition was an economic disaster. The utopia failed not because of lack of religion. It failed for many reasons, one of which was that it was politically and economically despotic, and another that there was no rule of law.

What was most shocking about this episode is how many people in the West, especially the well informed, believed that the Marxist philosophy was the answer. This showed with the utmost clarity that basic morality is a quality not necessarily understood by educated people nor by elites.

# The Advance of Secular Law

The fantastic growth of secular laws over the past couple of centuries shows how far religious codes have been left behind in terms of the law necessary to regulate our societies. Secular law has outstripped religious codes. In fact it is probably the case that secular law had outstripped the great religious codes by the time these religious codes came to be written down, at least in the case of Christianity and Islam. Legal morality preceded religious morality.

The code of Hammurabi, a king of Babylon, dated about 1732 BCE, carved on a stele now in the Louvre in Paris and unearthed in 1902, has 282 articles which show a lively comprehension of legal concepts. This remarkable and original code appeared long before the Ten Commandments, the Christian Gospels, the Koran and the crystallisation of the Hindu codes of conduct. It covers an enormous range of subjects—false accusation, theft, methods of proof, mercenaries, tenancy of land, debt, flooding, grazing rights, agents, tavern keepers, custodianship of goods, slander, adultery, divorce, murder, incest, dowry, inheritance, widows, adoption, the duties of children, slaves, servants, barbers, builders and shipbuilders, maritime law, and a great many others.

In accordance with the time, most crimes carried a death penalty and, in the case of women, being 'thrown into the water'. But it is not all primitive darkness. Here are two articles about wives:

> **142** If a woman quarrel with her husband, and say: 'You are not congenial to me', the reasons for her prejudice must be presented. If she is guiltless, and there is no fault on her part, but he leaves and neglects her, then no guilt attaches to this woman, she shall take her dowry and go back to her father's house.

> **145** If a man takes a wife, and she bears him no children and he intend to take another wife: if he take the second wife, and bring her into the house, this second wife shall not be allowed equality with his wife.

Hammurabi was enormously proud of his code. He said:

> I have in Babylon ... in order to bespeak justice in the land, to settle all disputes, and heal all injuries, set up these my precious words, written upon my memorial stone, before the image of me, as king of righteousness.

Then there follows a couple of pages of the terrible things which will happen if anyone changes his code. (Cited from a translation in 1915 by LW King, *The Code of Hammurabi*, on the internet.)

In fact, an earlier code has been unearthed—the laws of Eshnunna—maybe two hundred years older than Hammurabi's code. The earliest extant legal code we have is even older—the Code of Ur-Nammu (c 2100 to c 2050 BCE). The oldest legal code we have heard of from references, although we do not have the original, is the Code of Urukagina, about 2380 to 2360 BCE. All these codes were from Mesopotamia, present-day Iraq. The law of Moses was at least a thousand years later.

The Greeks wrote about the philosophy of law generically, but, unless lost, did not produce a work on practical legal science. That was left to the Romans.

We know little about the Twelve Tables of the Romans, said to have been compiled around 450 BCE, but Roman law was well developed by the time of Christ. By the time that the lawyers of Justinian, the emperor of the eastern empire in Constantinople, now Istanbul, came to codify Roman law in around 533 CE in the form of the Digest and Institutes (the Institutes are a commentary), these codes were arguably ahead in terms of scope and sophistication, richer, than the law set out in the Judaic Torah, the Christian New Testament and the Muslim Koran put together. The Koran was written down more than a century later than Justinian's codification.

The Institutes rely heavily on the Institutes of Gaius completed around 161 CE as a student textbook. A 5th or 6th-century copy was discovered by a German scholar in 1816 underneath a text of St Jerome in the cathedral library in Verona. This text was further authenticated by fragments of the same text found in Egypt in 1973.

The Digest was a huge intellectual achievement. It covered thirteen centuries of the development of Roman law, although 95 per cent of it was from authors writing between 100 and 250 CE. It was the work of 16 men plus their leader Tribonian, and was completed in an astonishing three years. These lawyers condensed over three million words into 150,000 lines which is one-and-a-half times as long as the Bible.

The compilation was introduced into Europe probably via the Arabs in Spain around 1100 and worked on mainly in Bologna University: the leading teacher was Irnerius. The teaching spread to Paris and Oxford. The corpus of Roman law formed the foundation of the law in continental Europe and was highly influential in the development of common law in England. For three hundred years this compilation was studied by law scholars—Glossators and post-Glossators, prestigious lawyers such as Accursus (active 1250) and Bartolus (1314–57). There was a medieval jingle, '*Nemo romanista nisi bartolista*'—'If you are not a follower of Bartolus you're not a scholar of Roman law': see JM Kelly, *A Short History of Western Legal Theory* (Oxford University Press, 1992) p 122. We will see that these European legal systems were adopted later in practically all the countries in the world—around 85 per cent of jurisdictions. The Digest was a piece of rationality which out-distanced the moral codes in the religions and had probably a most profound influence in our societies than any other legal codification.

The religious books were no doubt not intended to be codes of secular law, but the difference shows how the gap between secular and religious law was widening from early on. The gap is now an unbridgeable gulf.

When we come to describe the bare bones of the scope of the great religious codes, we must not expect too much of religious moral systems which were written fifteen or twenty centuries ago. As mentioned, until quite recently views about crime and punishment, misconduct causing harm and breach of contract, sex and family, bankruptcy and non-payment of debts, were very different and these differences were reflected in the religious codes of the times.

The Old Testament bible prescribes the death penalty for adultery, for cursing your parents, and homosexuality: Leviticus 20. Picking up sticks on the Sabbath also carried the death penalty: Numbers 15. The Koran prescribes dire penalties for conduct now considered completely acceptable. For example, Islamic sharia law forbids interest on loans, as indeed did the Roman Catholic Church until de facto relaxation in the 16th century. It seems not unreasonable that a lender should be entitled to charge for the hire of money just as for the hire of any other asset. Sharia law prescribes the cutting off of hands for theft and stoning of a woman for adultery.

One cannot reprimand religions for the barbarism of their moral codes in modern ages since they often represented the views of societies at the time which were also reflected in secular codes. Capital punishment for serious crimes was a standard feature of secular codes until quite recently.

The problem arises if, as is the case with both Christian and Muslim fundamentalists, devotees believe that these moral strictures still apply in the modern world on the basis that the scriptures are the unchangeable dictates of God, dictated by God himself to scribes and therefore permanently valid until God amends the text. Unlike this approach, the law is inherently capable of development and change to meet new circumstances. At times you could almost say that the legal sensitivity to change has been too quick and volatile.

One can sum up at this point by saying that modern law is the successor to religious law and probably also the predecessor of religious law, at least as regards the codification of legal principles.

My objective in the next series of chapters is to describe both the ethical and legal systems of the main religions and then to take you on a tour of secular laws so that we can compare. But first I must delineate the outlines of a foundation of secular legal ideology—the rule of law.

# 5

# *What is the Rule of Law?*

## Introduction

Many centuries after the foundation of our societies, there was another ideological development, an ideology which was extraordinarily slow in its arrival, which crept up only in tiny advancing waves over centuries, which is fundamental to our societies and our survival, and which practically everyone in the world aspires to and believes in. This is the rule of law.

Without the rule of law, we would live in primitive barbarism, a state of anarchy and fear. Any kind of prosperity or progress or safety would be impossible and our lives would truly be savage and stunted.

The rule of law covers, for example, freedom from arbitrary arrest, torture and state killings, freedom from uncompensated expropriations, and freedom from state-sponsored arbitrary violence. It covers the installation of an independent judiciary. By rule of law, I therefore mean, not the law generally, but basic constitutional and human rights.

## Law as a Source of Empowerment

The law is an instrument whereby we are empowered and liberated, whereby we can devise our own destiny.

If the rule of law prevails, then we can devote ourselves to peaceable enterprise and to the pursuit of happiness. The law empowers us to make contracts which are enforceable, to form a company which can own a business and protect us against the debts of the business, to vote in elections so as to participate in determining policy. The law protects our inventions and literary works by patents and copyrights so that our inventiveness and creativity are not taken from us. The law protects our private property so that it is not despoiled by government expropriations or private theft. The law provides the legal framework for money so that we may use it as a means of exchange or store it. The law strengthens us and makes possible what was previously impossible.

So the law is not just a system of restrictions backed by force. The law delivers freedom and enhances our potential to control our destiny. If the law chains us, it does so in order to liberate us.

Our duties to those who come after us and the preservation of their future and our duties to resolve the puzzles and riddles of our existence so that we can redeem ourselves requires both the restriction and the liberation of the law.

# Essence of the Rule of Law

One of the central concepts of the rule of law is that nobody is above the law, an idea which appeared in the writings of the ancient Greeks and Romans. As a commentator said, 'Be you never so high, the Law is above you'. Hence it does not matter whether you are a king, a president or a prime minister, or a chief justice of the Supreme Court, you are subject to the law like everyone else. As stated by Tom Bingham in his excellent and succinct book, *The Rule of Law* (Penguin, 2010), the core of the principle is that all persons and authorities within the state, whether public or private, should be subject to and entitled to the benefit of laws publically made, taking effect (generally) only in the future so they are not retrospective, and publicly administered in the courts by an independent and impartial judge in accordance with natural laws of due process. It follows that even the sovereign who makes the laws is subject to the laws. The English philosopher John Locke said in 1690 'Wherever law ends, tyranny begins': Second Treatise on Government, chapter XVII s 202 (1690). Tom Bingham was, among other things, Lord Chief Justice of England and senior Law Lord of the United Kingdom. I draw freely on his book in parts of this chapter.

The rule of law includes such principles as that the law should be accessible and predicable so that people know what to do and so that they can enter into transactions involving great amounts without the result being speculative, that public officials should exercise their powers within the law and not as a matter of arbitrary or unreasonable discretion, that generally the law should apply equally to all except where obviously different, such as children. It should be possible to resolve disputes fairly without prohibitive costs or unreasonable delay. There should be an international legal order including civilised principles of law.

Hence the rule of law is a set of ethical and moral principles.

# Historical Origins of the Rule of Law

Plato, not otherwise renowned for his views on free market economies or democracy, in his *Laws* makes the main speaker say:

> For wherever in a state the law is subservient and impotent, over that state I see ruin impending; but wherever the law is lord over the magistrates, the magistrates are servants to the law, there I descry salvation and all the blessings that the gods bestow on states (*Laws*, 715d).

We do not hear much about a separate profession of lawyers in ancient Greece or the development of a separate study of practical law. Rome was wholly different. Here is Cicero on the law:

> [L]aw is the highest reason, implanted in nature ... Law is understanding, whose natural function is to command right conduct and forbid wrongdoing ... The origin of Justice is to be found in Law, for law is a natural force (*De Legibus* 1.6. 18–19).

Later he said that 'laws were invented for the safety of citizens, the preservation of states, and the tranquillity and happiness of human life' (*De Legibus* 2.5.11). He added that a state without law would be like a human body without a mind and that we obey the law in order that we may be free.

Anglo-American principles of the rule of law start with the astonishing Magna Carta, the Great Charter signed by King John at Runnymede by the Thames under pressure from the barons in 1215, a document frequently quoted in the US Supreme Court as in the English courts. A translation of chapters 39 and 40 sets out principles of profound emotional power:

> 39. No free man shall be seized or imprisoned or stripped of his rights or possessions, or outlawed or exiled, or deprived of his standing in any other way, nor will we proceed with force against him or send others to do so, except by the lawful judgment of his equals or by the law of the land.

> 40. To no one will he sell, to no one deny or delay right or justice.

Although King John took no notice of Magna Carta, it stuck. It was subsequently backed up with compulsory orders for the release of suspects who had not been charged—the writ of habeas corpus—literally meaning 'that you have the body'. This was followed by the Bill of Rights 1689 signed by the new King William III on expulsion of James II after the English Revolution of 1688–89, and by the Constitution of the United States. This announced that man had certain inalienable rights, among them life, liberty and the pursuit of happiness, and that the purpose of government was to guarantee those rights. This was followed by the French Declaration of the Rights of Man and the Citizen 1789, by the first Ten Amendments to the US Constitution taking effect in 1791 and known as the American Bill of Rights, by major developments in the law relating to war and led mainly by Grotius (1583–1645), by the Universal of Declaration of Human Rights adopted by the General Assembly of the United Nations in Paris in 1948, and by many other regional declarations of human rights and other expansions of the basic text. The UN Declaration was not legally binding but it was the inspiration for the European Convention on Human Rights 1950.

The theory of natural rights has not gone without its critics. The philosopher Jeremy Bentham (1748–1832) wrote an impassioned attack on natural rights in 1791, apparently as a put-down of the *Rights of Man* by the American revolutionary Tom Paine. He insisted that the purpose of government was to restrain selfish passion but that the grant of natural rights would only add force to those passions which were already too strong. Others since have ridiculed decisions of quixotic human rights courts and attacked societies which think more of their rights and entitlements than their duties. There are constant arguments over the collision between an individual's rights and the protection of the state, between freedom of speech and the ban on religious or other discrimination. The field is often highly politicised. Happily these hot debates are catered for by the right to freedom of expression.

# A Codification of the Rule of Law

These days, the rule of law is largely identified with the human rights summarised in the various declarations and conventions. I summarise in outline the terms of the European Convention on Human Rights of 1950 because it is legally binding and because it represents a succinct statement of the state of the art. It has been signed by over 40 European states and there is a European Court of Human Rights. It might just as well have been called the Rule of Law Convention.

**The right to life** 'Everyone's right to life shall be protected by law' except, for example, when taking life is absolutely necessary to defend another person: article 2. If you do not have a right to be alive, then you can enjoy no other right. This right is implemented by, for example, the criminalisation of murder and the prohibition on euthanasia. It forbids arbitrary executions and genocide.

**The prohibition of torture** 'No one should be subjected to torture or to inhumane or degrading treatment or punishment': article 3. One of the main objects was to prohibit torturing of suspects in order to extract a confession. The rule is absolute and admits no exceptions.

In former times, torture was routinely used by the authorities in criminal trials around the world in order to get confessions and in some parts of the world it still is. Torture was abolished in England in 1640 by case law (subsequently confirmed by statute) in France in 1789, in certain Italian states between 1786 and 1859, in Prussia in 1740, in Denmark in 1771, in Russia in 1801 (but occasionally used until 1847) and in the United States from 1791.

In 2000 the Human Rights Court held that the deportation of a woman to Iran who would have been at risk of punishment by stoning was a violation. There have been many similar such cases.

**Prohibition of slavery and forced labour** 'No one shall be held in slavery or servitude ... No one shall be forced to perform forced or compulsory labour': article 4. There are some exclusions, such as work in prison and compulsory military service.

**Right to liberty and security** 'Everyone has the right to liberty and security of person': article 5. There are exceptions relating to a detention on court order following conviction and the like. The right to security requires the state to seek to protect the personal security of individuals from riots, gangs, arbitrary police brutality, civil disorder and the like, ie, the maintenance of a non-violent society.

**Right to a fair trial** In civil and criminal trials 'Everyone is entitled to a fair and public hearing within a reasonable time by an independent and impartial tribunal established by law. Judgement shall be pronounced publicly [subject to exceptions] ... Everyone charged with a criminal offence shall be presumed innocent until proved guilty according to law': article 6. The accused has certain minimum rights, such as a right to be informed promptly of the accusation, to have time and facilities to prepare a defence, to have a lawyer, to examine witnesses and to have an interpreter.

This right to a fair trial is at the heart of the rule of law and is often referred to as due process. The judiciary must be free from political interference and bribe-taking and there must also be an independent legal profession which is not subject to political pressures. Those accused of criminal offences are entitled to disclosure of material favourable to them which the prosecution has—'cards face up on the table'. There are many cases where these protections are not observed, particularly in relation to regulatory law where the criminal and due process requirements are often ignored.

**No punishment without law** 'No one shall be held guilty of any criminal offence on account of any act or omission which did not constitute a criminal offence under national and international law at the time when it was committed': article 7. The rule is clear and has been around since the Romans: you should not be punished for an act which was not criminal when you did it.

**Right to respect for private and family life** 'Everyone has the right to respect for his private and family life, his home and his correspondence': article 8. This is a right to privacy. But there are wide exceptions. Article 8(2) provides that there should be no interference

> by a public authority with the exercise of this right except such as is in accordance with the law and is necessary in a democratic society in the interests of national security, public safety or the economic well-being of the country, for the prevention of disorder or crime for the protection of health and morals, or for the protection of the rights and freedom of others.

Accordingly there are three conditions. The reality of the application of this article is no longer that 'a man's house is his castle' and that people's privacy is protected against intrusive surveillance by the government. Not long ago an English pamphlet described 266 ways in which the state can enter your home—a large underestimate.

**Freedom of thought, conscience and religion** 'Everyone has the right to freedom of thought, conscience and religion', subject to exceptions such as public safety, public order, health or morals or the protection of the rights and freedom of others: article 9. The origin of this principle lies in the terrible wars of religion and the sectarian violence of past centuries, wars and violence which are still with us. In addition the article underlies the idea that you should have the freedom to choose your own ethics provided that it is not harmful to others. Although courts have sometimes struggled to decide which religions qualify for protection, the main intent is clear. These exceptions set limits on these freedoms so that, for example, all Western societies do not permit human sacrifice or the duty on widows to throw themselves on the funeral pyres of their husbands or female genital mutilation. However Sikhs who have to wear a comb in uncut hair and so wear a turban are in England exempt from the general requirement to wear a crash helmet when riding a motorcycle. The freedoms include the freedom to change or manifest your religion.

**Freedom of expression** 'Everyone has the right to freedom of expression': article 10. Censorship is prohibited. There are wide exceptions on the lines of those in article 8 and article 9. One of the most urgent issues is whether freedom of expression includes the right to insult religions and also the protection of confidential information. Another issue is libel. The freedom of the press is essential for democratic societies, notwithstanding occasional abuse.

**Freedom of assembly and association** 'Everyone has the right to peaceful assembly and to freedom of association with others', subject to the usual exceptions: article 11. In other words, we can socialise with whom we like and form pressure groups with whom we like. People are social animals who live in villages, towns and cities. You can't be ordered to live alone without company, without any social contact, as a quarantined hermit on a pole. The freedom to seek good company or the company of those of similar views is basic to a happy life and it is also necessary for society to function.

As the philosopher-theologian St Thomas Aquinas commented 'One man alone could not provide himself with all his needs; one man, of himself, could not live an adequate life. It is therefore natural to man, that he should live in a society of many' (*De regimine principum* I.I).

**Right to marry** 'Men and women of marriageable age have the right to marry and to found a family, according to the national laws governing the exercise of this right': article 12. A state may regulate age, capacity and procedural rules but otherwise there are no exceptions. This article targets the prohibition of marriage between those of different races or religions or castes and also forced sterilisation.

**Right to an effective remedy** 'Everyone whose rights and freedoms as set forth in this Convention are violated shall have an effective remedy before a national authority notwithstanding that the violation has been committed by persons acting in an official capacity': article 13.

**Non-discrimination** 'The enjoyment of the rights and freedoms set forth in this Convention shall be secured without discrimination on any ground such as sex, race, colour, language, religion, political or other opinion, national or social origin, association with a national minority, property, birth or other status': article 14. There are no exceptions. The list is non-exclusive but the violation must be within the ambit of a convention article.

The effect is to give compulsion to the principle of the equality of the law. It does not matter if you are rich or poor, or belong to an unpopular group, or are a far left communist or a far right landowner. It is precisely the unpopular minorities who have to be protected by the rule of law. History has many other examples of legal inequality—the legal subordination of women, the immunity of clergy, the exemption of nobles from taxation, and the exclusion of this religion or that ethnicity from official posts.

**Protection of property** 'Every natural or legal person is entitled to the peaceful enjoyment of his possessions. No one shall be deprived of his possessions except in the public interest and subject to the conditions provided for by law and by the general principles of international law': First Protocol, article 1. There are qualifications, for example, controlling the use of property in accordance with the general interest, such as planning restrictions.

This article prohibits the arbitrary confiscation of people's property or possessions without compensation. Expropriation, for example, to build an airport, is allowed everywhere provided there is prompt, adequate and effective compensation. It would be intolerable if a state official or some other person could lawfully occupy your house or drive your car around or help themselves to your food. 'Hey, pal, I like your jacket. Thanks a lot, better than mine, suits me, don't you think? Ah, what's this in the pocket? Keys to your house! Bigger than my one-bedroom flat. No need to remove your stuff, I'm happy to look after it all'.

The great religions were not generally hostile to private property or dogmatically communistic. Their ire was reserved for the uncharitable rich, commercialism such as usury and speculators.

One of the earliest justifications of private property was written by St Thomas Aquinas: *Summa Theologica*, 2a 2ae 57.2. The English philosopher John Locke (1632–1704) was one of the prophets of private property and the German philosopher Immanuel Kant in 1797 presented private property as necessitated by practical reason. The French Declaration of the Rights of Man 1789 enthroned property as 'an inviolable and sacred right'.

There has always from very early times been an anti-property cult, epitomised by the phrase coined by Pierre-Joseph Proudhon (1809–65), 'Property is theft'. Nevertheless even Proudhon denounced communism.

**Right to education:** 'No person shall be denied the right to education': First Protocol, article 2. But parents can choose education in conformity with their own religious and philosophical convictions. There have been many cases on such matters as compulsory sex education, religious education and corporal punishment. Effectively education up to a certain age should be compulsory and access to education should be open to all.

**Other rights** Other rights are often promoted, for example, the right to food, the right of self-determination and the right to free elections. But the above are the generally recognised core rights. An essential component of the rule of law in practice is democracy. Experience shows that it is generally not possible to realise the principles of the rule of law in an autocracy. This is a subject to which we will return later.

# The Rule of Law in Public International Law: The Law of Nations

As a general proposition, the law between states has principles, however diluted, which are on the above lines. It is certainly true that there are many violations of these rules by sovereign states but that does not mean that we do not have to have them. It is also true that the ability to enforce these internationally is limited by reason of the weakness of international courts, but again we still have to have the rules so that at least other means of pressure can be brought to bear.

The rule of law also extends to the law relating to war where again the principles are often not observed. The United Nations Charter forbids war in articles 3 and 4 except in self-defence. The basic idea is that the United Nations has a monopoly of the use of force. It often delegates the use of force to countries willing to undertake the task.

The International Criminal Court can hear cases regarding genocide, crimes against humanity, war crimes and crimes of aggression under article 5 of its 1998 statute. But not everybody is a member—not the United States, Russia or China. It has no powers of arrest, and no police force.

The International Court of Justice set up in 1945 is a continuation of the Permanent Court of International Justice established in 1921. But the ability of the ICJ to judge cases depends on the consent of the parties (article 36) so its powers are very much reduced.

The first great exponent of the law of war and peace was the prodigiously precocious Dutch Protestant Hugo Grotius (1583–1645) whose most famous work *On the Law of War and Peace* was published in 1625. The book was written after the outbreak of the Thirty Years War in Europe. Grotius explained his motives:

> I observed a lack of restraint in relation to war, such as even barbarous nations should be ashamed of; I observed that men rush to arms for slight causes, or no cause at all, and that when arms have once been taken up there is no longer any respect for law, divine or human; it is as if, in accordance with a general decree, frenzy had openly been let loose for the committing of all crimes (*Prolegomena*, 28).

The rules of law relating to war are now mainly contained in the Hague and Geneva Conventions, as well as other conventions, treaties and customs. They are principally designed to protect non-combatants, such as the wounded and the sick, prisoners of war and civilians; to ban certain weapons causing unnecessary suffering such as poison gases and dum-dum bullets; to prohibit the taking of hostages, the use of torture, illegal executions and reprisals; to outlaw the indiscriminate destruction of property; and to preserve cultural objects and places of worship. Accordingly, war is permitted within limits but the abusive extension of war to those not directly involved could attract a criminal trial, notwithstanding the patchiness of international criminal jurisdiction.

One of the main contemporary issues is whether terrorists should be treated as combatants so that the normal protections do not apply to them, as is the case in the United States in relation to the 9/11 terrorist attacks, or whether they should be treated as subject to the normal criminal law, as was the case with the treatment by the United Kingdom of Northern Irish terrorists in the last quarter of the 20th century. Benjamin Franklin famously observed that 'He who would put security before liberty deserves neither'. Another issue is official surveillance and the conflict with privacy. The basic issue is whether civilised states should demonstrate their civilisation and their rule of law, notwithstanding fearful threats of terrorism, or whether the threats are so severe that it is right to characterise the situation as war and to remove rule of law protections.

# Measuring the Rule of Law

We have seen that the rule of law includes such things as the absence of expropriations without compensation, governmental or judicial corruption, high crime levels and a lack of personal security, civil war or terrorism, political killings, arbitrary arrests, a lack of independence of the judiciary, political instability and the abusive exercise of power.

There is a difference between (1) the written or black letter law or what the law says—law on the books, and (2) how the law is applied and what the legal environment is like in practice, ie, the legal infrastructure of a jurisdiction, how the government behaves and adherence to the rule of law.

For example, as regards legal infrastructure, the basic law in Congo Kinshasa and Belgium derives from the same roots, but the application is very different. There are many similarities between the written legal systems of, say, Malawi and England (English common law), or Brazil and Portugal (French Napoleonic), or Turkey and Switzerland (Turkey borrowed Switzerland's commercial codes), but there are significant differences in doing business in these countries so far as the application of the law is concerned.

The conditions necessary for the rule of law to operate are hard to come by. There is a direct correlation between the observance of the rule of law and the wealth of a society, the freedom of the society from penury and destitution. This remarkable conclusion is dramatically shown by the country ranking tables compiled by organisations which prepare indexes which measure legal efficiency and the rule of law. Some of the most prominent indexes are the World Bank Doing Business indexes, indexes prepared by the Heritage Foundation on economic freedom and indexes prepared by the World Economic Forum on global competitiveness. There are also the corruption perceptions indexes prepared by Transparency International and the rule of law indexes of the World Justice Project.

| | 1 | 2 | 3 | 4 | 5 | 6 | 7 | 8 | 9 | 10 | 11 | 12 | 13 | 14 | 15 | 16 | 17 | 18 | 19 | 20 | 21 | 22 | 23 | 24 |
|---|---|---|---|---|---|---|---|---|---|---|---|---|---|---|---|---|---|---|---|---|---|---|---|---|
| | GDP | HDI | World Bank Doing Business 2013 | | | | | | | | | Heritage Foundation 2012 | | | | World Economic Forum 2013 | | | | World Justice Project 2012/2013 | | | | Transparency International |
| Hong Kong | | | | | | | | | | | | | | | | | | | | | | | | |
| New Zealand | | | | | | | | | | | | | | | | | | | | | | | | |
| Singapore | | | | | | | | | | | | | | | | | | | | | | | | |
| UK | | | | | | | | | | | | | | | | | | | | | | | | |
| Panama | | | | | | | | | | | | | | | | | | | | | | | | |
| Poland | | | | | | | | | | | | | | | | | | | | | | | | |
| Portugal | | | | | | | | | | | | | | | | | | | | | | | | |
| Turkey | | | | | | | | | | | | | | | | | | | | | | | | |
| Bolivia | | | | | | | | | | | | | | | | | | | | | | | | |
| Dom Rep | | | | | | | | | | | | | | | | | | | | | | | | |
| Ecuador | | | | | | | | | | | | | | | | | | | | | | | | |
| Philippines | | | | | | | | | | | | | | | | | | | | | | | | |
| Chad | | | | | | | | | | | | | | | | | | | | | | | | |
| Côte d'Ivoire | | | | | | | | | | | | | | | | | | | | | | | | |
| Eritrea | | | | | | | | | | | | | | | | | | | | | | | | |
| Zimbabwe | | | | | | | | | | | | | | | | | | | | | | | | |

**Legal infrastructure and rule of law table** A selective snapshot of some of these indexes, extracted from full tables which I and a colleague have prepared covering about 200 countries are shown in colour-coded form in the table on p 62. The indexes represented are set out in the table in the box as follows:

1. GDP per capita
2. Human development index

**World Bank Doing Business**
3. Starting a business
4. Construction permits
5. Employing workers
6. Registering property
7. Getting credit
8. Protecting investors
9. Paying taxes
10. Trading across borders
11. Enforcing contracts

**Heritage Foundation**
12. Investment freedom
13. Financial freedom

14. Property rights
15. Economic freedom overall

**World Economic Forum**
16. Property rights
17. Judicial independence
18. Court efficiency
19. Global competitiveness overall

**World Justice Project**
20. Stable laws
21. Expropriation
22. Independent courts
23. Overall rule of law

**Transparency International**
24. Corruption perceptions

The indicators chosen from the indexes produced by the Heritage Foundation, World Economic Forum and the World Justice Project are selected from much larger arrays. For example, World Economic Forum has 12 main sets which in turn are divided into nearly 200 variables.

The colouring method I use is chainsaw art. Each index is divided into four with the best at the top and the worst at the bottom.

— The top quarter is coloured blue.
— The next quarter is coloured green.
— The third quarter is coloured yellow.
— The final quarter is coloured red.

You could rightly say that there are many limitations to the indexes. Some of the judgements are subjective. The indexes often do not distinguish between black letter law (or the written law) and how the law is applied, so that there is a commingling of concepts. If one measures too many things at once, one might end up with simply a blurred noise without sharp tune. There are many exceptions and qualifications to the general picture.

But the fundamental result which leaps out from the colours is that the rule of law is correlated to wealth in most cases. The tables list the countries according to GDP per capita. The GDP tables group the high-income countries with a high GDP per capita as blue (shown in the first column), those with a medium to high income as green, those with medium to low income as yellow, and those with a low per capita income as red. They therefore compare the country rankings in the indexes of legal infrastructure or legal efficiency or the rule of law according to GDP per capita.

The tables show that countries which have a high GDP per capita tend to have a good legal infrastructure and rule of law. A blue GDP per capita produces mainly blues in the indexes. On the other hand, very poor countries have a weak legal infrastructure and weak rule of law. Red GDP per capita countries have a red legal infrastructure or rule of law. The other ranks in the middle—green and yellow—tend to follow the same pattern. Accordingly GDP per capita or wealth is a powerful indicator of the rule of law. Poor countries—those where the people are struggling to survive, where they are hungry, where they lack clean water and sanitation—have poor rule of law and legal infrastructure and rich countries have a sound rule of law and an efficient legal infrastructure.

Many have argued that the rule of law comes before wealth in the sense that progress depends first on having an adequate rule of law. One of the countries most cited is Britain in the industrial revolution. It is equally possible to argue that the rule of law depends on prosperity—the other way round. It seems most likely that the rule of law and prosperity go hand in hand, depending on the country. The need for the rule of law is what development economists (or some of them) have been saying all along.

## Conclusion on the Rule of Law

And so there we have it. All of this codification and the widespread (but not complete) international acceptance of the principles have largely been an achievement of the 19th and 20th centuries with much more ancient roots in a longer perspective. They represent a coming of age of the ideology of secular law and an assertion of the civilised values which are necessary to survive and which are necessary for happiness and prosperity. The presence or absence of the basic rule of law touches everybody in their daily lives in a way in which religion does not. Whether you live in a violent and lawless society or a peaceable one is the framework of your existence. That is why the principles of the rule of law are so deeply moving: these maxims, precepts, canons, commandments, so simple in their purity, illuminate our existence.

# 6

# *The Families of Religion: Western Religions*

## Introduction

In this and the next chapter I summarise the main religions in the world so that we start on a secure foundation of particularity. We have to understand the religions so that we can understand their role in morality and hence in ensuring our survival.

This is a tale of the rise of religions, a tale of their ascent to power and dominance. For a few religions it is also a tale of their collapse and virtual disappearance. For all it is a tale of the rise of doctrines, some of which the modern world questions. For those religions which have collapsed or are so diminished as to attract only a tiny following—for example, Zoroastrianism, Taoism and Jainism—the issue for us is whether there are lessons to be learnt from them as to the reasons for their collapse. The current threat to religions is not a new development. History is littered with the dusty ruins of fallen creeds about the gods.

I divide the families of religion into Western and Eastern traditions. The Western tradition comprises Zoroastrianism (which scarcely still survives), Judaism (a small national religion, important because of the role it has played in the development of other religions), Christianity and Islam.

In the next chapter I cover Eastern religions, Hinduism and Buddhism. In each case, I mention their main offshoots and sects but not in any great detail.

There are differences between the Eastern and Western traditions. The Western traditions are all monotheistic, that is, they have one god, and they all propose that the human soul will go to heaven or hell on death. On the other hand, Hinduism is polytheistic and in the case of Buddhism there is a question about whether the notion of God or gods is central at all. In both Hinduism and Buddhism, instead of the soul on death going to heaven or hell, the soul is reincarnated in another being, depending on how you behave in this life.

## Zoroastrianism: The First Religious Genius

We begin with Zoroastrianism because it advanced key ideas, is symbolic of what we are talking about and is extremely ancient—although we do not know

Zoroaster's dates for sure. It is true that Zoroastrianism is almost a dead religion with fewer than 200,000 adherents worldwide. Yet it was a crucial theology in the development of religion, a precocious philosophy which worked it out at a very early date and which deserved to survive. But it was defeated by history.

Very little is known about Zoroaster himself. The estimates of his date of birth vary by 1300 years—between about 1800 BCE and 550 BCE, with about 1200 BCE being a compromise date. The doubts arise because the dates of his life given by the Greeks of c 628 BCE to c 551 BCE are thought by some commentators to be a fiction invented by the Greeks to support the theory that the Greek mathematician Pythagoras studied astronomy with Zoroaster. They say that linguistic and other evidence points to a much earlier date. Zoroaster is a Greek corruption of the Persian Zarathustra. He seems to have been born and to have lived his life in the north-eastern part of Iran or in Afghanistan.

In order to put the date 1200 in historical context, it was about this time that the Trojan War was fought between the Mycenaeans and the Trojans, that the exodus of the Israelites from Egypt took place, that the Ten Commandments as the law of Moses were promulgated, that the Dorian Greeks arrived in Greece, and that the Shang dynasty in China gave way to the Zhou dynasty. Populations were small, cities were tiny and most of the people were pastoral or engaged in agriculture. Writing was primitive—a true alphabetical script was introduced in the eastern Mediterranean only around 1075 BCE. The year 1200 is about 45 lives of 70 years each back from now.

If the earlier date of about 1200 for Zoroaster's birth is right, then Zoroaster would be the first great prophet of the monotheistic tradition which led to Judaism, Christianity and Islam, all springing up in that region. It is true that the Egyptian pharaoh Akhenaten instituted a primitive monotheism for a short period in Egypt around 1363 BCE but this was deficient on moral teaching. It is also true that Moses, who crystallised monotheistic Judaism, was probably active around 1235 BCE and that the legendary figure of Abraham of Ur may have been alive around 1800 BCE. They may have a claim to precedence. It is always hard to work out who was first and who influenced whom in those obscure times without a properly recorded history. Unquestionably the tenets of the Zoroastrian belief look remarkably like the tenets of the three great religions of the region.

**Zoroaster's teachings** Zoroaster proposed that there was only one god called Ahura Mazda, meaning the Wise Lord, who represented the good and who was the creator of the universe. He was aided by a holy spirit and six holy immortals who were emanations of this one god—possibly a concession to polytheism. The forces of good were opposed by an evil spirit—the original Satan or Devil—called Angra Mainyu—'the Lie'. Life was a struggle between good and evil, to be fought out here on earth. Zoroaster may have come to this view by reason of the slaughter and injustice occasioned by the wars and tribal fighting which were happening around him in his younger days.

The value of that insight was that it pierced to the centre of what was really going on, the centre of what religions sought to do or should have sought to do, which is that survival depends on the triumph of 'good' over 'evil'. It recognised that good might not always win—something which was obvious then and has been obvious since then. It accorded with people's sense of reality, that people are a mixture of good and evil. It was a template of the most powerful and important idea in philosophy and the moral purpose of life, expressed with shattering simplicity and directness, the truth in one line, the meaning of life in a few words. And all that at a time when the rest of the world was befuddled and misled by any number of moral misconceptions put about by primitive religious elders and shamans.

Good was to be achieved by good thoughts, good words and good deeds. So the religion recognised the ultimate importance of private mental morality as the foundation of public morality. The ethical approach had two other things in its favour. First, the religion was life-affirming, rather than life-denying—it was not an ascetic cult which despised the world and withdrew from it. That must surely be right. Secondly, the religion believed in progress and improvement in the sense that the combined efforts of the righteous would gradually wear down and weaken evil so as to bring about the triumph of the good. That also must be right.

In addition, the one god was not a fairy in the sky but was imageless, a force, not a person. The battle against anthropomorphism was commenced in earnest, to be continued by Judaism and Islam. The anti-iconic concept was intelligent for the time because it stated that good is a moral concept, a force, not a human-like individual. It took exceptional boldness and originality to work that out. You could say that the dematerialisation was not complete and that later there were relapses, but the idea was there, though sometimes misted over.

Zoroaster expressed the forces of good and evil as the forces of light versus darkness, an astonishing intuition. Astonishing because the image expressed what we discovered only thousands of years later—that light was an electromagnetic force, an emanation of one of the four forces of nature, and that the atom is made up of positive and negative charges. It was almost as if Zoroaster knew, but could not justify. If that is right, then Zoroaster was the father of physics. 'At the beginning of time Ohrmazd created the world out of his own substance, which is eternal light'. This passage from a Zoroastrian middle Persian piece text on cosmology, the Bundahishn, compiled in the 10th century CE based on much older traditions, is a proto-scientific summary of the theory of creation which is still in vogue. See a letter from Professor Almut Hintze in the *Financial Times* in 2014.

The fundamental belief was accompanied by a vision of the end of the world in a mighty battle, the terrifying resurrection of the souls of all the dead, and a cataclysmic judgement day when the good would join the one god and live in eternal happiness, and the bad would be damned to live in eternal suffering, an idea picked up with vigour by the successors to Zoroaster.

The judgement day was presented in an image of great poignancy. This was the image of the Chinvat Bridge. This bridge stretched from the cosmic mountain, which is at the centre of the universe, to paradise. The souls are judged when they are at the bridge. If they have been good, they are presented with an image of a beautiful young girl. If they have been bad, the image is of a hag (in those days heaven seemed to be for men only). If they have been bad, the bridge narrows to a razor's edge and the bad souls slither off into the raging fires of hell. The good pass through to heaven. This image ranks alongside the sorrowfulness of Plato's image of the cave—we are all in a cave and can see the shadows of reality reflected on the walls of the cave, but not reality itself.

**The undeserved fate of Zoroastrianism** So why then did this religion not succeed when its competitors did?

At one point the religion did well. Generally for a religion to gain traction, it had to be backed by a strong secular power. Apart from the initial support of a local king in Zoroaster's lifetime, Zoroastrianism achieved that essential impetus when it was adopted as the state religion by the ruler Darius I of Persia (548–486 BCE) of the dynasty of the Achaeminids. It was Darius who was defeated by the Athenians at Marathon in 490 BCE, an event which inspired the marathon race.

The Jews were for a time subjects of the Persians because Babylon, where the Jews were in captivity, was a Persian possession. Both religions were mono-theistic. In 538 BCE Cyrus occupied Jerusalem and offered to let all the Jews in Babylon return to their native land if they wished. It is impossible now to know whether Zoroaster influenced the Israelites, or the Israelites influenced Zoroaster—unless we find something underneath the sands or in a cave in Iraq or Iran or Afghanistan.

The Achaeminid dynasty was defeated by the conquering Alexander the Great, a blow which weakened the religion. Subsequently the Parthians from north-east Iran adopted Zoroastrianism as their state religion too in the period from about 129 BCE to 224 CE, but it took the second Persian Empire of the Sassanians (224–651 CE) to reinvigorate the now somewhat adulterated religion.

The Sassanians compiled the teachings of Zoroaster, previously transmitted orally, in written form in 21 volumes, known as the *Azvesta*. All these were subsequently lost. There were attempts to rewrite the scriptures in the 9th and 10th centuries CE but the oldest surviving manuscript is dated 1323. The effect is that we do not know for sure whether what we have represents the original thinking or whether it was reformulated. By the time the confused priests of Zoroastrianism were asked by religious comparativists in the 20th century to explain, they had to admit shamefacedly that verifiable truth was all gone, and all that remained were traditions, oral testimony and belief.

The Sassanians in turn succumbed to the militant might of the Muslims, a new aggressive faith, which after another three hundred years or so dominated Persia. The persecution of the Zoroastrians forced a group of them to emigrate ultimately to India, just as later a handful of Puritans emigrated to America. In India they eventually ended up in the commercial centre Bombay (now Mumbai) as the Parsees (Persians), leaving behind an impoverished and oppressed rump in Iran. The Parsees under the British Raj built themselves up into a formidable group of elite businessmen and professionals. One could say, ditto the Puritans on *The Mayflower*. Except that the Puritans and their successors did rather better. The Indian business family Tata are Parsees, as was the singer Freddie Mercury, born in Zanzibar. Jinnah, the founder of Pakistan, had a Parsee wife and was looked after by a Parsee doctor in his battle against cancer during the negotiations for the partition of India and Pakistan on independence from Britain in 1947.

**Conclusion on Zoroastrianism** The teachings of Zoroaster were one of the seminal ideologies of ancient times, an extraordinary achievement. Yet, this groundbreaking philosophy has ended up with a few thousand devotees in India, a few thousand devotees in Iran and a scattered diaspora of emigrants elsewhere—a melancholy end. It was finally obliterated by the conquistadors of a new religion, Islam.

Or was it? The rituals, the priests and the formal denomination may have all but gone. But ideas are more powerful than ceremonies and names. The ideas live on, three thousand years later in Judaism and in the two most triumphant religions in the world—Christianity and Islam.

An offshoot of Zoroastrianism also appeared in the form of the Roman soldiers' religion Mithraism which was overturned by Christianity in the famous events of 312 CE, a fateful historical accident. Or stroke of destiny? That subject is for later discussion.

# Judaism: Religion as Identity

It would be difficult to overestimate the importance of the religion of the Jews in world history.

The religion of Judaism was a foundation stone of both Christianity and Islam, the two largest religious in the world. Christianity was initially a Jewish sect. It took over the basic precepts of the religion of the Jews as its base. The Muslim Koran reads like another version of the religion, updated to take into its scope the arrival of Jesus Christ—who was treated simply as another prophet—and then the life and teachings of Muhammad. All three religions were and are monotheistic—they have one god.

Christianity and Islam put together completely dominate the religious world in terms of numbers and impact on history. The wars of religion between these two faiths—or rather the lifestyles they represent—have an enormous impact on modern events and the dangers we face. The modern Jewish state, Israel, continues to stand in the eye of the storm.

The religion of the Jews raises a fundamental question. The Jews have been enslaved, persecuted or oppressed for most of the past three thousand years, with only occasional periods of independence. They have suffered terrible adversities, been victimised, ill-treated, scorned and spurned. Theirs is the history of the underdog, a powerless, helpless creature, beaten by its various masters as it pleased them. Yet they endured, kept their identity and their spirit—they survived.

Probably the main factor which preserved them and their identity was their religion, a religion of such power and rationality that it could withstand practically any kind of oppression. So the question that this religion raises is whether this is the answer, the solution, to the issue of how we survive—an ideology with the potency and survival capabilities of this kind of religion.

I will develop the answer to that question in this book, but first we need to get a brief idea of the history and precepts of this remarkable faith and of the people who formed it.

**Number of Judaic adherents** The number of Jews in the world is very small, the number of believing Jews even smaller and the number of practising Jews smaller still. The religion is a minnow compared with Christianity or Islam, Hinduism or Buddhism. We may take someone to be Jewish if they have a Jewish mother (at least according to Orthodox Jews), though that is becoming a weaker criterion as more and more Jews 'marry out'.

The total number of Jews in the world is about 14.5 million, about the population of Cambodia or Guatemala, a bit less than the Netherlands and a bit more than Los Angeles or Buenos Aires or Beijing. The largest contingent is in North America—about six million, mainly comprising those who fled to the land of freedom from the persecution elsewhere. The next largest group is in Israel—about 4.5 million. The total population of Israel is about 7.2 million. There are about three million Jews in Europe and about 500,000 in South America. The remaining numbers are spread around the world in such countries as South Africa where the Jews were in the forefront of the opposition to apartheid.

The religion is an ethnic religion. Maybe conversion is technically possible but in practice the devotees are Jewish, just as nearly all Hindus are Indian. This exclusivity was one of the keys to the survival of the Jews, the feeling that they were chosen of God and therefore special. It conferred an identity which spurred them to protect themselves as a group, wherever they might be spread.

**Abraham of Ur** The Jews trace themselves back to Abraham of Ur, near the mouth of the Tigris and Euphrates in present-day Iraq. Possibly around 2000 to 1800 BCE Abraham and his tribe were pushed out of Ur by local tribal fighting and they moved to the land around the Sea of Galilee and the Dead Sea in present-day Israel. This was around the time that the Minoan civilisation was well established in Greece and the time when the first pharaoh of the great Egyptian 12th dynasty came to power and completed the reunification of Egypt. The year 2000 BCE would be about 56 lives of 70 years each, laid end to end from now.

There seems no reason to doubt that there was a historical figure called Abraham: archaeological evidence supports the biblical thesis. The mythic legend relates that God did a deal with Abraham—that, if Abraham and his tribe honoured and obeyed God as the one god, then God would give Abraham and his tribe the Promised Land, ie, the land they moved to, an area somewhat larger than the current Israel. We may doubt the deal, but there is no reason to doubt the historicity of Abraham. I don't see why we should regard all ancient historians as fabricators.

**Egypt, Moses and the temple** Later in that millennium, the Hebrews were enslaved by the Egyptians—for perhaps four hundred years. It is hard to tell when this oppression started in the seven hundred years between the departure of Abraham from Ur and subjection of the Jews to Egyptians. At any rate, the enslavement happened at least during the reign of Rameses II of Egypt

(1304–1237 BCE) who was the most prolific builder since the pyramid pharaohs and needed slave labour. Around 1235 BCE the Jews escaped and were led by Moses into the Sinai desert.

Moses is unquestionably one of the most influential men ever to have lived, one of the greatest lawgivers and philosophers the world has ever seen. He was in substance the founder of the religion and hence of Christianity and Islam. It was he who delivered the Ten Commandments (supposedly handed down to him by God on Mount Sinai) and it was he who crystallised the monotheistic beliefs and the deal with God.

The great King David—the David who slew the Philistine Goliath with a sling-shot—established Jerusalem about 1000 BCE, ruled until about 966 BCE and was succeeded by his son Solomon who died in 926 or 925 BCE. Solomon built the lavish and costly first temple of the Israelites in Jerusalem, an architectural triumph which presaged the great cathedrals of Christendom and which became the centre of the religion. It was around this time that the Phoenicians founded their alphabet, that the Indians first used a symbol for zero and that the Homeric poems and the Indian Vedas were recited orally.

After attacks on the Hebrew tribes by the Assyrians and the Babylonians, King Nebuchadnezzar of the Babylonians conquered Jerusalem in 597 BCE and the temple was destroyed in 586 BCE. The Jews were taken into captivity in Babylon. This time the captivity was less than 50 years and was ended when Cyrus II of Persia overcame the Babylonians and allowed the Jews to return to Palestine. They returned in waves from 538 to about 433 BCE and re-established the temple.

**The diaspora** Alexander the Great gained control of Palestine in the early 330s BCE but the Jews were tolerated and entered a period of prosperity. But in 63 BCE the Romans appeared under Pompey and conquered Judaea. Various revolutionary movements started up and a cult was commenced by a troublesome character called Jesus. A Jewish revolution against the Romans broke out in 66 CE. The Romans decided that this time they would deal with the situation firmly and destroyed the Jewish temple in 70 CE. The Jewish diaspora began and the Jews were out of Palestine for just under 1900 years, left to wander the world as exiles and rejects. Their religion was marginalised by Christianity and the Christians became a foe, not a friend. The more tolerant Muslims overran their lands after the death of Muhammad but the Jews were still subordinated. A mosque was built where the temple was on the Mount in Jerusalem. King Herod, who died in 4 BCE, had enhanced the temple but the only part of King Herod's temple still in existence is the Wailing Wall (now the Western Wall) at the foot of the Mount.

**Pogroms** Then the horrors began. There were massacres and pogroms in England in 1144, 1190 and 1290, under the Crusaders in 1096, in Germany from 1348 to 1350, in France in 1306 and 1394, in Sicily and Spain in 1492 when the Jews were expelled, in Lithuania in 1495, in Portugal in 1497, in Provence in 1498, in Naples in 1561 and 1591, in Russia in 1648, among others. The Jews were the Christ-murderers. Also, even more fatally, since both the Christians and Muslims banned interest, it was the Jews who lent money and became the creditors. In those days creditors were despised—an emotion which is widely found even in the 21st century.

The Jews ended up in ghettoes in European cities. A respite came after the European Enlightenment of the 18th century. France in 1791 was the first country in Europe to treat Jews as full citizens. Britain had a Jewish prime minister in the nineteenth century, though he was baptised a Christian (Disraeli). But the emancipation came in fits and starts with many retreats and much back sliding. This favourable trend was terminated with the Holocaust of the Second World War when nearly one-third of Jews in the world were exterminated—about six million of them.

It was just not going to work. In 1948 the British honoured their pledge from 1917 to hand over part of Palestine to the Jews as the new Jewish state of Israel, displacing many Palestinian Arabs. This new state faced almost continual war and insurrection from the Palestinians and other Arabs. Israelis realised that their 4000-year struggle to survive was not over. They became a nuclear power. The old underdog, now triumphant, was faced by a new underdog, the Muslim Palestinians.

**Jewish sects** Like most religions, the Jews have sects. The two most important groups of Jews were originally the Ashkenazim and the Sephardim. The Ashkenazim lived in Central and Eastern Europe and spoke Yiddish. The Sephardim lived in Spain and Portugal and spoke Ladino under the Muslims.

The Hasidim are an ultra orthodox group. They have a strict dress code for the men—a wide-brimmed black hat, a black coat and curled locks or ringlets hanging down by each ear. They emphasise the mystical side of religion based on the Kabala. The Kabala is a mystical interpretation of scripture which explores symbolic, secret and allegorical meanings. It was written between the 13th and 16th centuries and called the Zohar. Apart from the esoteric symbolism, it teaches love for fellow human beings and the development of ecstatic love for God through meditation.

Reform Judaism was begun in 19th-century Germany. It held that the basic scriptures—the Torah, which for example contained the book of Genesis—did not require strict and literal interpretation. The ritual practices, the dietary laws and even the laws themselves were not literally binding. The stories were symbolic where they did not fit modern science. The books reflected ancient times when things were different. It was not necessary for religious services to be in Hebrew. The congregation did not have to be separated into men and women. One did not have to believe in a messianic age. If parents were divorced by a civil divorce, the children of the second marriage could still be legitimate, even if there was no religious divorce. Female rabbis are allowed.

Conservative Judaism was a reaction to the Reform movement and ended up midway between Orthodox and Reform Judaism. There are various other sects.

Most of the disagreements between the sects are not about fundamental theology. They are about lifestyle, rituals, dietary laws, marriage, divorce and the attitude to females.

**Rites of passage and festivals** Like other religions, Judaism has rites of passage. Boys are circumcised when they are eight days old. They are initiated as full members of the religion at 13 years—the Bar Mitzvah. There is a Bat Mitzvah for girls. Marriages are in the synagogue with traditional ceremonies. Funerals are usually within 24 hours of death. Orthodox Jews do not practise cremation. Burial should take place in a Jewish consecrated cemetery.

The main festivals are the Passover, celebrating the Exodus from Egypt, the New Year and Yom Kippur, which is a day of atonement when God forgives sins. The main rituals are performed on the Sabbath which to Orthodox Jews is a strict day of rest. Jews are expected to pray three times a day.

**Dietary laws** The dietary laws list eligible animals, birds and sea creatures which can be eaten, require the removal of blood and are very detailed, for example, no eating of meat and drinking of milk together. There is much emphasis on hygiene, for example, the washing of hands before meals, after sleep and after the toilet. These rules were driven by medical views and hence were survival rules.

**Basic beliefs** Judaism is monotheistic in the tradition of Zoroaster. The religion, like Islam, originally rejected graven images and therefore rejected the quasi-pornography of the fertility cults. It is imageless, iconoclastic. This view gave rise in early Christian times to a prejudice against representational art and a taboo about idols and graven images, a distancing from the Christian icons—seen as idolatrous—a distancing from statues and paintings in Christian churches. The attitude may have given rise to the Jewish emphasis on music and singing.

The basic tenets of the religion were summed up and codified by Maimonides (1135–1204). He was born in Spain but later fled and spent most of his life in Egypt. His analysis of the 13 fundamental beliefs of Judaism are more or less an official creed.

The first five fundamental beliefs are about God. God is the creator of all things, he is incorporeal (ie, having no material or physical substance), eternal and is alone to be worshipped—the only God.

The next four fundamental beliefs deal with how God revealed himself to the Jews. God revealed himself though the medium of the prophecy of the prophets. Moses was the greatest prophet. The first five books—the Torah—of the scriptures are unchangeable and God will not supplant them by another revelation. The Torah is therefore set in stone. Most of the controversy between the sects has been about this literal interpretation of the Torah, for example, that God created the world in seven days, contrary to Darwinian evolution.

The tenth and eleventh fundamental beliefs are that God knows all the deeds of people and is concerned with them; and that he rewards and punishes people for their good or evil deeds. The belief therefore has a personal god and a salvationist view.

The final twelfth and thirteenth fundamentals deal with the coming of the Messiah, a descendant of King David, who will usher in the messianic age and the resurrection of the dead. Whatever one makes of these beliefs, they certainly include the immortality of the soul.

Subsequent codes were written by the Rabbis Caro and Isserles in the 15th and 16th centuries respectively. Modern writings are mainly commentaries on the old texts.

**Ethical and legal codes of Judaism** The basic scriptures of the Jews are called the Torah, meaning the 'Law'. The Torah has five books—Genesis, Exodus, Leviticus, Numbers and Deuteronomy. Genesis covers the creation of the universe and stories of the patriarchs from Abraham onwards, including Noah and the great flood. Exodus deals with the flight from Egypt and the delivery of the Ten Commandments to Moses. Leviticus is a law book setting out laws, including laws about rituals and sacrifices. Numbers is a census of the peoples and reiterates the laws and the keeping of festivals. Deuteronomy contains the sermons said to have been preached by Moses. These five books are the first five books of the Christian bible.

There are other books which do not have the same authenticity, for example, the Prophets, Psalms and Ecclesiastes. There are 24 books in all.

Subsequently there was a large number of commentaries, such as the Mishnah dated about 200 CE, all collected in the Talmud in the 5th and 6th centuries CE. Actually there were two Talmuds—the Babylonian and the Palestinian Talmud of the 4th and 5th centuries, but the Babylonian Talmud is three times as long and the most authentic version. This huge compilation of about four million words deals with aspects of daily life—agriculture, festivals, marriage, divorce, civil law and criminal law—in quite fantastic detail, although antiquated.

**The Ten Commandments** We may now turn to one of the most famous law codes in the world—the Ten Commandments.

The Ten Commandments are contained in Jewish books Exodus chapter 20 and Deuteronomy 5. They were said to be delivered to Moses by God on Mount Sinai hewn into two tablets of stone. The Exodus version of the Ten Commandments is as follows (the various transcriptions differ in detail):

1.  I am the Lord your God, who brought you out of the land of Egypt, out of the house of slavery. You must have no other gods before me.

2.  You must not make for yourself a carved image, or any likeness of anything that is in heaven above, or that is in the earth beneath, or that is in the water under the earth. You will not bow to them or serve them, for I the Lord Your God am a jealous God, visiting the iniquity of the fathers on the children to the third and the fourth generation of those who hate me, but showing steadfast love to a thousand generations of those who love me and keep my commandments.

3.  You will not take the name of the Lord your God in vain, for the Lord will not hold him guiltless who takes his name in vain.

4.  Remember the Sabbath day, to keep it holy. Six days you will labour, and do all your work, but the seventh day is a Sabbath to the Lord your God. On it you must not do any work, you or your son, or your daughter, your male servant, or your female servant, or your livestock, or the sojourner who is within your gates. For in six days the Lord made heaven and earth, the sea and all that is within them, and rested on the seventh day. Therefore the Lord blessed the Sabbath day and made it holy.

5.  Honour your father and your mother, that your days may be long in the land that the Lord God is giving you.

6. You must not murder.
7. You must not commit adultery.
8. You must not steal.
9. You must not bear false witness against your neighbour.
10. You must not covet your neighbour's house; you must not covet your neighbour's wife, or his male servant, or his ox, or his donkey, or anything that is your neighbour's.

These commandments were probably written down in the 900s BCE and may have represented previous traditions. Various other dates have been suggested.

Out of the Ten Commandments, only three deal with secular law—6 banning murder, 8 banning theft and 9 banning perjury and lying. The first four deal with belief in one God and the celebration of God on the Sabbath. The remaining three deal with personal morality—respect for parents in 5, the ban on adultery in 7 and the prohibition on envy in 10. Hence the legal coverage is extremely narrow.

Broadly the Decalogue deals with the most fundamental rules, for example, the greatest injury you can do to a person is to murder him or her, the greatest injury you can do to the family is to commit adultery, the greatest injury you can do to the law and to commerce is to commit perjury (bear false witness). The Ten Commandments were elaborated into the 613 commandments of the first five books of the Bible, mainly Leviticus.

**Expansion of Jewish law** The Jewish legal commentaries contained in the Mishnah are dramatic in their intrusion into private life. They are obsessed with details of how we should behave. For example, we should never sit down to eat a meal until we have fed our goats and our camels and that we should invite any widows in our communities for dinner every springtime. It prescribes how often we should have sex (once a day for men of independent means, twice a week for labourers and once a week for donkey drivers—taxi drivers, take note): Alain de Botton, *Religion for Atheists* (Penguin, 2012) p 71. The law is concerned only with action which harms others and is not usually concerned with private matters.

The Hebrew bible allows for justified killing in the case of warfare (Kings 2), capital punishment (Leviticus 20) and self-defence (Exodus 22).

The commandment against idolatry was subsequently used by Christians to justify various outbursts of iconoclasm justifying the smashing of images, pictures and statues of God, Jesus and the saints. This violent iconoclasm was a feature of the Christian Church in Constantinople in the 700s CE and again of the hardline Protestants at the time of the Protestant Reformation. The Roman Catholic Church took the view that icons were fine so long as they were not worshipped.

Hebrew law is otherwise dominated by rules about sacrifices, about the priesthood, what you can eat, hygiene and uncleanliness and rituals. There are rules about sexual behaviour in Leviticus 18 (including rules against sex with various relatives and with animals and a ban on homosexuality) and various laws of conduct in 19. Penalties for grave crimes are set out in 20. Leviticus was a major source of Jewish law.

Leviticus in 19 sets out a miscellany of laws—including, do not steal, do not lie, do not deceive others, do not defraud or rob your neighbour, do not hold back the wages of a hired worker overnight, do not pervert justice, do not show partiality to the poor or favouritism to the great but judge your neighbour fairly, do not go about spreading slander among your people, do not do anything that endangers your neighbour's life, do not hate a fellow Israelite in your heart, do not seek revenge or bear a grudge against anyone among your people, but love your neighbour as yourself, do not degrade your daughter making her a prostitute, show respect for the elderly, and do not use dishonest standards when measuring length, weight or quantity. It also contains a rule about the treatment of foreigners—when foreigners reside among you in your land, do not ill-treat them. The foreigner residing among you must be treated as your native-born. Love them as yourself, for you were foreigners in Egypt.

Subsequent Jewish law dealt with marriage and divorce and with civil and criminal law. The fields belong more to legal anthropology. Only a few of the most orthodox sects actually study or apply ancient Jewish law. There is some genuflection in the direction of this corpus of law in the Israeli legal system.

**Conclusion on Judaism** Moses and Zoroaster agreed on fundamental propositions—that there was only one God and that this god was not a marvellous human-type character in the sky, but an imageless being without physical form, incorporeal. This was an extraordinarily inventive and original insight for the time, not understood by the Chinese or the Greeks or the Romans. It was almost as if they were presaging the search of the 20th-century scientists from Einstein on to find the single grand universal force which combined and explained all forces—the electromagnetic force, the strong and weak nuclear force and gravity.

Judaism showed enormous resilience in enabling the Jews to endure the hardships they faced and seemed to be the chief factor giving them the fortitude and national will to survive. It showed the power of ideology in the endeavour to stay alive, the power of ideas. The strictness of the rituals was a daily reminder of the arduous efforts required to hold to the path, to endure; they symbolise struggle and discipline. Their community, spread across many nations, is a demonstration that a common will and identity does not have to be tied to some territory but can be international and bind peoples brought up in different cultures, dressing differently, speaking different tongues, being poor or rich.

So on the one hand one can say that the Jews were narrowly exclusive. On the other hand one can also say that they showed the fundamental potency that a universal philosophy can have.

# Christianity

**The unusual religion** Christianity is one of the world's two largest religions in terms of numbers and the largest by far in terms of geographical presence—see chapter 11 for an analysis of the numbers. Yet it is an unusual religion.

Christians believe in one God, but in fact the one God is divided into three, God the Father, God the Son (Jesus Christ) and God the Holy Spirit. Christian theology has been greatly vexed by the efforts to explain why this trinity of three is really one so as to conform to the concept of monotheism. Lurking malevolently in the background we also have Satan or Lucifer or the Devil—this chuckling but wicked creature has many names. To some Roman Catholics who are not as attentive to the theological detail as they should be, the mother of Jesus is as near to a goddess as you can get.

The doctrinal explanation of the concept of three in one, of singularity in severality, is that the one God has other manifestations but they are all of 'one substance'. This idea of the many in the one is not without religious precedent elsewhere. For example, Hinduism developed the doctrine early on that a god can have numerous other versions or appearances, including incarnations in flesh and blood—called avatars. One of the leading gods Vishnu boasts several such beings which are part of an elaborate pantheon. Unlike the Christians however, the Hindus did not seem to be troubled by this proliferation. An alternative Christian explanation is that one person can have many relational roles—parent, child and companion. The Trinity is three ways of knowing God.

Christianity must seem strange to outsiders. Its logo or main symbol is a man hanging nailed to a cross. The centre of its main ritual ceremony involves the symbolic eating of the body and drinking the blood of the son of its God.

God the Son, Jesus Christ, was born of a virgin around 3 BCE in Palestine. He performed many miracles and gathered around him a group of 12 disciples. As a result of his teachings he was crucified on a cross in Jerusalem in about 30 CE by the Jewish authorities, rose from the dead three days later (the resurrection) and ascended to heaven. The resurrection was treated as a sacrifice to redeem mankind from its sins. In due course the world will come to an end and there will be a last day of judgement conducted by the Christian God. The good, if they were believers, will go to heaven and live there for ever as immortals. The wicked will be sent to burn in hell for all eternity.

The main denominations are (1) the Roman Catholics based in Rome and the original Christian Church, (2) the Eastern Orthodox who split off in the 11th century, and (3) the Protestants who splintered into numerous sub-sects from the 15th century onwards—for example, Anglicans, Calvinists, Presbyterians, Baptists, Congregationalists, Reformed, Methodists, Quakers, Lutherans, and subsequently the ecstatic Pentecostalists, plus a number of fringe and eccentric sects such as the Mennonites, the Christian Scientists founded by Mary Baker-Eddy (1821–1910), the Mormons founded by Joseph Smith (1805–44) and the Jehovah's Witnesses founded by Charles Taze Russell (1852–1916). There are now thousands of these Protestant sects. Many of them appeared in the United States where they proselytised with enthusiastic zeal. There is a largish Christian community in South Korea.

The main source of this religion is the New Testament which has four versions of Christ's life (the Gospels) and various other texts, notably letters mainly from Paul of Tarsus, a convert, to early Christian communities explaining the religion, a supplement to the third Gospel (Acts of the Apostles) and a largely prophetic work—the Apocalypse or Revelation of John. The religion was considered a continuation of Judaism and therefore adopted the main Judaistic books in the form of the Old Testament. The New Testament was probably completed by at least 100 CE.

The morality was based on the Old Testament, notably the Jewish Ten Commandments, but with a special emphasis on loving your neighbour as yourself. **Reasons for success** Many adherents to other religions, especially Muslims, found the Christian story to be implausible, bizarre. Yet it had and has colossal appeal and emotional power. The religion was enormously successful.

Why was this?

— **The religion of Rome** The first reason was that it got established in Rome as the official religion in the early-300s CE. All changed after the persecutions of Christians by Diocletian (ruled 284–305). They had been persecuted because the Christians had insisted that their allegiance was to Christ and therefore they could not participate in the civil religion of the state cult which required veneration of the genius or sprit of the emperor. They often refused to undertake military service which was a further aggravation and so they were regarded as disloyal and dangerous. But when Constantine was emperor he had a dream in 312 CE that he would win a battle the next day over control of the empire (his opponent ended up drowned in the River Tiber) if he supported Christianity. In his vision he saw a flaming cross inscribed, 'Through this sign, you shall conquer'. There are various other versions of this story which is quite common in most cultures. Luckily for Christianity he did win the battle (the Battle of Milvian Bridge near Rome) and so he at first tolerated and then gave favours to the Christian Church. By the time of Emperor Theodosius, Christianity was well and truly established when the emperor declared Christianity to be the only legal religion in 393, although other religions were suppressed before that. Around that time, it is thought that probably 30 million Romans had converted so the religion was growing extremely rapidly. Constantine was baptised only on his deathbed.

— **Economic success** The fact that Rome was part of the West was key. The reason was that the West was destined to dominate the entire planet in terms of wealth and technology so that the religion was on the side of the economic winners who thereby became the territorial winners as well. Although in the early days the West was in decline during the Dark Ages, the atrocious conditions probably helped to spur the religion along as a source of comfort.

Christianity was the religion of the Roman Empire. It became the religion of most of the world by reason of Roman imperialism in Europe and subsequently by European imperialism over the rest of the world from 1500 onwards.

By 1830 the West controlled practically the entire world. Their wealth far surpassed that of the rest of the world. As shown in chapter 3, even by as late as 1995, if world GDP was divided into three football fields of ten trillion dollars each, the West had two of them—the United States one football field, the EU and its offshoots the second football field, while the rest had the third football field. Half of the third football field was occupied by Japan and the four Asian Tigers, so that Africa, Latin America, China and the others were squeezed up into the squashed-up half of the third football field on the end.

— **Religious vacuum** Christianity attracted converts in Rome possibly because there was a religious vacuum for ordinary people. Its competitors were emperor worship, the old gods like Jupiter and a debased form of Zoroastrianism called Mithraism, appealing mainly to the military.

— **Universal appeal** Christianity appealed to everybody including simple ordinary people. It appealed to women who as mothers would pass the religion to their children. The fact that everybody was in charge of their own destiny, because if they were good they would go to heaven and have eternal bliss, meant that everybody had a chance and the individual was not at the mercy of some arbitrary and capricious god.

— **God sacrifices himself** The central imagery of the cross and of sacrifice was exceptionally striking. The idea, however hard to understand, that God would send his son to earth to die for the rest of the people so that they could be saved was a concept of huge potency and power. It came across as the extreme sacrifice, the most extreme act of selflessness and charity, it appealed to the most profound and primitive emotions—one of the most ancient religious rituals, the ultimate sacrifice to the gods.

— **Death** The religion honoured the dying and the dead with respectful ceremony. The dead were not just cast off hastily into an unmarked grave as if they were polluted poison.

— **Guilt** The religion also dealt with guilt, the guilt towards ancestors, the guilt towards those you loved and betrayed. It redeemed guilt. You were entitled to forgiveness of your wrongdoings and a new start. It was salvationist, you had a chance. God was no longer some vindictive and menacing authoritarian figure intent on punishment.

Sexual guilt was not part of the original concept. Jesus said practically nothing about sex. It was only later that it became a central preoccupation of the church.

— **Weak competitors** In the Dark Ages, the religion did not have any competitors which convinced. The barbarian religions were a jumble. Christianity had prestige. It had books, it had writing. It was associated with the former glory of Rome and later the glory of Constantinople, the former Byzantium. It had an organisation, a leader (the pope), missionaries and priests. It had a programme and a plan. It was not tribal.

The only potential competitor was Islam. Bur Islam was too late. It only arrived in the middle of the 700s so far as the West was concerned and by that time the Arabs were the enemy. Therefore their religion, however pure and attractive, was the religion of the enemy. The West was not going to convert to the religion of the enemy. So from that time on, the Muslims were infidels. Christianity got there first and it was backing what became the best economic horse in the race—for a time at any rate.

By 1830 the Islamic countries were in severe decline. They were poverty stricken and backward. They had a tiny fraction of world GDP.

— **Power and protection** The Christian religion gave power and protection against enemies in a very dangerous world. The enemies were both natural enemies and spiritual threats. The source of this power came from one comprehensible God. There was a well-organised church, with its saints and martyrs to guarantee this protection. In addition, the Christians were a much larger group and had a larger identity which would tend to underline the authenticity of the power and protection. This is particularly the case when the idea of a Christian Roman empire was revisited in the Holy Roman Empire of Charlemagne who was crowned in 800. In addition, the Christians developed a strong monastic movement which were centres of intellectual learning which gave the church a single language and which strengthened a united liturgy and the central authority of Rome. The monastic movement was begun by St Benedict (c 480 to 542).

— **Empathy of Christ and emotional morality** The Christ of the four Gospels comes across as showing exceptional empathy with ordinary people. By comparison the Koran insisted on a central message of the belief in one God in order to defeat polytheism and did not give priority to developing doctrines of love to one another. Jesus Christ was living in a society where that battle against polytheism had already been won by the Jews and so he could concentrate more on the loving kindness aspect of religion. The morality of love was emotionally potent.

— **Imagery** The Christian Church wholeheartedly embraced pictorial imagery, crucial for an illiterate population. In this respect it was unlike Judaism and unlike Islam where there is a rejection of human images, mainly because of the threat that people might treat the images as God, when God was not capable of representation because of the threat of polytheism. Judaism and Islam are imageless. Islam came across as abstract, unfeeling, theoretical. I have already mentioned the power of the images of Christ on the cross. In addition one of the most pervasive other images was that of a virgin and child, both of which expressed femininity, the family and an exquisite purity.

The Eastern Church flirted with iconoclasm in the 8th century. Later in the Reformation English Protestants in the 1540s smashed idolatrous images, destroying a large part of England's Christian art, and, under the Long Parliament in the 1640s, some Puritan sects went around smashing stained glass windows in churches and destroying religious icons. But these were exceptions. Hinduism, and Buddhism to a lesser extent, also exploited the attraction of images and sought to portray their beliefs in representational art.

Christian theologians may claim that the source of the success of Christianity was that God was on the side of the religion. However, the historical record shows good reason why the religion did triumph, at least for now, without the necessity for divine intervention.

**Some historical events in the advance of Christianity** Some key historical events in the progress of Christianity are worth mentioning. In the very early days—around 45 CE—the Christians at a meeting in Jerusalem agreed to accept non-Jews into the religion without circumcision and without any requirements to fulfil Jewish ritual law. This bypassed the whole problem of the reception of Jewish converts and was a major step in the advance of Christianity as a universal religion. Faith in the Christian God took priority over ethnic and national bonds. It was lucky also that this step was taken when it was because Jerusalem was destroyed by the Romans after rebellions in 70 CE and the 130s which involved the destruction of the temple, the devastation of central Jewish areas and the end of the Jewish model of Christianity. Christianity had already broken out into foreign parts and so it no longer relied on the Jewish centre.

There is no question that the leading figure in the early spread of Christianity was a rabbi called Saul who also happened to be a Roman citizen. He was not an apostle of Jesus and had at first actively opposed the movement. But after a dramatic vision on the road to Damascus, he converted and took up the name Paul. He travelled all across the present-day Turkey and the eastern Mediterranean as well as Eastern Europe and Rome itself, introducing Jesus to overseas Jewish communities and converting the Gentiles. I have already mentioned the endorsement of Christianity by the Roman emperors which was followed by a council in Nicea in 325 called by Emperor Constantine to settle the whole question of whether there was one God or three. This matter caused enormous controversy and was sorted by a form of words which was considered to solve the matter.

After the ultimate fall of the Roman Empire in 476, Christianity became the religion of the barbarian tribes but still with the centre of authority maintained in a hugely diminished Rome and kept alive in the great monasteries. These barbarians were not without enthusiasm. The religion received another shot in the arm when Charlemagne, king of the Franks (768–814), effectively founded the Holy Roman Empire and imposed the faith on the conquered Saxons. The Franks had been united by Clovis (466–511) in 496. He was said to have been converted by his wife and was the founder of modern France. The Franks sent church missions elsewhere, a tradition which led to the mission of Pope Gregory the Great to southern England in 597.

In North Africa the barbarian and Arab invasions meant that Christianity had almost died out altogether in its region of origin but it kept going in Constantinople. In 988 Christianity was proclaimed the official religion in Kiev: this laid the basis of Russian Christianity which was the main support of the Eastern Orthodox Church in its subsequent travails, including the conquest of Constantinople by the Turks in 1453. The formal breach between Constantinople and Rome came in 1054 and was sealed without possibility of return when in 1204 crusaders from the West looted Constantinople and desecrated its churches. The Holy Orthodox Church survived in Russia, Greece and all the Balkan countries, except Albania, and most parts of Croatia and Bosnia.

The first really major challenge to Christianity came at the time of the Reformation when the Protestants broke away from Rome, out of resentment about the corruption of the clergy and out of disagreements on doctrinal points, all inflamed by nationalism. The leading Protestant reformers were Martin Luther (1483–1546), Huldreich Zwingli (1484–1531) and John Calvin (1509–64).

In fact it was not a setback because the Protestant Reformation coincided with the voyages of discovery by the Western Europeans to North and South America and the Caribbean, to Cape Town, India and the Far East and the beginning of Western imperialism over practically the entire world. The Christians had a strong missionary objective of converting the people in the countries they conquered, a process which led to some disgraceful atrocities. Not all of the imperial powers had a missionary motive. For example, the British East India Company which ruled India explicitly maintained religious neutrality and sought to avoid any public alignment with Christianity. Their objective was to not disturb trade.

The settlement of what was to become the United States by Christians resulted in one of the most Christian countries in the world. The subsequent division of Africa between the imperial Western powers also led to the Christianisation of large parts of Africa, except the Muslim north, through in part the activity of missionaries such as David Livingstone whose avowed purpose was to bring 'commerce and Christianity' to the native people. On the other hand Christianity never got established in China or South-East Asia or Japan, notwithstanding the existence of some Christian communities there.

**Ethical and legal codes in Christianity** Christians originally made very little contribution to law on their own and Jesus Christ did not appear to consider himself a lawgiver. The things that were Caesar's were irrelevant, the legalism of the Pharisees arid. He was interested instead in the ideology of love.

Christians took over the Jewish Ten Commandments. They mostly believe that the Ten Commandments are a summary of God's law which has to be observed. They added a further commandment, ascribed to Jesus by Matthew's Gospel (but found much earlier in the Jewish scriptures)—'You must love your neighbour as yourself', a message subsequently taken up vigorously by Paul in his letters to Christian communities. Jesus chose the love of God and the love of your neighbour as the two great commandments.

Other statements of a moral code are contained in the Sermon on the Mount, best read in Matthew's Gospel 5. This celebrates the poor and meek, those who hunger and thirst for righteousness, the merciful, the pure and the peacemakers. It is particularly notable for the precepts that if anyone slaps you on the right cheek, you should turn to them the other cheek also and that you should love your enemies.

There is a Code of Canon Law of 1983 containing 1752 canons and binding on the Roman Catholic Church, mainly to do with church matters and church doctrines on family and sex, such as the celibacy of the clergy, the prohibition on contraception and the prohibition on divorce. The Anglican Church also has an organised Canon Law.

It is worth quoting two of the most important Christian prayers which give a good feel of the religion.

The first is the Lord's prayer which was taught by Jesus to his disciples and reads as follows (the last sentence is a later addition):

Our Father, which art in heaven,
Hallowed be thy Name.
Thy Kingdom come.
Thy will be done on earth,
As it is in heaven.
Give us this day our daily bread.
And forgive us our trespasses,
As we forgive them that trespass against us.
And lead us not into temptation,
But deliver us from evil.
For thine is the kingdom,
The power, and the glory,
For ever and ever.
Amen.

The second prayer—or rather a statement of belief—is the Nicene Creed which was settled in 325 at a Christian Council at Nicaea (now Iznik in Turkey) to resolve disputes about the nature of God. This short creed, as amended at the Council of Constantinople in 381, reads as follows:

We believe in one God, the Father Almighty, maker of heaven and earth, and of all things visible and invisible.

And in one Lord Jesus Christ, the only-begotten Son of God, begotten of the Father before all worlds, God of God, Light of Light, Very God of Very God, begotten, not made, being of one substance with the Father by whom all things were made; who for us men and for our salvation came down from heaven, and was incarnate by the Holy Spirit of the Virgin Mary and was made man, and was crucified also for us under Pontius Pilate. He suffered and was buried and the third day he rose again according to the Scriptures and ascended into heaven and sitteth on the right hand of the Father. And he shall come again with glory to judge both the quick and the dead, whose kingdom shall have no end.

And we believe in the Holy Spirit, the Lord and Giver of Life, who proceedeth from the Father, who with the Father and the Son together is worshipped and glorified, who spoke by the prophets. And we believe in one holy catholic and apostolic Church. We acknowledge one baptism for the remission of sins. And we look for the resurrection of the dead and the life of the world to come. Amen.

There are various other versions differing in detail and translation. Most modern versions use 'I believe' rather than 'We believe'. There are other scattered affirmations of belief.

**Conclusion on Christianity** There is no question that Christianity has so far been the most important religious force the world has ever seen, followed by Islam. Jesus Christ, regarded at the time as a minor nuisance, has turned out to be one of the most influential men in history and possibly the most influential man ever. Quite apart from the fact that Christianity was the religion of a triumphant group of Western economies, it had a lot going for it in terms of its appeal and its extraordinary ability to combine redemption with a refreshing and potent morality. Its emphasis on loving kindness to all people is one of the most fundamental contributions to a universal morality of survival: in one powerful phrase it replaces oceans of treatises on ethics.

# Islam: The Last Great Religion

**Introduction** We now come to the last of the great religions—Islam. The arrival of Islam signalled the end of more than 2500 years of the invention of Big Religion. Thereafter, it was all filling in—redoing the pointing, adding an outbuilding, sometimes rebuilding bits of the edifice or subdividing it.

The speed and conviction with which Islam established itself and spread its visionary message were spectacular.

**Muslim population** Islam is one of the two largest religions in the world with Christianity. The largest populations are in Asia, mainly Pakistan, Bangladesh, Malaysia and Indonesia. Indonesia has the largest Muslim population in the world. There are large numbers of Muslims in the Middle East and North Africa. The largest Arab-speaking congregation of Muslims is in Egypt. I deal with the numbers in chapter 11.

**Life of the Prophet** Islam means 'submission'. Its founder Muhammad was born in Mecca in what is now Saudi Arabia in 570 CE, a member of the Hashim clan. His father died before he was born and his mother died when he was six, leaving Muhammad as an orphan. His grandfather looked after him and then his uncle.

The Arabian tribes in the region were grouped around oases and wells and otherwise were nomadic. In Mecca trade was important because it was located on caravan routes. In addition Mecca was a religious centre because it was host to a religious shrine called the Kabaa. The religions were polytheistic.

Probably because of Muhammad's evident talents, a wealthy commercially inclined widow called Khadija put Muhammad in charge of one of her caravans. In due course the boss married the servant when Khadija was 40 and Muhammad 25.

Muhammad used to spend some of his time off meditating in a cave. When he was about 40, he had a vision. And then more visions. Muhammad announced that the angel Gabriel spoke to him and instructed him to record the revelations which came direct from God. He memorised these periodic revelations throughout his life and then they were committed to writing, probably by his followers. These writings became the Koran ('to recite') during the caliphate of Uthman (644–56). Since they were delivered by God, they had divine authority, just as the Jewish Torah had divine authority, just as the Hindu Vedas were divine. Something dictated by God could not be changed and must be infallible. Some Muslims consider that it is wrong even to translate the Koran. Devout Muslims attempt to memorise the whole corpus. An English translation is over 400 pages so memorisation is quite a feat.

Around 613, Muhammad began to preach his message to the public in Mecca. In particular, he said there is only one God. Muhammad's teachings caused offence in Mecca. This may have been because the new message threatened polytheism out of which some Meccans were doing well, or because the teachings cut across fierce tribal loyalties regarded as immeasurably more important than loyalty to this new god, or because the families and clans and tribes were innately quarrelsome and resentful of somebody else's pre-eminence and claims to being directly in touch with God. The cheek! Whatever the resentments were, they led to trouble for Muhammad and his followers.

Fortunately for Muhammad visitors from the nearby town of Yathrib, which is about 340 kilometres (210 miles) north of Mecca, were sufficiently impressed by Muhammad to ask him to act as an intermediary in resolving a dispute between two tribes in Yathrib. So in 622 most of the Muslim community in Mecca decamped to Yathrib, leaving behind Muhammad, his cousin Ali and his friend Abu Bakr who was later to become his father-in-law and to play a major role in the future of Islam. Later in that year these three also escaped to Yathrib. This escape is known as the Hijira and was regarded as so important that the Muslim calendar is dated from 622 CE. Muhammad had only ten years to live. Later Yathrib changed its name to Medina—'the City of the Prophet'.

Once in Medina, Muhammad married Aisha, who was the daughter of his uncle Abu Bakr we have already heard about as staying on with Muhammad in Mecca. He also married Hafsa, the daughter of Umar.

Tribal warfare broke out between the cities of Mecca and Medina and, after some to and froing of armies and fighting, in 630 Muhammad marched on Mecca with a large army and the Meccans surrendered. Muhammad entered Mecca without violence. Having achieved this coup Muhammad returned to Medina. The Meccans in due course converted to Islam.

In early 632, the year of his death, Muhammad retuned to Mecca where he delivered his Farewell Sermon, as it turned out. This journey became the model of the Muslim pilgrimage or hajj to Mecca. Muhammad died a few months later in 632, aged 72. This is about 19 lives backwards from now of 70 years each, laid end to end.

**The first caliphs** Then the complications began. Abu Bakr, Muhammad's uncle and father-in-law, was chosen as successor, the first caliph ('successor'). The problem was that this choice overlooked another contender. Muhammad had a daughter by his first wife, the wealthy widow Khadija. This daughter was called Fatima and Fatima married Ali. Ali was the son of one of Muhammad's uncles and had been brought up in Muhammad's household from a young age. He was said to be the first convert to Islam at the age of 12. Ali had supporters who considered that Ali should have been the first caliph. So it was Abu Bakr, the uncle and father-in-law, versus Ali, the son-in-law. As well as being a son-in-law, Ali was also a cousin of Muhammad because Ali was the son of Muhammad's uncle. It was all in the family. Maybe the senior man should have won anyway but the Ali team were indignant. After all, Fatima was in the direct blood line from the Prophet and, in view of the fact that she was a female, her husband ought to have succeeded by right.

This disagreement and resentment had immense future consequences for Islam. It was the foundation of the division of Muslims into Sunnis and Shiites. That is why we are labouring though these intricate relationships which require a genealogical genius to understand them, but Sunnis and Shiites understand them only too well. Shiites are instructed in them from an early age.

The Shiites insisted that Ali should have been the first caliph, whereas the Sunnis disagree. The immediate family quarrels grew even worse. Abu Bakr was caliph for a mere two years from 632 to 634 before his death. Umar then became caliph and lasted for a respectable ten years. Umar, it will be remembered, was the father of one of Muhammad's wives, Hafsa, so he was another father-in-law of Muhammad, as in the case of Abu Bakr. If one believes in the family tradition, it made sense that he was next. Incidentally in those days, marriage was a way of cementing alliances, as in the case of European princes in the medieval era—nothing personal. By this time the Muslims had taken control of vast territories—Egypt, Palestine and Syria, Mesopotamia and central Iran. They had seized the beautiful island of Cyprus. They had defeated the Persian Empire controlling Mesopotamia and central Iran. Umar was murdered by a Persian slave.

Uthman succeeded Umar and was himself assassinated in 656, but not before the Muslims had expanded west towards Tripoli, north to the Taurus and Caucasian mountains and east to what is now Afghanistan and Pakistan, So by 650—a mere 18 years after the death of Muhammad—the Muslims had successfully subdued a gigantic territory.

Ali now had his chance and became the fourth caliph. This was not satisfactory to some and there were revolts. One revolt was led by Aisha, the daughter of Abu Bakr and former wife of Muhammad. Another revolt was led by Muawiyah who was a relative of the assassinated caliph Uthman and the governor of Syria. Ali was assassinated by a secessionist extremist in 661 and Muawiyah became the fifth caliph. So in the 29 years since the death of Muhammad we had three assassinations out of the four rulers. Arabia at the time was a chronically violent society.

After Ali's death, Muawiyah had persuaded Ali's first son to retire to Medina, no doubt with a nice pension. But now Ali's supporters wanted his son Husayn to be caliph. That did not happen because soldiers supporting the Umayadds killed Husayn in 680 at a battle on the plain of Kerbala which became a symbol of infamy for the Shiites. The effect was that Ali and his successors were deprived of the caliphate which the Shiites maintain was a grave injustice. This was basically a bloody family quarrel, the most virulent of all quarrels because it is seen as involving treachery between blood companions who, of all people, should play fair.

**The Umayyad dynasty** The fifth caliph Muawiyah founded the Umayyad dynasty (661–750) which had its headquarters in Damascus in Syria. In 711, about a hundred years after Muhammad first began preaching in Mecca, the Muslims conquered the rest of North Africa and entered Spain. In the east they crossed the Indus River into the Indian subcontinent. They spread up to Tashkent. They seemed unstoppable. Back in the West the Arabs got up to Poitiers in France.

That was the limit. They were defeated in 732 by Charles Martel, ten years before the birth of Charlemagne.

**The Abbasid dynasty** The Umayyad dynasty was succeeded by the Abbasid dynasty (750–1258) based in Baghdad from 752. Their first step was to massacre all members of the Umayyad family, just in case. They subjugated the north of India in 1193. So the Arabs ruled a huge empire from the Pyrenees to Bangladesh. It was baffling that a small town in the Arabian Desert could conquer such a massive empire. That does not mean that the religion was militaristic. You do not need religion as the commander to terrify vast territories. Compare the Huns who terrorised the Roman Empire, the Vikings who terrorised Europe and the Mongols who terrorised Asia and more.

Islamic culture went from strength to strength, their golden age. Their greatest caliph was Harun al-Rashid, a patron of learning. They were far ahead of non-Islamic Europe in science, astronomy, mathematics, literature and non-fiction writing. Great Arab philosophers of the period included al-Farabi from Turkey (born c 870), the founder of Arabic Neo-Platonism, Ibn-Rusd, also known as Averroes (died 1198), who battled with the relationship between faith and reason, revelation and rationality, and Ibn-Sina (died 1037), also known as Avicenna, who wrote an encyclopaedia of Greek and Islamic learning up until then, including philosophy, mathematics and science. That golden age is almost forgotten, unaccountably left behind.

The Crusaders from the West took Jerusalem in 1099 but lost it in 1187 to the chivalrous Saladin.

The Mongols from the East attacked Baghdad in 1258 and laid it waste. That finished the Abbasids and their culture. The empire broke up into independent Islamic territories, a process which had already begun before the Mongol onslaught as early as the 930s. By that time the local rulers had sidelined the caliphs who retained only symbolic power. Ironically by 1300 all four of the new Mongol empires in Asia had converted to Islam, at least theoretically.

**Subsequent expansion of Islam** The Muslims reached their zenith of expansion in the 17th century and thereafter were blocked mainly by the Europeans. It is true that by 1492 the Christians had retaken Spain but that was a special case. In the 14th century, the Ottoman Turks, the leading Muslim power in the world, crossed into Eastern Europe and took over most of the Balkans. Their dynasty was founded in 1288 in Anatolia. Constantinople fell in 1453, to the horror of Christian Europe and was renamed Istanbul. Despite a major defeat in the great sea battle of Lepanto in 1571, in 1683 the Ottomans were at the gates of Vienna and deep into the present Ukraine. They were in charge of Egypt, North Africa, Eastern Europe and the Fertile Crescent. In the 15th and 16th centuries, the Muslims founded three new empires—the Ottoman Turks in Asia Minor and Eastern Europe, the Safavids in Iran and the Mughals in India. The apogee of the Ottoman Empire was reached under Suleiman the Great (1494–1566), the 'Lawgiver', who issued a new legal code alongside sharia law and presided over a cultural renaissance. The prolific and justly famous court architect Sinan died in 1578. In India Akbar the Great (1542–1605), one of the most renowned rulers of the Mughal dynasty, enlarged the empire, patronised culture and promoted religious tolerance.

But the unsuccessful Ottoman siege of Vienna in 1683 was the turning point and by the 19th century, the tide had turned. The Ottoman Empire was the Sick Man of Europe and easily outclassed by the Europeans. The Ottomans were pushed out of most of Europe and most of North Africa. After the defeat of Turkey in the First World War the caliphate was abolished in 1924. Turkey was now run by the modernising and secular Kemal Attaturk. The strict Muslim state of the Kingdom of Saudi Arabia was founded in 1932.

By the end of the 17th century the Mughal Empire in India controlled all the subcontinent of India, in addition to present-day Afghanistan, Pakistan, Kashmir and Bangladesh. The last Mughal emperor was deposed by the British in 1858, in the middle of the decline of the Ottomans in Europe.

Islam also spread to Malaya and Indonesia, to Saharan Africa and to West Africa. In practice the conversion of the populations to Islam was a much slower process than the conquest of territory by the Muslims.

**Modern events affecting Islam** In the 19th and 20th centuries, Islam was faced by major challenges. The first was the scientific and rational modernity of the Europeans and their massive technological superiority, accompanied by European colonialism over nearly all Islamic countries in the 20th century. The lack of modernity led some leading Muslim theorists to advance the view that the Koran was not to be treated literally and that Islam and modernity were not incompatible.

The second challenge was socialism or its more fanatical cousin, Marxism. This view of politics was espoused initially as an economic saviour and altruistic utopia, but later was seen to be just another despotism and an economic disaster.

The third challenge was secularism. Turkey was secularist from 1924. The communist governments in the Central Asian republics of the USSR were secularist. The Pahlavi dynasty in Iran, founded in 1921 and lasting until the revolution of 1979, was secularist. Twentieth-century rulers in, for example, Egypt (Nasser, died 1970), Ayub Khan's government in Pakistan (from 1958 to 1969) and governments in Algeria and Iraq (Saddam Hussein) were secularist. In the Middle East the struggle between secular modernity and traditional Islam has not been resolved.

Islam was fundamentally affected by the two World Wars, by the collapse of the Ottoman Empire, by the withdrawal of the European colonists, by the fall of communism in 1989, by the rise of the feminist movement, by a revolution in the West of ideas on sexual morality, by the fall of the paternalistic family in the West, by the huge advance of science and technology, and by all the cultural and other shifts which have taken place over the past century or so.

Other important political events were the founding of the new state of Pakistan in 1947 (from which Bangladesh later split off), the rise of the political power of some Islamic states through their oil and gas resources, the establishment of the state of Israel in 1948 which led to constant battles between Arabs and the Israelis, the Islamic revolution in Iran in 1979 which brought Ayatollah Khomeini to power as head of a theocracy, the invasions of Iraq and Afghanistan led by the United States in the 2000s, and the heightening of Islamic terrorism and shocking jihadist atrocities in the past few decades.

In 2013 there was an apparent democratic 'Arab Spring' which succeeded in Tunisia but nowhere else, not even Egypt.

**The beliefs of Islam** Islam is a monotheistic faith with one God who is the creator of the world and all that is in it. On the last day of judgement, all people will be judged. Those who were good will enjoy the pleasures of the Garden of Paradise. Those who were evil and followed Satan will be punished by eternal hellfire. This is the simple system of reward and punishment.

The Koran is a continuation of the Jewish Torah and the Gospels of Jesus, except those inconsistent with Islam, such as the Christian assertion that Jesus was the son of God. Moses and David were earlier prophets. The last prophet is Muhammad. The overall effect is that Islam adopts the fundamental views of Zoroastrianism, Judaism and Christianity about the one God, the Day of Judgement, the resurrection of the dead and their allocation to heaven or hell. What is common to these religions is greater than what divides them.

The percentage of strictly legal text in the Koran is quite small. The book contains about 6200 verses and out of these only 100 deal with ritual practices, 70 verses discuss personal laws, 70 verses civil law, 30 penal laws and 20 judicial matters and testimony. These verses tend to deal with general principles, such as justice, kindness and charity, rather than detailed laws.

These statistics are from *The Qur'an*, a new translation by Muhammad Abdel Haleem (Oxford University Press, 2004). This author himself learnt the Koran by heart from his childhood.

The Koran is a remarkable work. One of its most insistent themes, which appears on practically every page, is the admonition to worship only the one God and to remind the people that if they do not worship Allah only, then they will be punished in hell and be unable to qualify for the bliss of heaven. This underlined the importance to Muhammad of ensuring that the current polytheism was defeated, a message so urgent that Muhammad remorselessly and relentlessly maintains the pressure throughout the work.

The description of Heaven is quite specific. I quote from the first paragraph from *Sura 56* entitled 'That which is coming' from Professor Abdel Haleem's translation. The Sura refers to those who are faithful and believe in God and confirms that their lot after death will be as follows:

> On couches of well-woven cloth they will sit facing each other; everlasting youths will go round among them with glasses, flagons, and cups of pure drink that causes no headache or intoxication; [there will be] any fruit they choose; the meat of any bird they like; and beautiful-eyed maidens like hidden pearls: a reward for what they used to do. They will hear no idle or simple talk there, only clean and wholesome speech ... they will dwell amid thornless lote trees and clustered acacia with spreading shade, constantly flowing water, abundant fruits, unfailing, unforbidden with incomparable companions We have specially created—virginal, loving, of matching age.

As for the unbelievers, they will dwell amid flames, scorching wind and scalding water in the shadow of black smoke.

**The rituals of Islam: the Five Pillars** Muslims have five principal rituals which have to be observed.

The first is the profession of faith in the following form—'There is no god but Allah and Muhammad is his messenger'. This is the monotheistic assertion.

The second pillar is the duty to pray five times a day, kneeling or prostrate and facing in the direction of Mecca, after a ritual washing—at daybreak, mid-day, the middle of the afternoon, at sunset and during the evening. On Fridays, you should attend the prayers at noon at the mosque where the imam says the prayers. The most important Islamic prayer, an obligatory part of the daily prayer, repeated several times a day, is the opening few lines of the Koran (from Professor Abdel Haleem's translation):

> In the name of God, the Lord of Mercy, the Giver of Mercy! Praise belongs to God, Lord of the Worlds, the Lord of Mercy, the Giver of Mercy, Master of the Day of Judgement. It is you we worship; it is You we ask for help. Guide us to the straight path: the path of those You have blessed, those who incur no anger and who have not gone astray.

The third pillar is to give alms—between 2.5 and 10 per cent of one's income according to the community. Sometimes this is distributed directly by the giver or by the mosque or collected and distributed by the government as an official tax backed by state tax-collecting powers. Only a few states, such as Saudi Arabia, have retained this religious tax. In most of the others the tax has been replaced by secular taxes.

The fourth pillar is to fast (no food or drink) during the month of Ramadan from sunrise to sunset for 30 days. It is hard not to have something to drink in a hot country during daylight. It is typical for Muslims to have a meal before sunrise and after sunset during Ramadan.

The fifth pillar is to make a pilgrimage to Mecca at least once in your life—the hajj.

Islam is treated by Muslims as a total way of life—the law, family life, business, what you eat, what you wear, your personal hygiene.

**Sunnis, Shiites and other sects** The Sunnis are the main Muslim sect. Around 90 per cent of Muslims are Sunni. The largest minority group are the Shiites—from the 'party of Ali', the cousin and son-in-law of Muhammad. They were originally a tribal group which backed Ali and his descendants as the only legitimate successors to Muhammad as the head of Muslims. Ultimately the sect centred mainly in Iran and developed different theological doctrines and rituals. Iran became Shiite under the first Safavid emperor Ismail (died 1524) who brutally suppressed Sunnis.

The majority subgroup of the Shiites—the Twelvers—hold that there is a direct line of infallible imams (a 'leader' or 'guide') traced back to Ali. The twelfth disappeared around 879 and a body of religious scholars—the ulema—took his place until his return as the Mahdi, meaning 'the Rightly Guided One'. Ayatollahs, meaning 'signs of God', regard themselves as caretakers of the office of imam who will return at the end of time.

A minority subgroup of Shiites is the Ismailis or Seveners who had a different view about the succession. This sect established the Fatimid dynasty in Egypt

(909–1171). One of the offshoots of this group is led by the Aga Khan. The Druze of Lebanon is another split-off from the Ismailis.

It is a puzzle that a disputed succession in the year 661 should lead to violent clashes for 1300 years so far. We are invited to conclude that there is some other explanation which is nothing to do with theocratic leadership so many centuries in the past.

Syncretic sects include the Babis and the Bahai'is whose roots go back to Persia of the 19th century.

The Wahhabis were a revivalist movement starting in the late-18th century and named after Bad-al-Wahhab (died 1792) who preached a return to the original beliefs and practices prevailing at the time of Muhammad. Their ultra conservative views were espoused by the subsequent rulers of the Kingdom of Saudi Arabia, established finally in 1932.

**Sufism** An adherent of this early sect seeks a direct understanding and experience of God. Sufism is an ascetic sect which rejects worldly goods and worldly desires. Sufi comes from 'wool', referring to the simple woollen cloth worn by early Sufis. The practice involves meditation or other rituals such as the repetition of one of the names of God over and over again, leading to the annihilation of the self, a concept similar to the Buddhist idea of enlightenment. One of the most famous Sufi mystics was Al-Ghazali (died 1111) who was born in Iran and ultimately established a Sufi community in Iran: he rejected the idea of becoming one with the deity as contrary to monotheism and rejected the veneration of saints. Unlike other Muslims, Sufis use music and dance in their rituals. Some would break out into unrestrained ecstasy and hence this branch became known as the 'drunken Sufis'.

**Sharia law** Sharia law is the traditional Islamic law in its state of development about a thousand years ago. Most Muslim states do not follow this old law, regarding it as out of date, for example, Indonesia and Malaysia. A few states still base their legal systems on the old sharia law on the basis that the Koran mandates these laws and, since the Koran is the word of God, it is not possible to change the law. The law is immutable, fixed forever. An example is Saudi Arabia. There are many hybrids and in-between solutions. On a scale of ten, very few countries are firmly ten (they include Saudi Arabia, Iran, Brunei and Sudan) but many are around five, for example, Qatar and Bahrain. A number of countries swing periodically between one approach and then another, for example, Pakistan and the Yemen.

The chief features of fundamentalist sharia law that differ from the views of modern Western societies are:

— The complete subjugation of women.

— In the sphere of criminal law, the imposition of draconian punishments, such as the stoning to death of women for adultery, the cutting off of the hands of thieves, the execution of those convicted of apostasy or blasphemy, and severe flogging to the point of death for drunkenness.

— In the sphere of commercial law, the rejection of interest-bearing transactions, such as loans where the borrower has to pay interest to the lender, the rejection of insurance and the obstacles in the way of the transfer of debts and receivables, such as the unpaid sale price for goods. Islamic finance transactions are very common in modern international capital markets for sale to devout Muslims. They use structures which were used by Christian financiers in the Italian Renaissance and before to avoid the Christian prohibition on usury.

— An uncompromising prohibition on alcohol and drugs (most Western states agree on drugs).

— Non-democratic government where the rulers are theocratic caliphs or ayatollahs.

Note that the above is the approach of fundamentalists, not Muslims generally. Nearly all of these doctrines, except the more violent punishments, were at one time a feature of some Christian societies in the medieval era.

Apart from the above, conservative Muslims are horrified by what they regard as the moral degeneracy of the West—the tolerance of sex before marriage and sex outside marriage threatening marriage and the family, the triumph of female liberation and open sexuality, the wild sensual abandon of pop music and clothes, the dethronement of the authority of the patriarchal father, the legalisation of homosexuality, the recognition of same-sex unions, and apparent widespread drunkenness and drug abuse. They fear that the adoption of Western morality and progress carries with it a threat which would annihilate the morality encased in their religion. The sexual threats create a deep sense of dread in young men. It is these emotions, among others, which inflame fanatical and extremist jihadists.

Historically it soon became apparent in the years after the death of Muhammad that the law propounded in the Koran did not give all the answers and that the answers given by various Muslim communities were different. The great Muslim lawyer al-Shafii (died 820) proposed a solution which amounted to a hierarchy of authenticity.

At the summit was the Koran. Next was the actual behaviour or conduct of Muhammad, what he actually did and said—the sunna, preserved in accounts called the haddith ('story', 'tradition'). Six multi-volume canonical collections were compiled in the 9th and early 10th centuries. The third technique was reasoning by analogy. The fourth technique was the consensus of the entire Muslim community. Since it was impracticable to discover this, the scholars of jurisprudence took over.

The result was that today there are four main Sunni schools of sharia law: (1) the Hanafis, founded by Hanafi (died 769) and dominant in Turkey, Pakistan and Central Asia, the most lenient sect; (2) the Malikis, founded by Malik (died 795) and dominant in upper Egypt, the rest of North Africa and Saharan Africa; (3) the Shafis, founded by Shafi (died 820) and dominant in lower Egypt, Syria, Malaysia and Indonesia; and (4) the Hanbalis, founded by Hanbal (died 855), dominant mainly in Saudi Arabia, the most strict and puritanical sect and the most insistent on the literal interpretation of the Koran. The main Shiite school is Imami.

The Koran is specific on some laws dealing, for example, with marriage, divorce, inheritance and food. It also makes it clear that certain practices, such as usury, eating pork, drinking wine and gambling, are bad. The Koran encouraged modesty in female dress, but appears not to have required that women wear a veil covering their face. A man must provide living expenses to wives, unmarried daughters and, in some cases, certain female relatives. A man can have up to four wives but a woman can have only one husband. A man can divorce a wife more easily than a woman can divorce a man. Both may remarry after divorce, but a woman must wait three or four months—because of the importance of knowing the paternity of children. Sons inherit twice as much as daughters, but at the time daughters inherited nothing and men were not responsible for the living expenses of their wives and other females. The dowry previously went to the bride's guardian (typically her father or a brother) but in the Koran it went to the bride and became her permanent property. In general the Koran improved the rights of women compared with previous customs and indeed compared with the customs of many contemporary Western countries, but whether these improvements were observed in practice is another matter.

**Impact of Islam on economic progress** There has been much debate about whether the relative lack of modernity of Muslim countries and whether their relative lack of economic development is due to religion or some other factor, such as climate or desert, or in some countries to the complacency and absence of competitive spur caused by vast quantities of oil. Is it the religion or is it geography or is it the general culture, the habits of the people? From the 18th century onwards, nearly all scientific progress was led by Western Europe and its offshoots. The leading Muslim power, the Ottoman Empire, fell far behind and scientific progress was virtually non-existent. In 1515 a decree of the Sultan threatened the death penalty on anyone found using the printing press. In 1518 the Sultan ordered the demolition of a groundbreaking observatory built by one of the most renowned intellectuals at the time from Istanbul. They did not build another observatory in Istanbul until 1868. A later commentator observed that while the Ottoman Empire was subject to sharia law, the Europeans had laws and rules invented by reason. The first printing press was introduced in the Ottoman Empire in 1727. It took the authority of the revolutionary Kemal Attaturk to establish Turkey as a secular state separate from religious authority. The caliphate was abolished in 1924, the religious courts were shut down and sharia law was replaced by a civil code based on Switzerland which had the latest code.

It was Attaturk's view that the main reason for the failure of the Ottoman Empire to advance in the realm of science was religious interference. This is an argument that has often been made but the Ottoman Empire was not the only society to turn its back on science. China did so in the 15th century and Japan a century or so afterwards. In the 20th century Mao's China also sought to reverse intellectual advance, as did Pol Pot in Cambodia in a more gruesome way in the 1970s. The lesson from this is that it can be too easy to point to religion as the cause of a backward-looking attitude which seizes a whole country. The cause seems much deeper and has a lot to do with the vulnerability felt by absolute rulers to innovation and the fact that these rulers tap into a general hostility to innovation among the population at large. So it is hard to lay the blame only at the door of Islam which had in the 9th century already shown what a precociously scientific and forward-looking religion it could be.

Moreover many other countries throughout the world were and are undeveloped compared with the West—in Africa, South America, South-East Asia and India. One cannot blame religion for this slower advent of modernisation. For example, many of the countries concerned are Christian and it is clear that Christianity in whatever form has not been a serious brake on progress in modern times.

**Conclusion on Islam** There is no doubt that Muhammad was a truly outstanding genius—a merchant, a diplomat, and above all a visionary thinker and the founder of a hugely successful religion, a remarkable achievement.

The religion has an intense purity and rationality in its resolute monotheism and its insistence on the imageless abstraction of God, a being or force which is not capable of representation and is beyond understanding. If you accept the idea of a supernatural god, then Islam is arguably the most intellectually logical of the universal religions. Its original message had a striking simplicity and directness, free of theological intricacy and metaphysics. The combination of these features propelled the religion forward as an indelible and compelling ideology.

The downside of the religion is the atrocious conduct of its fanatical terrorist wing, conduct which is a shocking violation of the most basic shared morality of all the great religions.

All three of the main Western religions expanded their legal texts after the initial foundation of their religions—Judaism in the Talmud, Christianity in canon law and Islam in sharia law. Only sharia law remains as a significant source of ordinary law in the modern day world.

For the great mass of devout Muslims, one suspects that many of them want both religion and modernity. There is no reason why they should not have both.

# 7

# *The Families of Religion:*
# *Eastern Religions*

## Introduction

We now come to the two main Eastern religions: Hinduism, which is almost exclusively an Indian religion and Buddhism, which is the third largest universal religion. I also include some notes on Jainism, Sikhism, Taoism and Shintoism which are not mainstream religions but which are worth a mention.

## Hinduism: Religion Without Leadership

**Introduction** One of the most striking features of Hinduism is that it was and is a religion without leadership. It had no founder in the sense that Zoroaster, Siddartha Gautama, Jesus Christ or Muhammad were founders of a distinct faith, no centralised leader, such as the pope or a caliph or an archbishop, no ordained and centrally trained priesthood, only an hereditary caste of brahmins, no conventions or councils or synods or gatherings of the leading priests to settle a common doctrine or creed with the concentration with which the Christians settled their creed at Nicaea, no single code or short statement of belief so that the people could be taught, hardly even an agreed canon of the sacred scriptures, no explicit and agreed summary laws of the succinctness of the Ten Command-ments, and no central site, such as the Jewish temple or the Vatican in Rome or Mecca. It just grew up, almost spontaneously, the work of the people over many centuries of custom and consensus.

The result was that there are many gods and many beliefs. Some say the beliefs are so disparate that Hinduism is not even a single religion, but rather many reli-gions, any belief that each individual or group likes. Yet, although there is much fragmentation, there is a common core which is recognisably Hindu and which provides the bond and link between Hindus, the fundamental identity which gives them meaning and cohesion.
**Transmigration of souls** Although there are many gods, there is a core belief that each person has a soul and that this soul will, after death, transmigrate to another being in an endless cycle of birth and rebirth until the individual achieves

enlightenment and joins in union with the ultimate soul, a sort of incorporeal god. If you are good in your life, you will have more status in the next life. If you are bad, you will end up possibly an untouchable or even worse. So Hinduism satisfies the basic requirements of religion in that it has supernatural beings who are interested in humans and each person has an immortal soul which survives death. It also has rituals and ceremonies to be practised. The core belief, the basic proposition, is not particularly complicated or mystical or occult. The key difference compared with the group composed of Judaism, Christianity and Islam is that advent to heaven is postponed until your soul has earned it—which could take many lifetimes.

**Not a universal religion** The religion is now national and territorial, apart from Indians living abroad. It is the religion of Indians. After a short sojourn in other territories in South-East Asia, it retreated under the impact of Buddhism or Islam. So it never claimed universality like Christianity or Islam. It was left to its main offshoot—Buddhism—to become an international faith on a large scale. It may be that Hinduism's very disorganisation made it hard to sell to other peoples, even though the priests did sell it very successfully to the whole of India with its numerous languages and different ethnicities and cultures. It was also hard to sell something which was written in ancient Sanskrit. It was hard to sell something which was a whole library of scriptures, like English case law.

**Number of Hindu adherents** Because India is so populous, Hinduism is nominally the world's third largest religion after Christianity and Islam. The population of India is about 1.32 billion (of whom a large proportion are Hindus) compared with China at about 1.4 billion and the United States (third) at about 316 million. The population is forecast to overtake China by 2050 (1.6 billion). The land area of India is around 3.3 million square kilometres which is a third the size of China or the United States and somewhat smaller than Europe but has nearly three times the population of Europe. Hindus are nominally about 80 per cent of the population of India. Muslims are nominally about 14 per cent (150 million) and are a majority in Kashmir. The 23 million nominal Christians have a 2.2 per cent share of the national population. These figures do not represent practising adherents.

Most of Nepal's population of 23 million are nominally Hindus. There are about one million Hindus in the United States and just under one million in the United Kingdon, although many are non-practising. The rest are scattered around the world, for example, in Bali and East Africa.

So from the top of the Indian subcontinent—from Tibet (Buddhist)—down to the tip but not including Sri Lanka, the former Ceylon (also Buddhist)—the people are Hindus apart from a few outposts, such as Muslim Hyderabad and Kashmir. To the west there is Islam in the shape of Pakistan. To the east there is Muslim Bangladesh and Buddhist Burma. As before, the real number of true practising Hindus is not available and so the numbers are nominal at most.

About 80 per cent of Indians live in villages. There are about 500,000 villages. Most of the villagers are extremely poor. They seek a practical religion, not metaphysical lore.

Hinduism is an extremely ancient religion. Whether it is the world's oldest existing religion is another question. Zoroastrianism could have been formulated by 1200 or even 1500 BCE and Judaism certainly crystallised its doctrines by the time of Moses, not later than 1220 BCE. Although the oldest scriptures of the Hindus go back possibly to 1500 BCE, these were very sketchy in terms of doctrine and the religion possibly only took its present form around the time of the Upanishads composed between 600 and 200 BCE. Nevertheless the religion is of great antiquity.

The historical evidence suggests that a people called the Aryans arrived from Iran and Central Asia in the Indus valley around 1500 BCE. The Indus valley runs up the middle of present-day Pakistan. They overran the excising Harappa civilisation, one of the great civilisations of the ancients existing from about 2300 to 1500, whose main cities were Mohenjo-Daro and Harappa, now excavated. In due course the Aryans established themselves in northern and central India.

**Authentic Hindu scriptures** It was these Aryans who produced the sacred Vedas over the period from 1200 to 200 BCE. The Vedas comprised chronologically (1) probably between 1200 and 800, the Vedic Samhitas which were hymns of praise to various gods, including fire and sun gods, most of whom have disappeared from the Hindu pantheon, plus mantras to be chanted, especially the Rig-Veda, (2) probably between 800 and 500 BCE, explanations of various rituals called the Brahmanas, (3) probably between 400 and 200 BCE, works on philosophical and contemplative themes, called the Aranyakas, and (4) probably between 600 and 200 BCE, the much more important Upanishads. All these dates are very approximate.

Many of the Upanishads were conversations between a devotee and his master on religious subjects. They developed the core beliefs of Hinduism. The old gods were not swept aside but were regarded as reflections of the one God, the Brahman—the monistic idea that everything is one, an idea which was to cause much ideological trouble later—and also the idea that everybody had a soul, an *atman*. The soul was the true self, what we now call consciousness. The Upanishads further developed the central idea of the transmigration of souls (*samsara*), ie, that after death your soul lives on in some other being.

The above texts are known as the *sruti* texts, ie, the texts 'heard' by the ancient sages and revealed by the gods to these sages. Being divine in origin they were regarded as infallible and unchangeable, the fundamental Hinduism, just as the Torah, the four Gospels of the Christians and the Koran are treated by some devotees as divinely inspired and not to be challenged or reinterpreted. All the other texts were *smrti* texts, ie, 'remembered' or written down from memory and not divinely inspired.

Books within the *smrti* tradition, ie, those which did not have divine origin, included the great epics which contain much didactic material as well as grand legends and which are told and re-told, enacted and re-enacted in story, dance, drama and art. The Ramayana were written between 500 BCE and 400 CE recording an oral story thought to be about 2500 years old. The Ramayana is a violent and poignant tale of the seizure of a king's kingdom by an enemy, the abduction of his wife, her subsequent doleful banishment by the king and their ultimate reconciliation, followed by universal harmony. The epic Mahabharata was also recorded between about 200 BCE and 200 CE. This deals with a confrontation between good and evil by exploring the relationship between two rival family factions. The most important part of this epic is the Bhagavad Gita or Song of God, which effectively contains a summary of Hindu beliefs.

**The Hindu caste system** Much earlier on the Hindus had developed the caste system. Many societies had a quite rigid system of social classes—typically, priests, nobles, warriors, merchants and the rest, a categorisation which has lasted in Western societies at least into the 20th century—but nobody produced a caste system, backed by divine commands, with quite such relentlessness as the Indians. At one time there could have been nearly three thousand castes and sub-castes.

At the top were the priests—the *brahmins*, a scholarly caste. One of the things which made the brahmins so powerful is that they insisted that they knew all the correct sacrifices, hymns, chants and rituals. If you did not get these matters exactly right, then the gods would be upset which could be a disaster for you. After the brahmins came the rulers and the warriors—the nobles, called the *kshatriya*. Third were the tradesmen and craftsmen in metals—the *vaishiyas*. Fourth were the *shudras*—the peasants, the lowly workers, the serfs. And then right at the bottom, so horribly polluted as to have to live outside the village, were the untouchables—grave-diggers who touched corpses, latrine cleaners, sweepers, tanners of leather and also their families. In 1950 untouchability was abolished by law, but often the legal wand, though waved, disturbs nothing but the air.

This stratified hierarchical society advantaged those at the top, the brahmins, who thought of the idea, and was justified as improving social cohesion and giving identity to the people who otherwise might be alienated by not knowing their place. You were born in your caste and there was no way you could move up. There was no such thing as a meritocracy. You were tied to your job which was hereditary, whatever the religion had to say about your soul moving up if you were good. It was not done to marry out of your caste. The hierarchy was backed by religious commands: you had a positive moral duty to perform the functions of your caste and to not step out of place. Since the brahmins were at the top and since they wrote the rules, change was not going to be likely. The caste system is still strong in India and a great barrier to advancement.

**The main Hindu gods** The ancient Vedic gods, such as the god of fire, have more or less disappeared from the line-up. The most popular gods were and are Vishnu, Shiva and Shakti the Mother Goddess. Each male god has a consort who might be worshipped in her own right.

Vishnu was originally god of the sky but is now the sustainer, the preserver. This god fights against evil and promotes law and righteousness. His consort is Lakshmi. Vishnu can be incarnated and appear on earth as an avatar, meaning 'down-coming' or 'descent', to guide people when they are in danger There are ten avatars of Vishnu of whom only one is still to come and of whom the most important is Krishna, recognisable by his blue skin and often also worshipped in his own right. The idea of the avatar is similar to the idea of Jesus Christ being God incarnated on earth. Those who worship only Vishnu are virtually monotheist.

The second most important god is Shiva, the destroyer. This extraordinary god is the god of destruction, sexuality, fear, the mystical forces of the psyche, life and death, eternal rest and ceaseless activity—a god of many paradoxes and opposites, divine and demoniac. Shiva is often represented by a stylised phallus or the yoni-lingam (vagina-penis) which is a stone or wooden stylised sharp-ended penis lying in a round female organ and worshipped as an object of veneration. His consort is Shakti.

Shakti is the third of the three pre-eminent gods, representing female energy in creation. She comes in many forms, both horrific and benign, and has many names of which the Mother Goddess or Parvati (mild) are the most common.

Brahma, the creator, used to be regularly worshipped in classical times but has now faded from attention. It is worth noting the distinction between *Brahman*, who is the one supreme reality, the creator god *Brahma*, and the *brahmins*, who are priests. Brahman is the one eternal God, without attributes, all-knowing, all-powerful, all-pervading—an idea developed in the Rig Veda and the Upanishads. Brahman was too abstract to worship—hence the development of gods who have form and attributes.

The statues of the above gods in the home or in the temple are often accompanied by either or both of Ganesh, an elephant-headed god, who is seen as the god of good luck and remover of obstacles, and Hanuman, who is a monkey god representing physical strength. Both have a mythical genealogy.

In addition villages may have thousands of other local gods—a god of a river, a lake, a tree, a mountain. Gods may be represented by statues or icons of birds, flowers or snakes, sometimes deities, sometimes just an aid to worship.

**The Bhagavad Gita and Hindu beliefs** We can now get back to the Bhagavad Gita composed perhaps between 100 and 200 CE and probably the most important Hindu religious text. The Gita has been translated about 1800 times into about 75 languages. An English prose translation is about 80 pages.

Two great armies face each other on the battlefield. They are led by cousins and are made up of rival factions in the same family who fell out with each other. The warrior Arjuna is the leader of one of the armies. He commands his charioteer to drive him between the armies to view them. He is horrified to see so many relatives and family members facing each other for battle, so horrified that he decides not to fight. But it turns out that his charioteer is in fact Krishna who is the avatar or incarnation of the god Vishnu. Krishna convinces Arjuna that this is a just war because the opponents tricked Arjuna's family out of their kingdom and because Arjuna as a member of the warrior caste has a sacred duty to fulfil the responsibilities of his caste. This rejection of pacifism may have been a side-swipe at Buddhism. In the main, the moral lesson is that a just war is legitimate and that moral ideology overcomes tribal and family allegiances.

In the course of their conversation, Krishna succinctly and clearly states the main tenets of the Hindu faith.

Each individual has an immortal soul which cannot be killed. This soul is continuously reborn in a cycle of reincarnation until the soul achieves liberation or freedom from the cycle. This enlightenment is called moksha. Only right living and good conduct can lead to enlightenment and hence to unity with the Absolute (Brahman), the source and soul of all creation. Because this notion of some great soul is so abstract some devotees believe that each god has its own heaven for those who make it and that there is a hell where you get tortured if you don't make it. This concept of the transmigration of souls does not fit with modern genetics since genetics establishes that you inherit the genes of your father and mother without intermixture of some third force. Some Hindus explain this away by arguing that the soul somehow homes in on your father and mother. Anyway this concept of transmigration of souls, called samsara, is the big idea.

Two other concepts are relevant, for both of which the Upanishads are important sources. The first is the notion of karma, which means 'action'. If your actions, your karma, are bad, you will be reborn in a lower level of society or even as an animal. Even worse things could happen to you. The results of karma can last for several lifetimes. We would now say that we are moulded by our genetic inheritance and our environment—our nature and our nurture.

The second further concept is dharma, which broadly means the 'law' but has a range of meanings—truth, providence, ethics, religious or social duty or the moral force which holds the universe together. Dharma is the duties which individuals have to fulfil to comply with the whole order of the universe, the moral order, the social order, such as caste, and personal righteousness or ethics. For example, you must not lie or cause injury. You must be charitable. You must follow the customs of your caste. You must honour the brahmins.

Krishna explains that the four main goals of life are (1) to perform your duties (*dharma*), (2) to achieve liberation from the cycle of birth and rebirth, (3) to accumulate material things, wealth and power (another dig at ascetic Buddhist monks?)—called *artha*, and (4) to achieve personal gratification, in particular sexual pleasure and the love of beauty—*kama*. A life-affirming creed, which may help to explain the popularity of the Bhagavad Gita. As a way of living, the code is not bad.

Krishna added that there were three paths to enlightenment. The first was the path of knowledge, for example, of the scriptures and understanding Brahman, the universal soul. The second was action or *karma*, the performance of duty, selflessness and the carrying out of rituals. The third was the path of devotion (*bhakti*), ie, a selfless love of god and enjoyment of his presence. God in turn helps the soul towards liberation. Hindus can choose the gods to whom they offer this devotion or *bhakti*. It follows from this that the religion puts great emphasis upon worshipping and honouring the gods.

The above epics were not the only *smrti* texts. There are also the Puranas (meaning 'ancient'), which are mainly collections of stories about kings, gods, wise men and heroes. There are 18 major Puranas and 18 minor. They were probably written between 500 and 1500 CE. In addition there is a vast number of other texts, including the Tantras which were manuals or handbooks produced between the 6th and 7th centuries CE.

**The Dharmasastras** And then finally there are the law books, the Dharmasastras which were preceded by the Dharmasutras and of which the most prominent are the laws of Manu. These could have been written between the 6th and 3rd centuries BCE. They were not really law books of secular law, but set out religious life and duties. The main obligation was to fulfil one's duties and the right way of living appropriate to one's caste. The books deal with domestic rituals, rites of passage, sin, expiation, pollution, ritual purification and other aspects of the religious life.

The later legal texts were written in metered verse between about 200 BCE and 1000 CE and expanded in voluminous commentaries over the next few centuries, so much so that the British regarded them as an entire legal system. The 18 titles of Hindu substantive law covered an assorted range including the non-payment of debts, sale, partnership, breach of contract, boundary disputes, verbal assault, physical assault, theft, sexual crimes against women and inheritance.

One can see that this is a somewhat haphazard collection of topics. The question of whether these laws were ever implemented is debatable. Anglo-Indian law preserved family law areas—marriage, child marriage, polygamy, divorce, maintenance and the like, but the rest was replaced by colonial British law. Post-colonial Indian law included statutes on family subjects and also inheritance.

**The later classical period** One of the greatest dynasties of classical times was the Mauryan dynasty founded by Chandragupta Maurya (reigned 321–297 BCE). Hinduism received a setback when his grandson Asoka (reigned c 271 to c 231) converted to pacifist Buddhism after a bout of remorse at the casualties suffered in a battle. Nevertheless Hinduism ideas had spread. By 500 BCE Sri Lanka was in the sphere of influence of Hinduism and over the next eight hundred years Hindu kingdoms were established in Burma, Cambodia, Sumatra, Thailand and Java. The splendid Khmer kingdom based on Angkor Wat in Cambodia was Hindu.

The golden age of Hinduism came into its own at the time of the Gupta Empire from about 320 to 480 CE when the status of the brahmins was at its height. The Gupta Empire was destroyed by a Hunnish invasion in 480 CE. Buddhism faded, so much so that by the 12th century it had almost disappeared from India.

In 713 CE the Muslims ominously appeared in Sind in present-day Pakistan.

**Yoga** Around the 2nd century CE the religious leader Patanjali developed the yoga school which has been so influential in Indian history. Yoga focused more on the spiritual side than the gymnastics. It advocated the use of meditation and exercises to achieve concentration and to escape the whirlwind of thought so as to quieten thoughts and see the unity of all things—a state of higher consciousness and illumination. To achieve this, posture and breathing were important as aids to concentration and detachment from the world. Patanjali described the eight steps of yoga which included non-injury of others, speaking the truth, celibacy and the rejection of greed and theft—a rather different set of moral priorities than that propounded by Krishna in the Bhagavad Gita—with its acceptance of the accumulation of wealth and the enjoyment of sex.

**The Muslims** The Muslims made inroads over centuries. The great Sultanate of Delhi of 1208 to 1526 was displaced by the Mughal Empire, founded by Babur (reigned 1526–30) who was a descendant of Genghis Khan. By the time of Akbar the Great (reigned 1556–1605), the Empire stretched almost to the southern tip of India. The artistic splendour of this dynasty was beautifully demonstrated by the Taj Mahal built by Shah Jehan (reigned 1628–58) in honour of his dead wife. Hindus were persecuted by Aurangjeb who reigned from 1658 to 1707 but already something else alarming had happened.

**From Taj to Raj** The Portuguese arrived in India in 1498 and by 1510 they had taken Goa. The East India Company was established in England in 1600. In 1661 the English had taken Bombay, now Mumbai. Their main competitor was France. The French were defeated finally at the Battle of Plessey in 1757 by Clive (1725–74). By the middle of the 19th century the East India Company controlled 60 per cent of India but was displaced in its sovereign responsibilities by the British Government in 1858 after the Indian Mutiny of 1857. The British brought English law, railways, British administration and their language. They did not bring their religion because the British East India Company thought that missionary activity would upset the inhabitants and get in the way of trade. So unlike Africa where the Christian missionaries, such as David Livingstone, brought Christianity and commerce, the British in India brought just commerce.

One reaction to the British religion was to try to update Hinduism. The main leader here was Ram Mohan Roy (1772–1833). Roy was an early universalist who endeavoured to blend Hinduism with Christianity but succeeded with neither. He founded the Brahmo Samaj or Divine Society. He attempted to expurgate Hinduism of its supposed superstitions, objected to image worship and rejected reincarnation. Appalled by the practice of suttee whereby a widow was supposed to throw herself on to her dead husband's funeral pyre, he successfully campaigned to have the practice made illegal.

A very different reaction was that of Dayananda Sarawati (1824–83) who called for a return to the classical Vedas and a return to the old faith. If you are faced with a new threatening culture, you either join them or you go back to your basics. He also rejected image worship, the belief in avatars and the caste system.

The 19th century was a time of religious reawakening, driven by a new nationalist consciousness aroused by the presence of the British. There were many other Indian religious reformers at work. Vivikananda (1863–1902), for example, expressed a religious universalism which saw Hinduism as at the forefront, rather than backward.

Certainly Hinduism became more confident and self-assertive. In one extraordinary episode Madam Blavatsky, the founder of the Theosophical Society, arrived in India in 1877 with her successor Annie Besant. They travelled around praising all things Hindu. This was a good example of the fascination of many people in the West with Hindu mysticism, a fascination which gave rise to the Hare Krishna movement of the 1960s and Transcendental Meditation. The Western devotees, including the Beatles, in their wide-eyed wonderment at the mystical metaphysics of these movements, evidently did not know anything of the robust Hinduism of the Bhagavad Gita with its emphasis on material things and its plain philosophy.

Nationalist pressures intensified in the 20th century, greatly assisted by the work of Mahatma Gandhi (1869–1948). Gandhi trained as a barrister in London and qualified in 1891. He worked as a lawyer in Durban in South Africa where he was active in combating racialism. He returned to India in 1915 and became involved in the independence campaign. He adopted the principle of non-violence in the promotion of his political protests. He proposed to teach the materialist West some of the spiritual values of the East. A great reformer, he rejected caste. Economically he looked back rather than forward, objecting to large-scale industry in favour of a simple village-based economy. He was a pacifist. He was assassinated in 1948 by a Hindu radical who was enraged by the belief that Gandhi had abandoned traditional Hinduism.

**Independence of India** In 1947 Britain granted independence to India which split up into Hindu India led by Nehru (1889–1964) and Muslim Pakistan led by Ali Jinnah (1876–1948), amid great bloodshed and mass migrations. India and Pakistan fought over Kashmir in 1947 to 1949, in 1965 and 1971. In 1971 East Pakistan became independent as Muslim Bangladesh, amid atrocities.

India assumed joint leadership of the non-aligned world and developed close relations with the USSR. Indira Gandhi, who was Nehru's daughter and Prime Minister from 1966, was assassinated in 1984 by one of her Sikh bodyguards. In 1991 her son Rajiv who succeeded her as Prime Minister was assassinated by a Tamil Tiger suicide bomber. Subsequently violence between Hindus and Muslims increased over a campaign, begun in 1990, to build a Hindu temple on the site of a mosque in the holy city of Ajodhya. There were numerous terrorist attacks in subsequent years. India embarked on a process of market reform and privatisation from 1990 onwards.

The subsequent political history of India saw a rising nationalist side to Hinduism, opposing the secular state, illustrated by the success of the Bharatiya Janat Party which was first in power from 1998 to 2004, having defeated the dominant Congress Party. There was a spread of fundamentalist groups.

India exploded its first nuclear device in 1974. Pakistan carried out nuclear tests in 1998.

**Hindu rituals and festivals** Hinduism must be one of the most ritualised of all the major religions. The whole of secular life is governed by rituals. The first reason for this is that, if something goes wrong, it is because you have neglected the gods. The gods need an offering to sort the matter out. Or there is some evil spirit which has to be bought off. Or it is the evil eye. Whatever it is, money has to change hands and food handed over. If the rituals are not performed precisely as required, the god will be incensed and you are in even more trouble.

In the second place many rituals are driven by cleanliness, hygiene and the avoidance of pollution—a simple health measure, observed by Hindus where they can in their personal lives (if there is any clean water around), but abysmally observed at the municipal level in terms of adequate sewers and waste treatment.

The act of worship is called *puja*, mainly image worship. This could be a visit to the temple or just lighting a lamp. Most Hindu homes have a shrine—in a niche or on a shelf in the kitchen or in the hallway, say—with statues of the favourite gods. The members of the family pray at this shrine. In the temples the act of worship is generally to treat the god as a human—the god has to be woken, cleansed, dressed and fed. Devotees offer food—such as fruit or sweets, flowers and money, all of which no doubt ease the hard path of the priests.

Domestic rituals included five daily obligatory offerings: (1) offerings of food to the gods, (2) a brief offering to 'all beings', (3) a libation of water and sesame offered to the spirits of the dead, (4) hospitality, and (5) recitation of the Veda. There are also morning and evening adorations.

All human emissions are regarded as polluting—saliva, urine, faeces, sweat, semen, menstrual flow and the afterbirth. There are elaborate rituals to cope with these pollutants. Cows are sacred. Killing a cow is not permitted. There are at least 40 rites of passage, all attended by their own rituals. The dead are cremated. Pilgrimage is not obligatory, as it is in Islam, but is very common. There are dozens of top pilgrimage sites—rivers, mountains, springs.

There are numerous festivals of which Diwali, the New Year Festival, is the most important. Diwali is a family occasion and involves the giving of gifts and many other ceremonies. The festival of Holi is a saturnalia, usually connected with the spring equinox.

**Hindu attitudes to family and women** The extended family is common in the villages and even in the cities. The family is generally male dominated and feminism has some way to go. Women have the right to inherit property equally with their brothers as a result of secular legislation. It was hard to get this through because it meant that a daughter would on marriage take family wealth to her new family, thereby rendering family farms in the villages less economical. A Hindu man traditionally has a duty to marry and weddings are often lavish affairs, staged at huge expense. The legal prohibitions on dowry are widely ignored. Remarriage of a widow is now lawful. Child marriage is illegal. Suttee was outlawed in 1829 by the British. Battles to promote female education were largely won in the 19th century. There are virtually no female priests. Some marriages are arranged. There is quite a high rate of female abortion. Divorce is legal and is governed by the Hindu Marriage Act 1955.

**Conclusion on Hinduism** The core of the religious beliefs shows great subtlety and exhibits a strong sense of the need for a code of survival. The system of reward and punishment for violations of the moral code in the form of the transmigration of your soul is as weak or as strong as the alternative of heaven and hell. As with other major religions, Hindu law does not deliver a comprehensive modern legal morality but otherwise seems on a par with other moral codes pronounced by religion. The Bhagavad Gita version of morality is life-affirming and sensible in its recognition of the real world.

Hinduism has a continuous history longer than any other large religion and enormous staying power. It fought off all its rivals—the religion of the Buddha who introduced a Reformation in India but then lost the battle, the religion of the Mughal conquerors and then the religion of the European conquerors. The religion may have failed to be truly international, but it still is at least the third largest religion in the world in terms of number of nominal adherents.

# Jainism and Sikhism

I deal here with two offshoots of Hinduism—Jainism and Sikhism. Neither of them is mainstream or universal but they both have some interesting features.

**Jainism** Jainism is almost totally an Indian religion. There are between five and six million nominal adherents, which is about 0.5 per cent of the population of India. The religion was started by Mahavira whose dates were probably 599–527 BCE although some scholars suggest that these dates are about 50 years too early. He was born in what is now Bihar State in India.

It is doubtful that Jainism is strictly a religion because they do not believe in a supreme deity or in divine intervention in human affairs or in a creator of the universe. But they do believe in the Hindu ideology of transmigration of souls on death, according to your conduct during life.

Mahavira was roughly a contemporary of Siddhartha Gautama, the Buddha. There are two sects, one of which comprises wandering naked ascetics and another whose adherents wear white robes. Each sect has its own canon of scriptures. They stress your personal responsibility for your ethical conduct. They have a doctrine of extreme non-violence which extends to all creatures, insects and even plants, all of which have souls. Some ascetics will sweep the ground before them so as to avoid trampling on any creature and will wear masks so as not to swallow insects. This doctrine meant that they could not get involved in any form of agriculture which might for example lead to the killing of worms. As a result they ended up as businessmen and professionals and were and are quite influential in the Indian economy. They had some very challenging views about the universe and the cosmos but at least they had a good sense of the length of the history of the earth and the fact that there are millions of micro-organisms in the soil and in the air.

**Sikhism** This is a hybrid offshoot from Hinduism spurred probably by dissatisfaction with the brahmins and Hinduism generally. In particular, it was probably driven by the intense nationalism of the Punjabis. There are about 23 million Sikhs and 80 per cent of them live in the Punjab region in the north-west of India. The Punjab was divided at the time of Indian independence on the division of India into India and Pakistan and the location has occasioned much sectarian angst.

Sikhism is a local belief and is not mainstream or universal. It nevertheless does have some extremely interesting features.

It was begun by Guru Nanak (1469–1539) after an intense spiritual experience. Nine additional gurus, making ten in all, followed until 1708 when this form of leadership came to an end. The religion therefore started at the same time as the Reformation in Europe and indeed the movement has a number of ideological parallels with the Protestants, including, for example, a direct personal relationship with God without priests being in the way, the open temples, the dislike of ritual, a pro-business orientation, an ethical duty to work to support oneself, and a duty to help support others. The main sins are lust, anger, greed or covetousness, excessive attachment to the world, pride and selfishness. The movement was not ascetic and did not encourage renunciation of the world, rather involvement in the world. It was not monastic.

The remarkable feature of this religion is that it is monotheistic, probably because of the influence of the surrounding Muslims. In other respects, the religion follows the Hindu tradition of transmigration of souls. Meditation is emphasised. One form involves simply concentrating on God so as to remove all other thoughts and another involves repeating the name of God over and over again like a mantra, again to clear the mind.

The dead are cremated. The Sikhs had a more welcoming attitude to the lower castes but otherwise they preserve the caste system, the traditional Hindu emphasis on the family and the subordination of women. Sikhs still tend not to marry out.

Among other features of dress, they are not to cut their hair, which is why they wear a turban, and they must carry a short sword. This symbolises the defence of their religion and also the sense of protecting the weak against the strong. In Britain, Sikhs are not obliged to wear a safety helmet when they are riding a motorcycle.

# Buddhism

**The split off from Hinduism** Buddhism was born in the north of the Indian subcontinent at the time of the mature development of the basic Vedic scriptures of the Hindus, around 500 BCE. It was an abrupt break with the Hindu ideology. Gone was the great Hindu pantheon of gods and the Vedic tradition, even the Ultimate Soul. Gone was the centrality of the transmigration of souls and the endless cycle of birth and rebirth. Gone was the draconian insistence on the caste system and your place in it. In their stead was the Buddha and his teachings, a way of life, only just a religion.

Almost all Buddhists are Asian—nominally about 350 million of them, but some estimates put the number of Buddhists as much higher. The actual numbers of practising Buddhists are guesswork and unverifiable. Two of the most thoroughly Buddhist countries in the modern world are Thailand and Myanmar (Burma).

**Siddhartha Gautama** Buddhism was founded by Siddhartha Gautama, who died probably in 483 BCE, as a breakaway religion from Hinduism. Unlike Hinduism, the religion had a founder. The story of Gautama seems credible, with some allowance for dramatic effect. He was born near Lumbini in what is now Nepal. He came from the warrior or noble caste. He was brought up as a prince in luxury and married a princess by whom he had a son. Growing tired of this bland existence, he journeyed outside his palace.

He was horrified to encounter an old man, a sick man, a corpse and an ascetic. His charioteer told him that he too would be old, sick and then a corpse. Life is transitory. His first reaction was to renounce life and become an ascetic, free of riches and status.

After years of fasting and meditation, he realised that he wanted to achieve enlightenment as to what things really are and freedom from suffering. He became the Buddha, so-called because his moment of understanding came when he was meditating under the bodhi tree, the 'tree of enlightenment'. He rejected extreme asceticism and chose the middle way. It is only when you feel no sense of self that you eliminate all fear of dying and loss, that you achieve nirvana— blissful enlightenment, serenity. Nirvana literally means 'cooling off' or 'going out'—like a fire or a lamp. He gathered a group of disciples and travelled around northern India. He died in the little town of Kusinara, aged 80, possibly from dysentery.

**Buddhism and the gods** Buddhism is often said not to be a religion since there is no god and no central creed. Nevertheless the religion does adhere to a reformulated idea of reincarnation and most Buddhists would agree that there is an omniscient being who is however beyond comprehension. There is no god who created the earth and the universe.

The core belief of Buddhism is that you can attain enlightenment or awakening or nirvana, a state of complete peace and escape from the circle of death and birth, by following various principles of ethics and conduct, including meditation and control of your internal thoughts. In that way, you can escape suffering, anxiety and dissatisfaction. So the emphasis is upon spiritual development, conduct and thought, rather than the supernatural.

It is hard to say whether Buddhism has a belief in an ultimate heaven. The religion does contemplate a pure abode inhabited by those of great spiritual attainment. The Pure Land School contemplated a paradisiacal pure land in the West. But the immortality of the soul is not a leading motif. The Buddha seemed to think that this point was just a distraction. He was non-committal. Buddhism did not deny the gods. They too are not eternal, but impermanent. Buddhism is the Middle Way, which includes the middle way between the personal immortality of the soul and the belief that death is the final end. In the end the Buddhist supernatural god is not central as a being to be worshipped and the soul is not the fixed self but is forever changing. The philosophy is only marginally a religion in that sense. You have only got to compare the Islamic insistence in the Koran on the absolute need to honour and worship one God to see the difference.

Even nirvana remains an elusive concept. It is not like going to heaven. The Buddha refused to answer the question of whether those who attained nirvana lived on after death—he dismissed the question as 'improper'. So on crucial questions the Buddha was enigmatic. It was almost as if Siddartha Gautama, unlike Moses or Muhammad, was insisting that Siddartha Gautama was in charge of the theology, not God.

Buddhism had a precocious concept of the universe which was on an enormous scale and was composed of galaxies and super-galaxies, each containing billions of worlds, a view far ahead of its time. The inferior levels of the universe included terrible regions populated by the dead, by animals and by hell's dwellers. There were also cold hells and hells between the universes. They thought, correctly, that the universe was likely to be extremely cold.

**Buddhist rituals** The devotional practices or rituals involve meditation, bowing, offerings, pilgrimage and chanting.

The meditation is essentially simple. One example is as follows. If you are sitting still or lying down, you concentrate on the tiny detail of the sense of each part of your body in turn, from your toes to your scalp, a minute for each part. What do they feel like, what sensations do you have? If you eat a piece of fruit, you gaze at the colours, you eat it, slowly and let the tastes infuse your mind. Be alert to the touch on your tongue, be aware of the act of swallowing. You apply the same concentrated awareness to everything you do, whether lifting your hand or walking down a path—be aware of your shoes touching the ground, the sensations in your leg muscles, so as to prevent harassing thoughts entering your mind. Similarly concentration on the repetitive rhythmic process of breathing induces calm and peacefulness in your mind. In this way, you come to observe everything, be aware of everything, see things as they really are. What was mechanical and automatic becomes rich and magical. This is mindfulness—a kind of insight and self-observation.

Meditation also included analysis of your thoughts. Thoughts, often disturbing, drift in and out of your mind. Note that they are impermanent. Note that they are not your true self since they are ephemeral. You don't own these thoughts. In the end, you then empty your mind of everything, you don't let your mind brood or worry about the past or the future or be inflamed by anger. So this is not something mystical or metaphysical or esoteric or occult. Meditation is simple.

Alternatively you can achieve the same effect of closing out harmful thoughts by repeating the same phrase over and over again—a mantra.

You become a Buddhist by committing to the Three Jewels—taking refuge in the triple gem, as it is called—the Buddha, the teachings and the community, ie, the *sangha*, or the assembly of Buddhist monks. The other commitments are to ethical precepts, to the development of mindfulness and the cultivation of higher wisdom, and various ritual practices and ceremonies.

Birth and marriage celebrations are secular, but there is an initiation rite for young boys. The dead are usually cremated. Worship is in temples or at home. There is an abundance of statues of the Buddha. Devotees bring offerings of food and flowers and prostrate themselves. Pilgrimage is not obligatory but is common. One of the most stupendous pilgrimage sites is at Borobudur near Yogyakarta in Java, Indonesia.

**Buddhist scriptures** The Buddha left nothing in writing, but a few months after his death his followers convened a council at Rajagurha to recite his teachings orally. Apparently there were a further three councils over the centuries up to 100 BCE to settle doctrine.

There are numerous texts but no single canon, unlike Christianity and Islam. The Theravada Pali Canon was finally committed to writing in the 1st century CE.

The scriptures of the Mahayana sect are mainly in sutras or verses, originally chanted and then written down, perhaps between 100 BCE and 100 CE. There are about six hundred surviving sutras. The Mahayana scriptures were subsequently expanded to include, for example, the Tantras using magical mantras and including a manual on sexual techniques to achieve spiritual enlightenment. Tantras were also a feature of Hinduism. The sexual tantras were largely techniques of prolonging and enhancing the enjoyment of sex. In substance they offered little more than you would find in a competent medical sex manual written by a clinical psychologist, though somewhat elaborated by rituals such as meditating in the lotus position. Buddhists in the lay villages and towns were not always impressed by this method of achieving divinity practised by monks in their monasteries, and so the tantras were not central by any means.

**Main Buddhist sects** The two main sects are Theravada Buddhism ('way of the Elders') and Mahayana Buddhism ('the Great Vehicle'). The split seems to have happened between 100 BCE and 100 CE. Theravada ('original teaching') is the most conservative and the closest to the original Buddhism.

Theravada Buddhism or Southern Buddhism is the dominant form in Cambodia, Laos, Thailand, Sri Lanka and Burma, with possibly about 120 million nominal adherents. Statistics as to the number of adherents are hard to substantiate and may be wildly inaccurate.

Mahayana Buddhism or Eastern Buddhism is the dominant form in Vietnam and Singapore and in China, Japan, Korea and Taiwan. It could have 100 million nominal adherents. The Mahayana sect regards the Buddha as not being merely human but as the earthly projection of an endless, omnipresent being who has no corporeal being, in other words, a god or a force or a Platonic form. The Buddha is like the Hindu avatar or Jesus Christ—a reincarnation of God on earth, but merely an appearance in a different form of a god, just as a goblin or imp is a manifestation of the same spirit. The Mahayanas believe that there are innumerable other Buddhas in other universes. Some sects come close to the idea of heaven in that they believe that you can be liberated on death into some pure blissful land. The Theravada Buddhists believe that the Buddha was not a god, but an ordinary man, just as Islam treats Jesus Christ as an ordinary man, but not a god.

Theravada Buddhism is heavily influenced by the monastic lifestyle. Mahayana less so.

Mahayana Buddhists also believe that there is a class of godlike figures or bodhisattvas who are on the path to enlightenment and who live in heavenly realms but can come down to earth, where they can be worshipped. So images of gods were reintroduced into Buddhism: the first statues appeared in the 1st century BCE. Mahayana can be virtually polytheist, as with Hinduism.

Tibetan Buddhism or Northern Buddhism is found mainly in Bhutan, Nepal, Tibet and Mongolia. It has up to 20 million nominal adherents.

Zen Buddhism emphasises meditation as opposed to the ethics and rituals of Buddhism. Zen Buddhism became popular in China, Korea and Japan.

**The spread of Buddhism** A critical event in the history of Buddhism was the conversion of the Emperor Ashoka of the Mauryan dynasty. He ruled almost all

India from about 269 BCE to 232 BCE. After his conversion around 263 BCE, apparently brought on by disgust and remorse at the huge number of deaths in a war he had waged, he propagated Buddhism internationally with great vigour. The war inspired his great monologue beginning, 'What have I done?' Ashoka summoned a further council of devotees to agree numerous Buddhist scriptures written in Sanskrit. Subsequently this remarkable character became the model of ideal kingship, the perfect philosopher-king. He set an example which resonates down even to us in the 21st century.

The support given by the local kings to Buddhism led to a close association between the religious and secular authorities. Even now, Buddhism is the state-supported religion of Thailand and the King of Thailand is both a secular and religious leader, as indeed is also the case in Britain in relation to the Church of England.

Apart from conversions by Ashoka emissaries to the west, the Theravada sect spread south in the 200s BCE to Sri Lanka and Thailand, Burma and Indonesia. Another school spread north at the same time to Kashmir, Gandhara and the modern Afghanistan. It was probably not until the 1st or 2nd century CE that the religion spread to China and in the 2nd century CE to Korea and Japan. By the 4th century, it achieved full official recognition in China and Korea. In the 8th century Buddhism was the state religion of Japan. In China Buddhism and Taoism merged into a melange of magic and the immortality of the soul, with nirvana converted into the more comprehensible conventional heaven. From the 700s CE, Buddhism spread to Tibet and Mongolia.

But these victories did not last. Buddhism began to decline in India after 500 CE and by 1200 CE, Buddhism had become virtually extinct in India having been reabsorbed by Hinduism. In addition, their monasteries were sacked by the Muslim invaders in the 12th century and, since Buddhism was largely a monastic movement, they never really recovered.

In China, towards the end of the Tang period (618–907 CE) Buddhists were persecuted (in 845) and from then on Buddhism lost ground. Buddhism was treated as a cult of foreign barbarian peoples and there was a backlash. The backlash was convenient for the emperor because Buddhist monasteries had accumulated enormous wealth. The closing of the monasteries and the plundering of their treasures certainly assisted the emperor's fiscal affairs. A similar development occurred in Korea and especially Japan much later. In Japan the Tokugawa regime took control of the Buddhist monasteries in the 17th century and after the Meiji restoration in 1867, Shintoism was revived at the expense of Buddhism. The religion was finally despatched in China by Mao's communism after 1949. In the late 1960s at the height of the Cultural Revolution, Buddhism was prohibited altogether, and its monasteries and temples closed and vandalised by Marxist fanatics.

Buddhism met a similar fate at the hands of communists in the Asian territories of the USSR, in North Korea, in Vietnam, Laos and Cambodia. The religion was crippled. In Central Asia Buddhism had been submerged by Islam from the 11th century onwards. In Korea Buddhism began to be edged out from the 1400s onwards.

Buddhism probably arrived in Tibet in the 640s CE, did reasonably well in the following century but was eclipsed after the break up of the Tibetan kingdom in 842, only to be renewed at the end of the 10th century. It continued to expand until the arrival of communism in China. The Chinese communists invaded Tibet in 1950. In 1959 the Dalai Lama fled to India and the Chinese imposed their own rule. During the Cultural Revolution, the Marxists destroyed Tibet's art, sculpture and architecture on a large scale. Burning embers of Tibetan Buddhism remain in Himalayan India, in Nepal and in Bhutan.

Buddhism was largely defeated by Islam in Malaysia and Indonesia.

The religion was thus rejected in numerous countries after very promising beginnings. In the pre-modern period one reason may have been that the Buddhists were mainly monks living separately from the people in wealthy monasteries. They therefore may have seemed an exclusive and powerful elite, even more to be suspected because of the foreign origin of their doctrines, the fact that they were alien. It is not surprising that they became the target of persecution and expropriations by reason of the greed and fearfulness of secular rulers who legitimised their views by nationalism. Another version of Henry VIII of England. A further reason is that the theology was abstruse and easily swept aside by the simple monotheistic salvationism of Islam. In the modern period, the atheistic philosophy of communism or its cousin, military socialism or an inflamed nationalism completed the destruction.

**Ethical and legal codes in Buddhism generally** The way of life recommended by the Buddha was the Middle Way, that is, a way of life between extreme self-indulgence and extreme self-mortification and asceticism. The central teachings are contained in synthesised propositions—three of this, four of that, eight of the other, all conveniently summarised and codified, easier for the faithful to memorise than the Koran. Unlike Hinduism, the religion is packaged.

**The Four Noble Truths** The Four Noble Truths are (1) that suffering is an inescapable part of life (sickness, death, unhappiness), (2) the source of suffering is craving or desire, (3) it is possible to escape from suffering, and (4) the path to escape or cause the cessation of suffering is the Eightfold Path, also known as the Middle Way, discussed below. Nirvana is not a negation. It is a state of absolute happiness. The step by step reasoning is typical of the faith.

The appeal of Buddhism to the abject poor—the majority of its devotees—must have been the sense that, however destitute you were, however deprived, however hopeless, you still could by meditation achieve calm, peace, equanimity of mind, freedom from desire—all the components of happiness, they said. You could escape from the misery of the mind to tranquil bliss.

This nirvana was individual enlightenments. Buddha did not see it as a unity with the ultimate eternal god or a personal god. Nirvana is not going to a conventional paradise or heaven. It is not annihilation. It can be experienced in one's present existence.

The Four Noble Truths and the Eightfold Path were enunciated in the Sermon of the Turning of the Wheel of the Law preached by Gautama in the Deer Park at Sarnath near Benares in north-east India (now Varanasi).

The Buddhist view is that good skilful deeds and bad unskilful deeds come to fruition either in this life or in some rebirth. Each rebirth takes place in one of five or six realms, for example, a hell or an animal or lowly demons, or even as a human or with spirits or angels. The object is to avoid ending up in a condition of suffering, anxiety or dissatisfaction. These are said to be caused by a craving resulting from ignorance.

**The Eightfold Path** In order to escape craving and to achieve enlightenment or nirvana, the individual has to develop the eight factors which are:

1.  **Right understanding** This is viewing reality as it really is—its impermanence and decay—not just as it appears to be. Sometimes translated as 'right view'.

2.  **Right thought** This means having the intention of renunciation and harmlessness. It covers selflessness and compassion, and freedom from lust, ill-will and cruelty. Sometimes translated as 'right intention' or 'right aspirations'.

3.  **Right speech** This means speaking in a truthful and non-hurtful or abusive way.

4.  **Right action** This means acting in a non-harmful way, including abstaining from killing, stealing and sexual misconduct.

5.  **Right livelihood** This means having a non-harmful livelihood.

6.  **Right effort** This means the effort to overcome evil thoughts and to maintain good thoughts. It also covers temperance and moderation.

7.  **Right mindfulness** This is the awareness to see things for what they are with clear consciousness; being aware of the present reality within oneself, without craving or aversion, to pay vigilant attention to every state of the body, feeling and mind.

8.  **Right concentration** This is correct meditation or concentration.

The first two are regarded as wisdom. The next three, that is, numbers 3, 4 and 5, are classified as ethical conduct, and the last three as concentration.

These together are the way of living. Those capable of the necessary spiritual striving reach the end of the cycle of rebirth and are no longer reincarnated as human, animal, ghost or other being. The awakening or enlightenment results in freedom from craving (or greed), hatred and delusion—these are three key concepts of Buddhism. The point is that the cultivation of inward peace keeps the cultivator from rebirth in the four woeful realms of existence, but also encourages peace towards others.

The practitioner prays that all sentient beings should have happiness, be free of suffering, should have bliss without suffering, and equanimity, free of bias, attachment and anger. These are the four immeasurables.

In some respects Buddhism is similar in approach to stoicism, founded by Zeno of Cyprus (c 333 to c 264 BCE) and much favoured by the classical Romans. Both aim at serenity, inner independence in the face of adversity, indifference to good or ill fortune, accompanied by a streak of austerity and simplicity.

As with most of us, religions like lists: Moses with his ten. Muhammad with his five. Siddhartha Gautama beats all the others—four of this, eight of that, three of the other. Why not? Learning is lists.

**Three marks of existence** Buddhism proposes three marks of existence as an explanation of life. The first is that, because everything is impermanent including oneself, attachment to things is futile and leads to suffering. Suffering, which includes concepts of pain, sorrow, anxiety, dissatisfaction, misery and frustration, is the second mark of existence and is central to Buddhism: you have to accept that life can never give any fulfilment. The third mark of existence is no-self. You are made up of physical flesh and blood, feelings, perceptions, consciousness and the like, all of which are changing so that you have no fixed identity.

**Five precepts of morality** There are several levels of ethical behaviour to the five precepts of basic morality applying to lay people, the eight precepts of basic morality for ascetics, the ten precepts for novice monkhood and further ethical rules for monks. The five precepts of basic morality are:

1. To refrain from taking life, ie, non-violence towards all sentient life forms.
2. To refrain from taking that which is not given, ie, no theft.
3. To refrain from sexual misconduct.
4. To refrain from lying, ie, to tell the truth.
5. To refrain from intoxicants which lead to loss of mindfulness, specifically, drugs and alcohol.

The other precepts for ascetics and monks include celibacy, fasting, no dancing or music and the like.

The family is central. On the whole, Buddhism still gives a lower role to women.
**Conclusion on Buddhism** Buddhism shows that you can have a religion or a mass faith, without the supernatural. The supernatural is there in the practise of the religion by some sects, but on the whole the emphasis on the worship of a personal god and on the immortality of the soul is very much less than in other major religions. Despite this, the faith has all the accoutrements of a religion—devoted adherents, temples, images of godlike figures, prayers, rituals, festivals, and a moral code delivered by someone who was semi-divine. Although apparently ascetic, the Middle Way proposed by Gautama is life-affirming and the moral code is spotless. The common Western assertion that the religion is mystical and therefore superstitious does not seem to be true of the mainstream beliefs. The low emphasis on the supernatural makes the religion less vulnerable to the attacks of modern science.

The religion has had a considerable historical buffeting. It had international pretensions, but, like Christianity, it did not succeed in the land of its birth. Like Christianity, it failed to achieve permanent acceptance in some of the main cultures in Asia, notably China and India. Ironically it probably never occurred to the Buddha that in his revelation of the transience of all things, his own religion could also be transient.

The religion's popular appeal may have been compromised by the fact that Buddhism is essentially monastic, by the absence of an easy salvationist redemption in a heaven and by the relative intellectual complexity of how you escape suffering and achieve nirvana. It was going to struggle to appeal to large and often illiterate populations.

Buddhism sometimes comes across as quite narrow in promoting personal enlightenment through meditation as the chief solution to life and to the question of how we should live it. On the other hand the beliefs promote fortitude and a noble patience. It is the most serene of all the great religions.

The Buddhists may be right: everything is impermanent and ephemeral, including humankind. If that is the case, it is not only our religions which are impermanent—we too might ultimately be doomed.

# Taoism and Shintoism

Both of these Eastern religions are mainly of historical interest but each of them still has a following, although the actual number of adherents is virtually impossible to assess.

**Taoism** Taoism is a traditional Chinese religion, a nature religion full of animistic magic. There are possibly about 2.5 million practising Taoists, nearly all of them in China.

The founder was probably Lao-Tzu but this is uncertain and virtually nothing is known about him. Perhaps he lived between the 6th and 4th centuries BCE and therefore might have been a contemporary of Siddhartha Gautama and Confucius. Tao means the path or way and is a Chinese word for a physical path.

The main scripture is the Tao Te Ching which could be translated as 'The classic of the way and virtue'. This short laconic work is credited to Lao-Tzu. It is a collection of terse and pithy sayings and proverbs, some of which are occult and obscure. It is not easy to define exactly what the Taoists believed in with the same clarity that you could describe the beliefs of the Roman Catholics or the Sunni Muslims where the doctrinal creed is specific and clearly articulated for the benefit of the faithful.

Taoism went through many transformations and in later years was influenced by Confucius and Buddhism. The fact is that it did not really have an ideological leader like the Christian pope in the Vatican. Evidently people could just make it up as they went along and as they endeavoured to interpret the gnomic sayings of the master. In any event, there is a great emphasis on meditation and yoga through which devotees must improve their awareness of immortality and the wonder of all things. The approach is quite metaphysical and passive. There is withdrawal from the world, a desire for spontaneity and freedom from restraint, coupled with a degree of quiet non-action. There are several sects.

At one time believers believed in various gods. The religion has priests and rituals. As it is a nature religion, there is a degree of magic.

The religion was more or less killed off by the communists, although quite widespread until then. It achieved some popularity in US counterculture in the

1960s where it became an authentic hippy religion matching the anarchic freedom from restriction in the air at the time.

**Shintoism** This is a traditional Japanese religion stemming from very ancient times. There are probably only about four million practising Shintoists at the most—much higher figures have been quoted of nominal Shinto adherence, but in reality Japan is virtually a secular country.

There is no single founder and the religion emerged from ancient animism which believed in deities in trees, mountains, rivers, ancestors, the emperor, the sun and the moon—all have a soul or spirit in typical animistic style of ancient days all over the world.

Attempts were made to develop the religion in the 6th century CE, probably as a nationalistic reaction to the dominant foreign religions of Buddhism and Taoism coming in from China.

Shinto means 'the way of the gods'. The sun goddess Amaterasu is regarded as the deity who gave Japan its people and whose special charge is Japan. Hence the red sun symbol in the Japanese flag.

In rural areas, the religion exhibited a wide array of superstitious, necromantic and occult witchcraft. However, at the time of the nationalist Meiji restoration in 1867 the cult was seized upon as a source of emperor worship and from then on until the end of the Second World War, when the emperor lost his divinity, the religion had a strong nationalistic strain.

There are many nebulous sects, including ancestor worship.

Some scriptures were put together in the 8th and 9th centuries CE.

There is a remarkable emphasis on social harmony, order and loyalty to one's group—typical Confucian virtues which were probably widespread in Eastern societies and which are attitudes which play an extremely important role to this day in both China and Japan. Some commentators regard this extraordinary emphasis on the local team as being the root driver of the enormous economic success of Japan and China in modern times. It seems doubtful that this culture stemmed from religion, but rather that the culture came first and moulded the religion.

# Confucianism

A word must be said about Confucianism because it demonstrates how a very large society can operate without a supernatural religion but rather a philosophical system.

The philosophy was founded by Confucius in China. He died in 479 BCE, a few years after Siddhartha Gautama, the founder of Buddhism, 80 years before Socrates in Greece. Confucius took the 11th-century BCE Duke of Zhou as his paragon of goodness and sought to return to the virtuous morality of the Duke's time by reinstating the rituals of the period. One of the alternatives was the legalist tradition of which one of the guiding lights was Lord Shang who was a 4th-century BCE chief minister. For him, the aim was not humaneness, it was the enrichment of the state and the strengthening of the military capacity of the state. The legalists espoused a harsh Machiavellian view. They favoured comprehensive legal codes with brutal penalties and sought to impose their will by force. They were not interested in rituals or philosophy and adopted a deliberately authoritarian doctrine.

The great goal of the Confucian view was social harmony. Confucius therefore stressed the cultivation of virtue and the observance of ethics. He promoted altruism and humaneness, propriety, courtesy, integrity, filial piety, loyalty and righteousness. Confucius had much to say about government. In particular he advanced the proposition that a ruler could lose the right to rule if the ruler was inhumane or failed to rule with moral rectitude.

The philosophy did not include a supernatural single god but did recognise ancestor worship, ritual and sacrifice. These were really a recognition of existing Chinese folk religions. The philosophy was entirely secular. It did not call in the gods to help it.

We do not have to go along with Confucius' ideas about the patriarchal society and filial piety. But the basic premise that a society could govern itself morally in the interests of the survival of society without the sanction of the supernatural has much to say to the modern world.

With interruptions and some intermeddling at times from Taoism and Buddhism, Confucianism stuck it out as the official philosophy of China from 500 BCE to 1905. Not bad. Now Confucianism hardly exists, except as a subject of academic study.

# Other Religions

Of course there are many hundreds of other religions appearing throughout history—the animist religions of primitive people, the fertility cults of ancient times, the religions of ancient Mesopotamia, Babylon and Egypt, the classical religions of Greece and pre-Christian Rome, the thunderous gods of the Celts and the Germanic tribes, the pre-Hindu religions of the Harappans in the Indus Valley, the African religions and voodoo, shamanism, the ancient religions of the Pacific Polynesians and the Australian Aborigines, the religions of the Incas, the Aztecs and other native Americans, north and south, and numerous others of the period. Then there were the 19th-century religious revivals, such as Baha'i and then the late-20th century movements, called the new or renewalist religious movements such as Pentecostalism and including exotics like New Age and Hare Krishna. Alongside these there have always been paganism and devil worship which are so anxious to distinguish themselves from each other.

It is hard among the many hundreds of new religions to find anything which is not just treading water or adopting ecstatic or mystic or nature worship or meditative practices which have been around for centuries. It is certainly hard to find in them proposals for a convincing way for us to go forward now or which propose a meaning of life which makes sense for the whole planet, not just fringe people breaking free of the modern world.

Finally, there are cults led by dangerous psychopaths who have had apocalyptic visions and some of whom specialise in abducting and brainwashing children and young people so as to mould them to serve their murderous intent.

# Overall Conclusion on the Spread of Religion

In the year 900 you could not foresee the future of religions. Christianity was stagnant, hemmed in its peninsula off Asia, going nowhere. Buddhism and Islam were about to make huge leaps forward in Asia. But already Buddhism had begun its slow decline. By 1700 Islam reached its greatest extent but already its people were falling behind economically, sowing the seeds of the terrible conflicts of the ancients against the moderns in the 20th and 21st centuries.

In 1930 Christianity was its height in terms of population and territory. Yet already in the triumph of its flowering there was a worm, eating away at its centre in Europe, the continent of its supremacy, the worm of indifference and disenchantment.

Christianity modernised itself at the time of the Reformation but without the destruction of Roman Catholicism which reformed its organisation but only partially modernised its doctrines. Buddhism was a kind of reform and modernising movement within Hinduism. Only Islam did not go through a period of modernisation.

The religions were on the side of life. They said to us we could be redeemed, that we could live for ever in bliss, if we believed in their gods and if we led the good life. They promised us eternal happiness. If that reassurance is in vain, then we are left on our own to make of it what we will, whether to aim for survival or not to care, to let it slip away into oblivion. If, as I believe, survival is our fundamental aim, then it is to the law that we can turn for the means.

# 8

# *The Families of Law*

## Introduction

Now that we have recorded the rise of religions, this chapter charts the rise and rapid spread of the modern families of law. Formal law may have predated formal religion. Yet modern legal systems took shape much later than religions. Many centuries separate the last major articulation of the great religions and the advent of modern law. Christianity was more or less settled in its basics by the middle of the 4th century and its last great doctrinal upheaval was at the time of the Reformation in the 16th century. Islam's doctrines were crystallised by the 9th century as a result of the work of the sharia law schools.

By contrast, the sudden expansion of modern law in such key areas as corporations, bankruptcy and regulation took place in the 19th and 20th centuries, a thousand years after Islam decided its development work was done and 1600 years after Christianity added the finishing touches to its original model which still suffuses all the subsequent sects born in the shattering of the Reformation and after.

The constitutional law of democracies and the foundations of the rule of law, although discussed from early times, were developed in earnest from the late-18th century onwards and applied in practice on a much wider scale than at any time before. This is only about three lives of 70 years each, laid end to end from now backwards in time.

The effect is that most religion is ancient but most law is modern.

## The Triple Polarisation of Law

Just as the world is dominated by three universal religions—Christianity, Islam and Buddhism—so it is with families of law. There are three major families of law in the world—the common law jurisdictions championed by England and the United States, the Napoleonic jurisdictions championed by France, and the Roman-Germanic jurisdictions championed by Germany with others, such as the Dutch. Just as religions split into sects, so also with the families of law. If we reflect subdivisions, including sharia law, we end up with about eight groups, composed in turn of subdivisions of subdivisions.

Nevertheless the groups are completely dominated by the three major groups so that if you understand the fundamental approaches of these three major groups, then you discover the formula, the key, the code, the secret to understanding all of them. If we were to take a much broader brush and blur some of the lines between some jurisdictions and amalgamate others, then in very crude terms a division of the world into 40 per cent English-American common law, 30 per cent Napoleonic, 20 per cent Roman-Germanic and 10 per cent the rest would not be too far out.

# Export of Legal Systems

The universal religions were exported by a mixture of coercion—as where rulers decreed a state religion (Darius of Persia, Ashoka of India and Theodosius of Rome)—and voluntary conversion. So it was with legal systems. Both religions and legal systems had bouts of imperialism. Western Europe was economically the most dominant region in the world in the period around the 1830s, a period described by economists as the Great Divide when Western European economies pulled away from the rest. The Western European nations concerned exported their legal systems by imperialism, emulation or significant influence. About half the world's legal systems adopted a Western legal system voluntarily. Those who did took the latest model, for example, most of Latin America after independence from France, partly via Spain, in the 19th century, post-Meiji Japan from Germany in the early-20th century, and post-revolutionary Turkey from Switzerland in the 1920s. Following the collapse of the USSR in 1991, the new Russian civil code was influenced by the Dutch new civil code which happened to be the latest in the early 1990s. People buy the latest car. The result is that now out of the 320 or so jurisdictions, more than 280 draw their inspiration from three fundamental approaches developed originally by three jurisdictions—England, France and Germany (with others).

This is what I call the triple polarisation of law when the jurisdictions of the world consolidated into the three basic approaches introduced by imperialism and emulation of the West. These ideologies are now represented in more than 90 per cent of the world's territory, holding more than 95 per cent of the world's population and producing more than 90 per cent of world GDP.

History has seen many empires—Egyptian, Chinese, Greek, Persian, Roman, Arab, Ottoman, Russian, British, French and a multitude of others—all vanished, crumbled into dust, leaving behind sometimes nothing, sometimes something more than memories. Some of these empires were extremely long-lived. The Byzantine Empire lasted more than a thousand years from c 300 to 1453. Others lasted more than six hundred years—the Roman Empire, the Arab Empire of the initial caliphates after Muhammad's death followed by the Ummayad and Abbasid dynasties (632–1258), the Khmer Empire, the Ottoman Empire and the

British and French Empires. The longest of all—the Chinese Empire from about 200 BCE was really a unification movement.

The imperialism of Europe of the 19th century and before has come in for much adverse criticism. But there is no question that one of the best things the imperialists and settlers did was to deliver highly advanced legal systems which had been in the works for hundreds of years.

Centuries before, the universal religions—Buddhism, Christianity and Islam—also delivered brand-new religions

**Limited overlap between families** There is little overlap between the families of religion and the families of law. This is because the three main families of law were all disseminated around the world by European nations which were Christian. In some Islamic countries there is a battle for superiority between the received modern Western legal regime and ancient sharia law.

**Diversity of cultures within the legal families** History has thrown up some extraordinary alliances in the spread of religions. Thus the United States, Russia and Malawi are in the same Christian family of religion. Similarly in the case of the families of law the historical accident of the reception of legal systems resulted in some quite unexpected line-ups. The main legal groups include countries which are poor and rich, democratic and despotic, as with the religious groups. There are some other oddities. For example, why is China now so different from Russia? Both emerged from communist economies and reformed their private law at about the same time. Russia has a complex amalgam but China determined to adopt a system of business law which is uncannily like English law of the 19th century, ie, exceptionally liberal and pro-business, at least on paper. The initial surprise vanishes when one appreciates that China is a developing country now and so it is not strange that it should adopt business laws which are similar to the business laws of a major developing country in 19th-century Britain.

**Rejection of a foreign ideology** Some countries did not react well to a foreign religion. Buddhism was eventually seen as an interloper in both China and Japan. Christianity was a reject in most of Asia. The families of law have met with similar rejection. For example, in the decades after independence, India and Pakistan introduced business laws that more or less savaged the liberal English model which they had received, but Hong Kong and Singapore did exactly the opposite and welcomed English law with great enthusiasm. One can see the difference in economic performance, which one must admit did not result only from the legal system. India and Pakistan adopted socialism, which was anti-business. Hong Kong and Singapore supported business enterprise.

**Use of the maps** In the coming pages, I show some maps which exhibit the groups of jurisdictions. In teaching comparative law, I used to get the students early on to colour in a large version of these maps according to whether they thought the country was basically English, Napoleonic, Roman-Germanic or a mixture. The students generally had very little difficulty in identifying the right legal system, except that they almost always got Israel and Malta wrong.

# What is a Jurisdiction?

Legal provinces or jurisdictions range from enormous jurisdictions, both in terms of population and geographic size, like China and Brazil, to tiny micro states like Niue in the Pacific.

A legal jurisdiction is different from a nation state—there are currently just under two hundred sovereign states. The latest sovereign states to be formed and recognised are South Sudan, Kosovo, East Timor and Montenegro. There are others waiting in the wings. Many nation states have a large number of internal jurisdictions. Thus the United States has 51 (if we include the District of Columbia) and the British Isles has seven. The question of legal distinctness has nothing to do with who has overall sovereignty. The criterion as to whether a territory is a separate jurisdiction is whether the law is sufficiently different to merit separate investigation.

In lectures, I would also offer the students a reasonably large denomination note to any student who could correctly name the seven jurisdictions in the British Isles by the end of the lecture. Nobody ever got it right, but I gave away the note anyway. For those interested, the correct answer is England, Scotland, Northern Ireland, Isle of Man, Jersey, Guernsey, and Alderney and Sark, although knowledgeable lawyers in the Channel Islands may well dispute the last three. Scotland is basically a Roman jurisdiction with a direct view back to Roman law as codified by Justinian's lawyers by 533. The Channel Islands are as a matter of strict constitution not part of the United Kingdom but were islands belonging to the Duchy of Normandy before the Norman conquest of Britain in 1066 and therefore belong to the British Crown. Their law is largely based on pre-Napoleonic Norman law, though now much anglicised.

# Which Laws are Family of Law and Which Laws are not?

Some classes of law are determined wholly by the family of law, others not at all.

The family of law is an excellent indicator of commercial and financial law, such as contract, the sale of goods, insurance, intellectual property, real property, litigation and bankruptcy, and also torts or delicts (that is, civil wrongs and injuries such as motoring negligence or defamation). These are all mainly the province of private law.

It is generally true that in modern states the criminal law and the laws relating to the family, sex and inheritance are determined by the family of law. But this fit is weak in the case of divorce and in the case of legal approaches to sex, such as abortion, homosexuality, premarital sex and adultery. In these cases, the international scene is extremely complex, a violent confrontation.

Adherence to the rule of law tends to be determined by the degree of economic development of the country, not family of law. Rich countries generally exhibit a sound adherence to the rule of law, such as the independence of the judiciary and the absence of corruption and of expropriations without compensation. The observance by poor countries of the rule of law is generally not good.

The constitutional law of a country—whether a country is a theocracy or autocratic or a democracy—is nothing to do with family of law. All the families of law contain countries which are variously autocratic or democratic.

At one time comparative lawyers thought that the main differences between jurisdictions was the degree of codification and the adherence to the doctrine that lower courts should follow the decisions of higher courts so as to increase predictability. For various reasons, these formal traits are no longer considered to be major distinguishing characteristics and there are other much more important distinctions between the content of the law.

## The Eight Main Family Groups of Jurisdictions

We can now proceed to describe briefly the main family groups and indicate broadly who their members are.

The identity of the jurisdictions is shown in the accompanying 'Key map of jurisdictions' which is followed by the map 'Global jurisdictions' showing the main groups in a single map, which is in turn followed by maps showing the identity of the members of each group.

Altogether there are about 61 jurisdictions in the American common law group. They comprise the 51 American states and territories, most of which are based on English common law, plus a few outer jurisdictions, such as the Marshall Islands, Puerto Rico and (marginally) Liberia. Liberia is the only African territory which was not colonised by a Western power. Although originally Napoleonic, for most purposes Louisiana is now common law.

The population of the United States is around 316 million—the third largest after China and India. The population of the other ten jurisdictions is small. The United States has the largest economy in the world and is the fourth largest country in the world by size of territory—about 9.5 million square kilometres—after Russia, Canada and China, but this depends on the lake and coastal count.

Unlike the great legal empires of the past, this group is not a territorial empire. However in the law it is an empire of the mind, and it is the empires of the mind which matter.

The United States inherited its legal system from England and is a common law jurisdiction. American common law jurisdictions took over and developed the English legal system in their own direction with enormous energy and vigour. They took the trouble of synthesising the legal regime, mainly the result of the efforts of American academic scholarship of prodigious diligence. This systematic recording was achieved not only in the semi-official 'Restatements' of major areas of law by the American Law Institute but in a series of Uniform Acts

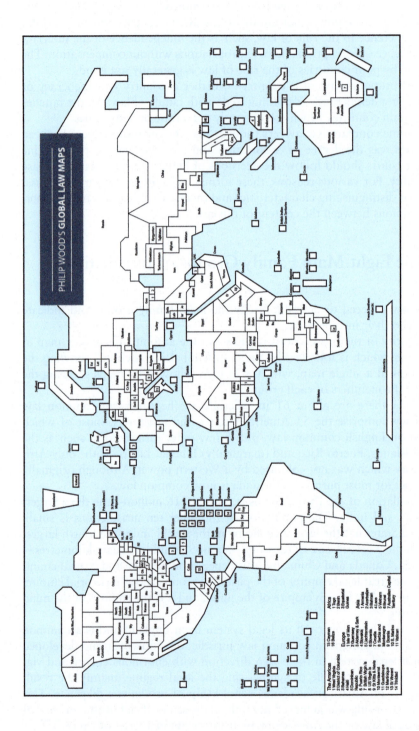

**Key map of jurisdictions**

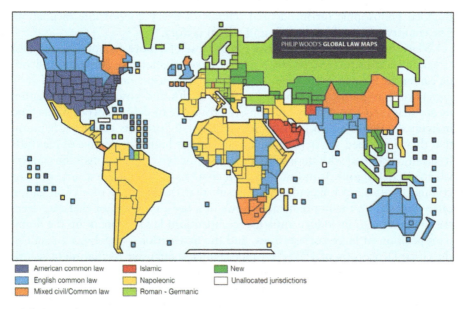

American common law

English common law

Mixed civil/Common law

Islamic

Napoleonic

Roman - Germanic

New

Unallocated jurisdictions

Global jurisdictions

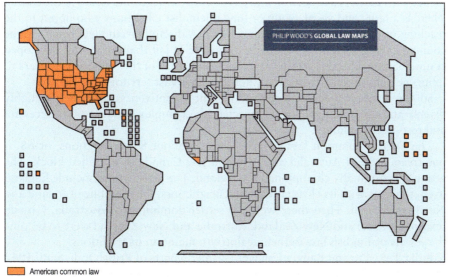

American common law

Other

1. American common law jurisdictions

and in the magnificent Uniform Commercial Code which was a partial codification of commercial law. Because the country is so rich in its legal cultures, its lawyers explored every possibility, tried everything, went down every path and founded philosophic jurisprudential schools of every conceivable inclination. The country is a legal laboratory and a legal factory.

US law differs from English law partly because of a more pronounced populist streak in US culture. Historically, this may have originated in American individualism or the Puritan spirit of equality, or from the suspicion, particularly felt by agricultural migrants, of authority, money, wealth and power. This inclination meant that their bankruptcy law is more protective of debtor corporations (and individuals) than English law—which traditionally protects creditors. It meant that they developed a system of litigation which is highly protective of plaintiffs (typically identified with poor individuals fighting big corporations): the country is extremely litigious. It meant that even civil trials still require a jury, not just criminal trials as in England, with a result that the outcome of civil litigation often depends on the unpredictable views of a lay jury. It meant that they were the first nation to introduce antitrust (competition) laws to break up the dominant position of large corporations, and the first nation—largely as a result of the Great Depression of 1929—to impose intense intrusive regulation of securities and banking. Regulation dominates the legal system and its enforcement can be aggressive. The result is that the legal system is not the free arch-capitalist legal system you would expect. That crown is taken by traditional English-based legal systems.

In addition, Americans are famously religious compared with Europeans. Hence such matters as abortion and gay sex are battleground issues in the courts. There is a large and vocal group of fundamentalist Christians who object to the teaching of Darwinian evolution in schools. A disciplinarian view results in the country having a higher proportion of people in jail than any other developed country. Some 32 states retain capital punishment. But the religiosity appears to influence only these narrow areas, not the other vast territories of the law.

So the result is a legal system of vibrant inventiveness and energy, highly diverse and noisy, sometimes unexpected, the complex product of a successful and resourceful country.

The English common law group comprises about 84 jurisdictions, or 68, if one treats each of Australia and common law Canada as a unified block. The group was originally championed by England. The jurisdictions include England itself, together with its close cousins and neighbours, the Republic of Ireland and Northern Ireland. Then there were the settler dominions of Australia, Canada (except Quebec) and New Zealand. Australia and New Zealand were to become the Jesuits of English law in their zealotry to maintain its traditions.

India, Pakistan and Bangladesh were formerly parts of British India until 1947 when the country broke up into two and later into three with the split off of Bangladesh in the east from Pakistan in the west. Pakistan has still not resolved the clash between English law and the Muslim sharia law while Malaysia took this in its stride. So all these jurisdictions joined the ultra free club.

The rest of the common law British Empire consisted of a large number of territories in Africa such as Nigeria, Kenya, Uganda, Tanzania, Zambia, Malawi, Uganda and the two Sudans, and a huge number of small islands scattered around the world.

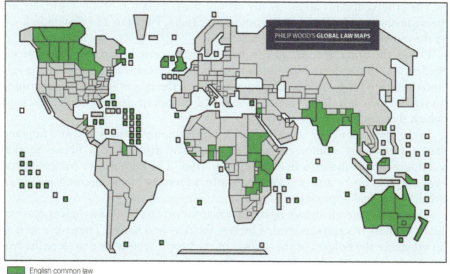

English common law

Other

## 2. English common law jurisdictions

There are hybrid French-English systems in Mauritius, St Lucia, the Seychelles and Vanuatu. Sri Lanka was originally Roman-Dutch and there are some differences, notably in relation to land law.

Britain had a mandate over Palestine between the wars: on independence Israel chose to adopt English law but Jordan chose to follow Napoleonic law, popularised in Egypt and more debtor-oriented than English law. Other escapees included the southern African countries, Quebec, the Channel Islands and, not to be forgotten, Scotland.

Most of the members of this group ended up as democracies but quite a few did not, especially in Africa. India remained a democracy (more or less) but Pakistan was only episodically democratic. A shaky democracy of a sort only triumphed in Bangladesh in 1986. In Myanmar, the former British Burma, democracy had not arrived by 2015.

There is little overlap with the religious families. Settlers in countries such as Australia, Canada and New Zealand, carried their Protestant Christianity with them so that both law and religion were majority English. Some parts of Africa were Christianised, such as southern Nigeria. Pakistan, Bangladesh, most of Malaysia and North Sudan were originally Muslim and remained so. Myanmar stayed largely Buddhist. Israel was resolutely Judaic. In effect the British were tolerant of established religions and did not embark on large-scale conversion except in African societies which were previously animist.

Some of the very small jurisdictions in the group are extremely important in financial and corporate law, for example, Singapore and Hong Kong, as well as the Cayman Islands.

The group contains about 30 per cent of the population of the world, largely because of the inclusion of such countries as India, Pakistan and Bangladesh—it is the most populous group in fact.

Unlike the other groups, all the jurisdictions received their legal systems via settlers and colonialism. England did not codify its legal system comprehensively and so did not have a marketable legal system in the eyes of jurisdictions wishing to reform their law. By contrast, continental Europeans had a codified package which they could deliver neatly.

In the 19th century Britain was the leading economy in the world and England had a precocious commercial and financial law attuned to a liberal market economy—well suited to developing countries. The enthusiasm for enterprise was not held up by any religious antipathy to money or the aggrandisement of wealth: the legal approach was secular.

This secular view is shown by the fact that the private legal system was dramatically friendly to capital provided by bondholders and banks. They were seen as in substance the holders of the savings of the people who were therefore the real creditors. The overriding desire was to use capital to bring prosperity—which is what they succeeded in doing. At the same time the private ordinary law was free, without bureaucratic restrictions, and backed by a judiciary which valued the freedom of capital but yet espoused austere Victorian views about morality in business conduct, an unbeatable combination. It is no surprise therefore that English law became an international standard, an international public utility for large financial and commercial contracts and one of the most important exports of the English. English law ranks in world importance only second after their greatest export, the English language. The legal system luckily enjoyed a greater rationality than English spelling.

The main challenges for members of this group are to retain the original radical simplicity, versatility and freedom.

When the French codes were written down, they were a masterpiece of legal style. They were economical, musical, elegiac. The Civil Code was initially prepared by the Duc de Cambacérès who, on the instructions of the revolutionary National Assembly in 1793, produced the first draft in six weeks, with a verve aided no doubt by the proximity of a fully operative guillotine. The Assembly, with typical client unreality, wanted it in a month. It was many years before it was finally settled. Portalis was a leading influence but Napoleon himself attended many drafting meetings. The Civil Code came into force in 1804, and the Commercial Code was completed in 1807.

The codes took an enormous hold on the imagination. They voiced a heroic liberalism generated by a prestigious European power, celebrating its intellectual might with convincing charisma. The 19th-century French novelist Stendhal is said to have read part of the Civil Code every day to refine his feelings for the language. Even now, the French lapidary and poignant style of drafting is exemplary and consistently better than anybody else's.

But notwithstanding the revolutionary intent of Napoleon and his admiration of capitalism and notwithstanding the radicalism of the changes in family law and the abolition of feudalism, when it came to commercial law the codes

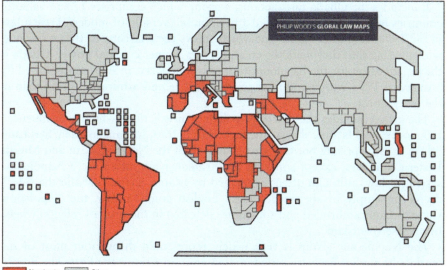

**3. Napoleonic jurisdictions**

largely codified Roman law, as transmuted by medieval and subsequent ideas. These reflected an agricultural economy and therefore tended to be pro-debtor and anti-money in their bias. The codes were written before the industrial revolution really got under way in France and so, unlike England, the approach crystallised before the demands of a developing country took over. Because they were such splendid legal codes, they were extremely attractive to other countries which rapidly imported them as the most civilised model which one of the most civilised nations in the world could provide. They were a neat package, ready to be used. It was not therefore surprising that they should have taken such a strong root which remains more or less unchanged to this day. The Napoleonic group is easily the second largest family of law in the world and covers a gigantic amount of territory.

Napoleon could truly say when he was in exile on St Helena 'It is not in winning 40 battles that my real glory lies, for all those victories will be eclipsed by Waterloo. But my Code civil will not be forgotten, it will live forever'.

This Napoleonic group comprises about 82 jurisdictions drawing their original inspiration from France.

The group includes the European Napoleonic jurisdictions, including Belgium, Italy, Luxembourg, Portugal, Spain and others; the French island dependencies in the Caribbean and elsewhere; and a large number of traditional Napoleonic jurisdictions which have hardly changed their law since independence, including such countries as Ethiopia, Angola, Mozambique, Egypt, Lebanon, Madagascar, Morocco and Tunisia.

It includes the Ohada jurisdictions, a group which comprises 17 sub-Saharan countries in Africa which adopted a harmonised version of modern French law in the 1990s and after—an event which shows the charisma of the codes, notwithstanding that they were the creatures of a former colonial power. Ohada is the organisation for the harmonisation of business law in Africa established by a treaty of 1993 with a common court of justice and arbitration in Abidjan in the Ivory Coast.

The group includes the sharia Napoleonic jurisdictions which are influenced by an overlay of Islamic sharia law, such as Iran, Iraq, Jordan, Somalia, Syria and others. It is surprising but true that nearly all of the North African and Middle Eastern countries, except some on the Arabian peninsula, have a Napoleonic system of law, although often submerged by Islamic sharia law and the ruler's decree or simply in abeyance. Unlike English common law, the Napoleonic Codes became embroiled and sometimes defeated in the wars of religion waged by an assertive Islam.

The Napoleonic group is very widely represented throughout most of the world, although it has very little representation in Asia or the East. The French did have a substantial empire in Indochina—in Vietnam, Cambodia and Laos—but they were forced to withdraw in the 1950s, and their efforts to implant French law were unavailing. They were pushed out by communism and some of the most atrocious rulers the world has ever seen.

The group's most populous member is Brazil which also is the fifth largest country in area in the world, after Russia, Canada, China and the United States. France is the largest country in the EU with a total area of nearly 550,000 square kilometres, one-and-a-half times the size of Germany, more than twice the size of the United Kingdom and four times the size of England.

Unlike the dissemination of English law, large parts of the world are Napoleonic voluntarily not by imperialism. This applies to the Latin American countries which desired unifying legal codes after independence in the 19th century and naturally turned to the main codes available at the time—from France. These codes continued to be influential in the 20th century, for example, in Kuwait, the United Arab Emirates and Jordan, partly by reason of the influence of Egyptian, Syrian and Lebanese lawyers, partly perhaps because the pro-debtor colouring of the approach appealed more to countries with Islamic objections to usury.

The group covers the largest land area of all the groups—nearly 35 per cent. As with the English common law group, there is no identity between the Napoleonic legal system and religions. The Napoleonic legal system covers both Christian and Muslim countries but not predominantly Buddhist countries. It has its fair share of democracies and autocracies.

The legal ideology was settled early on and in some respects there might be a case for re-storming the Bastille in the more traditional Napoleonic jurisdictions. Recent developments in France and Belgium in particular show a remarkable shift in the direction of protecting creditors in credit economies, as opposed to the traditional view of a debtor protection prevalent at the end of the 18th century when the codes were crystallised.

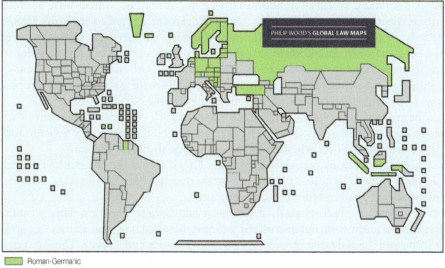

Roman-Germanic
Other

## 4. Roman-Germanic jurisdictions

The German Civil Code, the impressive BGB (*Bürgerliches Gesetzbuch*) was put together after the industrial revolution in Germany as a result of 13 years' work ending in the mid-1890s and came into force on 1 January 1900. The German Commercial Code (the HGB) stemmed from 1861 and the final version also came into force in 1900. The precocious German Bankruptcy Act was enacted in 1877 and not replaced until the 1990s which shows what an enduring law it was.

German ideas had advanced some way beyond the Napoleonic view in terms of economic development and prosperity. On the other hand the codes were strongly influenced by jurists who were steeped in Roman law, who brought juristic archaeology of the Roman remains to a new intensity and who, being academics, did not have a high regard for merchants and money. This explains why the German view was midway between the Napoleonic and English views.

In retrospect, it seems that the great German lawyer Friedrich Carl von Savigny (1779–1861) was right to stop the codification of German law when it was proposed by Anton Thibaut in 1814 and to counsel delay until the necessary research had been carried out to work out the *Volksgeist* or national soul of the peoples of the as yet non-unified Germany.

German writers sometimes bemoan the abstractness of their codes, their lack of poetry and their glaciality. They should not be so modest. They are beautifully and elegantly expressed; they are codes of stunning mastery of principle and detail and provide more solutions to more questions than any other. This was because, unlike the French before them, with their grand maxims and large principles, and the Swiss after them, with their realistic acknowledgment in article 1 of the Civil Code (drafted by Huber and subsequently adopted by

Kemal Attaturk in Turkey), admitting to gaps in the law which must be filled in the spirit of the legislator—an acknowledgement expressed in terms almost exactly echoing Aristotle and St Thomas Aquinas—the Germans set out to cover the field and to be as complete and comprehensive as possible. That they did so in a laconic manner with such meticulous elegance, without falling into the trap of the Prussian General Law of the Land of 1794 with its 17,000 paragraphs, was one of the greatest legal achievements of all time.

The group was strongly influenced by German 19th-century jurisprudence with significant contributions from, for example, the Netherlands and Switzerland. There are about 31 jurisdictions in this group, as shown in the map.

These jurisdictions include Austria, the Czech Republic, Denmark, Finland, Germany itself, South Korea, the Netherlands, Poland, Russia, Sweden, Switzerland, Thailand (doubtfully) and others.

The group is predominantly a northern hemisphere ideology with substantial representation in north-western Europe, Scandinavia, the Baltics, Central Europe and the Balkans, spreading through to Russia and Turkey. There is a gap in the Middle East, but substantial representation in East Asia including South Korea and Indonesia. China, Japan and Taiwan, though classified as mixed civil/common law, were strongly influenced by German law.

Apart from the southern African group of five jurisdictions south of the Zambezi River and stopping at the English jurisdiction of Zambia (the five are all treated as mixed civil/common law), there is virtually no representation in the southern hemisphere, with only Aruba and the former Netherlands Antilles in the Caribbean and with Suriname the sole representative in South America. There is no representation in North Africa.

The member with the largest population is Russia with around 143 million people. Germany has a population of about 82 million—the most populous state in Europe.

In GDP terms, the group probably has a higher proportion of jurisdictions with high capita income compared with the other two main groups.

Out of a total world land mass of about 148 million square kilometres, the group includes the largest country in the world—Russia at 17 million square kilometres. Germany, with nearly 360,000 square kilometres, is the fourth largest country in Europe after France, Spain and Sweden.

The German ideology was transmitted primarily by the strength of the codes which have been in the works for most of the 19th century. These codes formed the basis for the legal system in Japan some 30 years after the Meiji restoration in 1867. The codes then found their way to Korea by virtue of Japanese colonialism (1905) and then into China, largely by the reason of the influence of Japanese jurists in China in the 1930s and subsequently during the Second World War. It was this system which found its way to Taiwan, then called Formosa, partly by reason of Japanese conquests (1895) and bolstered on the ejection from mainland China in 1949 of Chiang Kai Shek and the Kuomintang by communist forces led by Mao Tse Tung.

The Netherlands contribution is also notable. The Netherlands was colonised by France in Napoleonic times but subsequently returned to its commercialised

Roman roots reflecting Dutch mercantile and financial supremacy in Europe in the 17th century and after. It was this system which was transmitted by Dutch settlers to the Cape of Good Hope and was in turn carried upwards to the rest of southern Africa. The Russian Civil Code is influenced by the Dutch Civil Code—the latest model in the early 1990s. Most of Indonesia was a Dutch colony.

The overall philosophy was midway between the English common law and the Napoleonic in commercial and financial law.

The member jurisdictions are nominally Christian, except mainly for Turkey and Indonesia which are largely Muslim. Nearly all the countries are broadly democratic which may be because the group has very few extremely poor country members.

The systematic working out of the ideology of this group was an extraordinarily intellectual feat. The ideology was, and still is, transmitted entirely by the quality of the product.

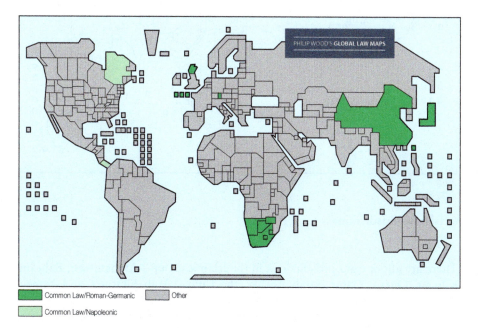

PHILIP WOOD'S **GLOBAL LAW MAPS**

■ Common Law/Roman-Germanic ☐ Other
☐ Common Law/Napoleonic

5. Mixed civil/common law jurisdictions

There are about 17 jurisdictions in this mixed group. All of them have continental European roots but they also generally have some common law features, typically the trust.

It is part of the ironic wit of history that this group should include countries as various as Swaziland, Zimbabwe, Panama, Scotland and Jersey. The fact that it also includes both China and Japan means that it is an extremely important group. The historical origins are in fact easily explicable if one follows colonial and economic history.

Japan's codes were originally German. The common law aspect resulted from US occupation after the Second World War.

South Africa and the other five southern African Roman-Dutch jurisdictions, including Zimbabwe, retained their Roman-Dutch law delivered by the Hollanders at the time of Rembrandt when Holland was a leading maritime power, but elements of this were anglisised after the British occupation of South Africa in the early-19th century.

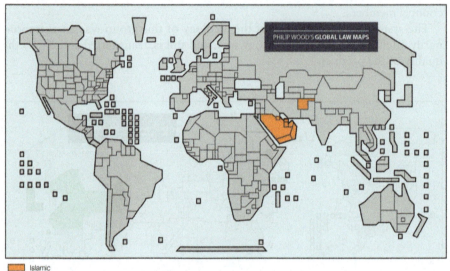

PHILIP WOOD'S **GLOBAL LAW MAPS**

▮ Islamic
☐ Other

**6. Islamic jurisdictions**

There are about eight jurisdictions in the Islamic group—Afghanistan, Bahrain, Kuwait, Oman, Qatar, Saudi Arabia, the United Arab Emirates and Yemen. In most, but not all of these countries, sharia law applies. The most relaxed is the United Arab Emirates probably followed by Bahrain and Kuwait. Some other countries where the underlying law is not Islamic, such as Brunei, Pakistan and Sudan (all submerged English common law), have an overlay of sharia law to a greater or lesser extent.

Bankruptcy laws of a sort are present in some of these jurisdictions but in most cases are inchoate and extremely slim—not surprising in view of the fact that in many of them there is a rejection of usury. The most legally ambitious jurisdictions are probably Dubai, Kuwait and Qatar. Both Dubai and Qatar have set up international financial centres. In Dubai, the laws applicable in this internal enclave are based on English law.

Effectively there is a war of religion going on in these countries and, as mentioned, in many Napoleonic countries in the Middle East as to whether sharia law or a modern Western legal system dominates. The state of the conflict differs according to the country.

Western law had its fount in the Fertile Crescent before the rise of the ancient Greeks—the first achievement of this group. The second achievement of this group was the development of a rich body of law in the 9th century. History does not stop now.

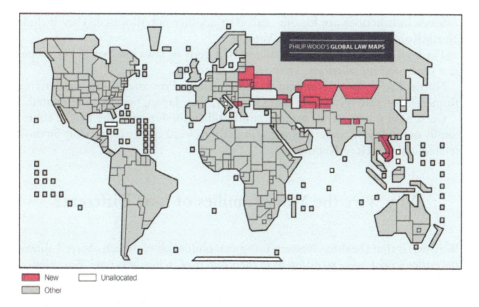

New       Unallocated
Other

**7. and 8. New and unallocated jurisdictions**

There are about 19 jurisdictions in the new category, sometimes called transition jurisdictions. With the exception of Bhutan and Nepal, they were formerly communist countries which subsequently adopted programmes of law reform to fill the vacuum left by the defeated ideology of communism. The sources of their new laws are heterogeneous but normally the new jurisdiction sought market-friendly laws. In many cases it would now be possible to ascribe these jurisdictions to one of the other groups.

The Eastern European jurisdictions are the most developed legally—these are Belarus, Ukraine, Moldova (a tiny country tucked into the side of Ukraine), then the Balkan countries alongside Greece—Albania, Macedonia—plus the three Caucasus countries of Georgia, Armenia and Azerbaijan. These countries are largely secularised as a result partly of communism.

Then there are the Central Asian former Soviet countries of Kazakhstan, Tajikistan, Turkmenistan, Uzbekistan and Kyrgyzstan, where the hold of formal law and observance of the rule of law are less convincing. The predominant religion is Islam, although there is a high degree of secularisation.

Sitting above India and the Himalayas are Nepal and Bhutan. Nothing much happens in either country in terms of legal change and they are virtually legal vacuums, especially Bhutan. Further east are the former Indochina countries of Vietnam, Laos and Cambodia. Of these, Vietnam has the most advanced programme of law reform. Nepal is Hindu; otherwise in these countries the most pervasive religion is Buddhism, although they are largely secularised.

The jurisdictions had many models to choose from. The problem for them is that the models presented to them did not speak in unison.

Seven jurisdictions are for one reason or another not allocated. They include North Korea, Antarctica and the Vatican.

The high seas and space is the subject of a body of laws but they are not separate territorial jurisdictions. They are the commons.

North Korea is a communist dictatorship. Presumably the underlying Roman-Germanic system, via first Germany, then Japan, has been obliterated.

Cuba has been governed by a communist dictatorship since the 1960s. Unless totally overruled by communism, the underlying legal system is probably Spanish related and therefore Napoleonic.

## Why were the Main Families of Law Different?

Why was it that the three Western European philosophies, which covered almost the entire world, were so different in their outcome in business law? Was religion responsible?

Although there were many influences and counter-influences, the reason for the difference between the three great groups based on England, France and Germany could be a much simpler historical circumstance.

This was the timing of the impact of the industrial revolution in relation to the timing of the crystallisation of the three great legal traditions.

The industrial revolution was first felt in England after about 1750. This happened at a time when the economic philosophy was one of laissez-faire as pronounced in Adam Smith's *Wealth of Nations* published in 1776. This propounded the theory of the invisible hand of the market. By the early-19th century when Britain had more or less been through the first stages of its industrial revolution, the ideas of total market liberalism were the prevailing mainstream consensus. The attitude was 'capital is king', 'the railways must be built'.

Hence if the banks wanted all of the corporate assets as security for a loan, they got it. If the banks then wanted to be able to enforce their monopolistic security in one hour after a default by the debtor by appointing a friendly accountant as a receiver, do go ahead. If the receiver fired all the directors and took complete charge of the company without any reference to the courts, please be my guest. These 18th- and 19th-century lawyers had got it into their minds that it made no sense to switch off a power station on an enforcement, and that the real creditors who were being protected were the depositors with banks so that protecting banks was in effect protecting the savings of the people.

However security interests under the French system were hugely different. It was not possible to cover all the assets and enforcement was difficult, involving applications to the court and long delays. There was no concept whereby a creditor could take over the management of the business through a receiver on enforcement. One may infer that when the Napoleonic codes were crystallised, which was in the last decade of the 18th century, the industrial revolution had not really hit France to any great degree. The people who were drafting the code were still living in the earlier agricultural world where moneylenders were small and an irritant and where trade and finance were somewhat contemptible. It did not occur to them that banks needed security interests to secure loans for giant power stations, nor did it occur to them that one needed some way of netting off exposures between banks in payment systems or between counter-parties in markets, if one of them became bankrupt, ie setting off debts owed to and from a counter–party so as to reduce the amount. Why would they? There were no big power stations requiring huge amounts of finance to be secured and there were no such things as large amount payment systems. Trade could get along quite well enough without these things.

When we came to the Roman-Germanic system, the industrial revolution had certainly swept through Germany—the codes were in the works from about 1850 onwards although only promulgated in 1900. However the really important law—the bankruptcy law—was enacted in Germany in 1879, at the height of the industrial revolution in Germany. It was no surprise therefore that the Roman-Germanic system, as evidenced in the great codes and in the bankruptcy legislation, had a distinct creditor bias in order to encourage capital. On the other hand the codes were drafted by conservative academics immersed in Roman law and it was the influence of this academic approach, with its some-what aristocratic disdain for trade and commercial business, which resulted in the Roman-Germanic system being somewhere in between the Napoleonic and the common law view on pro-creditor and pro-debtor attitudes.

It seems unlikely that religion was a major factor in the different approaches in England, Germany and France, ie, because the northern countries were Protestant and France was Roman Catholic. It is certainly true that Catholicism was more conservative on commercial matters and especially usury, but usury was abolished at the time of the French Revolution when the codes were being drafted. The explanation advanced by Max Weber that it was the Protestant ethic of hard work and thrift which led to economic advance seems doubtful as the main force underlying legal developments. Religion was just not a significant political influence on most secular law by this time. Law was promulgated by secular authorities, not by priests.

Why then did these 19th-century views cling on for so long—for nearly two hundred years now?

The reason seems to be that all three of the philosophies were extremely successful. A successful legal regime is almost as indelible in its basic propositions as a successful religion. Once the ideology takes hold—and especially if it originally had compelling content at its core—it becomes resistant to change, even if the case for change resulting from changed circumstances is overpowering. A detailed comparison of the three great camps shows an adherence to a historical tradition which cannot be explained by real differences in current need, or current economic circumstances, or current culture.

In any event, the differences between the originating countries—England, France and Germany—have now narrowed. The gulf between the ideologies is more perceptible in the case of emerging countries which received one of the legal systems and left it as it was.

# Conclusion on the Families of Law

Whenever in history an empire collapsed, there followed a period of decolonisation, as when the Romans withdraw from Britain in the 4th century. The decolonisation of the European empires began in the early-19th century with Haiti and the South American republics. It gathered speed in the 20th century, ending with the decolonisation of the Russian Empire in the 1990s.

If there was no modern legal system already in place in the former colonies, as in the case of Latin America and the USSR, the desire of the former colonists to install one was one of their first priorities, however difficult and time-consuming the work. Law was an urgent objective.

The export of religions over a period of some two thousand years was an event of staggering importance for the world.

The export of law in the last three hundred years or so has also been a major event in history. The rule of law and the laws embodied in legal systems are now the single most significant ideology in the world and the most important in terms of our survival.

# 9

# *A Brief Tour of Secular Law*

## Introduction

This brief tour through secular law will show how massive and intricate are the mansions of the law built up through the centuries by civilisations and how far these structures of the mind go beyond the legal structures of religions.

We will see later however that there are some dark rooms in the legal edifice.

We on this earth require a moral framework to protect ourselves from the miserable wasteland of destruction and devastation, rule by the most savage, the most ruthless. We need the ethical structures to enable us to survive so that we can take our destiny in our hands so far as we can, not leave it to fate heedlessly, not slipping blindly and carelessly into nothing.

Secular law is an advance on religious law for four main reasons:

1. Secular law covers a hugely greater range of topics. Religious law has only a tiny corner, a corner which is diminishing as secular legislatures insist on exclusive control of the laws.

2. Secular law covers the typical religious topics, for example, sex and family, in vastly more detail. The generic religious admonitions to love your neighbour, to be virtuous, to do to others what you would have them do to you, are too vague to provide specific guidance on the range of detailed situations which present themselves. Even murder, which gets only a few lines in religious codes, prompts whole books in secular law. These cover, for example, the threshold of child responsibility, insanity, abortion, euthanasia, suicide pacts, deaths caused by intent to cause serious harm like beating someone up, the impact of extreme provocation, failure to rescue someone, participation by others and complicity, corporate murder, conspiracy to murder, mistakes, the scope of self-defence, duress, coercion and the burden of proof beyond reasonable doubt, police shootings, the distinction between murder and manslaughter, the rules of evidence, due process, the protections of the accused, the grading of punishments—all in the most meticulous detail.

3. Secular law is on the whole reasonably up-to-date in most countries, for example, criminal punishment. Religious law is often at least a thousand years old. The sudden surge of modern law in the 19th century onwards caught the religions by surprise and they never regained their footing. Theologians of former times were indeed very interested in law—see for example the 1600 years spent by the Hindus on the Dharmasastras up until about

1000 CE, the probably equally long time spent on the Talmud of the Jews up until 600 CE, the Christian canon law perfected in the medieval period in the main, and the versions of Islamic sharia law produced mainly between 700 and 900 CE. All these codes now have little relevance in the mainstream modern world in terms of secular use, notwithstanding the attempts by some Muslim states to cling on to the sharia.

4.  Secular authorities elbowed out the control of the clerics over the administration of justice in almost all areas of law, especially the right to impose punishments for crime and the right to order compensation for civil violations.

Civilised secular law is based on ethics and morality as much as the morality of religions and in much wider contexts. It applies the principles of justice. The codification of the rule of law principles in human rights conventions is a set of profound moral principles attuned to our survival. The criminal law is morality at its most austere and pitiless. Even the ladder of the priority of payment of creditors on a bankruptcy expresses a view of the jurisdiction of just and fair preferences.

Even an apparently technical topic like taxation has a moral base because it involves a taking of the property of the individual by the state. Most religions endorse the giving of alms to the poor. They never envisaged anything like the scale of alms-giving enforced by taxation law which in many welfare state countries imposes taxes to redistribute to the poor a several times multiple of the religious tithes.

# Law and the Hierarchy of Legal Needs

The scope of secular laws may be illustrated by a hierarchy of legal needs based on the concept of a hierarchy of human needs developed in 1954 by the famous Californian psychologist, Abraham Maslow. This hierarchy also demonstrates the significance of the law of money, banks and corporations and similar areas of law.

Abraham Maslow produced the celebrated Hierarchy of Human Needs which showed his view of the ranking of human needs from the most basic and fundamental to the most refined and sophisticated.

At the base of the triangle were physiological needs, which he designated as food, water and oxygen. These were the needs which were absolutely necessary for survival of the organism.

Then one step up were safety needs which were designated as comfort, security and freedom from fear.

The next step up were belongingness and love needs (this was California, don't forget) which were named as affiliation, acceptance and belongingness, ie, the satisfaction of basic human desires.

The hierarchy then moved upwards through esteem needs, cognitive needs, aesthetic needs, and self-actualisation.

At the peak of the triangle's hierarchy were 'peak experiences' which were evidently not of the 'Puff the magic dragon' category but higher spiritual states of awareness of the type experienced by ecstatic religious mystics, presumably.

Similar principles of the hierarchy can be used in relation to legal needs, as shown in the figure 'Hierarchy of legal needs'.

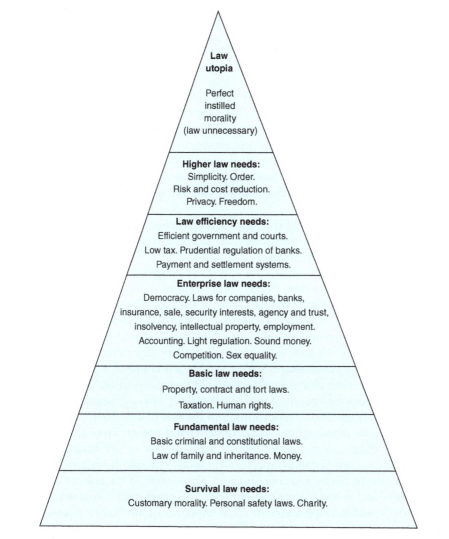

**Law utopia**

Perfect instilled morality (law unnecessary)

**Higher law needs:**
Simplicity. Order.
Risk and cost reduction.
Privacy. Freedom.

**Law efficiency needs:**
Efficient government and courts.
Low tax. Prudential regulation of banks.
Payment and settlement systems.

**Enterprise law needs:**
Democracy. Laws for companies, banks,
insurance, sale, security interests, agency and trust,
insolvency, intellectual property, employment.
Accounting. Light regulation. Sound money.
Competition. Sex equality.

**Basic law needs:**
Property, contract and tort laws.
Taxation. Human rights.

**Fundamental law needs:**
Basic criminal and constitutional laws.
Law of family and inheritance. Money.

**Survival law needs:**
Customary morality. Personal safety laws. Charity.

After Maslow 1954

Hierarchy of legal needs

**Level 1** The most fundamental and primitive of legal needs are those which go directly to survival, such as customary morality, personal safety laws and charity.

**Level 2** Fundamental law needs at level 2 include basic criminal and constitutional laws, the rule of law, and laws on family, sex and inheritance. The latter were originally the province of the great religions. I would include money and its attendant law in this range or step, ie, money appears at a fundamental level as a basis of societies in the sense that modern society goes nowhere if it does not have the institution of money.

**Level 3** Above this are basic law needs, at level 3, such as property, contract and tort laws, and taxation. Already we are in the sphere of commercial and business law and in areas mostly outside the religious domain.

**Level 4** Enterprise law needs appear next about halfway up the hierarchy, at level 4. This category would include laws for companies, banks and insurance. Most people in developed countries are either employed by a corporation or operate their business through a corporation. Corporations are fundamentally important in people's lives. This level would include accounting and sound money. It would also include bankruptcy or insolvency laws, as well as laws relating to employment and competition. We are now completely beyond the scope of religious codes.

**Level 5** The hierarchy would then proceed up through law efficiency needs, at level 5, such as efficient government and courts, and proportionate regulation, such as the supervision of banks.

**Level 6** Higher law needs are at level 6, which I designate as fairness, simplicity, order, risk and cost reduction, privacy and freedom.

**Level 7** Finally, at the top of the hierarchy in the peak of the triangle, at level 7, there would, as with Maslow, be a utopia, in this case a law utopia. In view of the inherent restrictiveness of the law, a law utopia would be a society where everybody has a perfect instilled morality and where law in its formal and written form would be unnecessary. Such a society is a chimera, a dream. We need not hold our breath in case this society should ever materialise. We have to have laws and sanctions for breach of the laws. Similarly laws are needed to empower us, such as contracts and corporations, and the rule of law itself.

This hierarchy demonstrates some fundamental points. First, the main religious codes either do not cover crucial areas of law or are hostile to them, for example, money. Secondly, the survival motive of law directly or indirectly applies to money, banks and corporations. These areas of the law are central to our societies and in one way or another have an impact on the lives of just about everybody. Good law applicable to them improves us all. Bad or excessive law prejudices us all.

**Amounts involved** The amounts involved in corporate and financial law and transactions are colossal.

**How much is a million, a billion and a trillion?** Since we are getting into figures, it is worth getting a feel at this stage for what is meant by a trillion.

— A million is a square piece of graph paper, as wide as a child's arms stretched out, finger point to finger point, a metre. A metre is a long step of the foot.

— A billion is that piece of paper a kilometre to the side—just over half a mile.

— A trillion is that piece of graph paper a kilometre to the side and a kilometre up.

So a billion is much bigger than a million. A trillion is much, much bigger than a billion. A trillion is an enormous figure.

The flows of financial assets are a large multiple of trade flows and the turn-over through payment systems and through foreign exchange markets is a many times multiple of world gross domestic product (GDP).

A useful although vague measurement of very large monetary amounts is the domestic GDP of a country—sometimes called 'grossly deceptive product' but nevertheless a reasonably workable measure of how big an economy is, even if crude. The world GDP around 2015 was probably around $73 trillion on a strict basis (technically, purchasing power parity).

Foreign exchange turnover on the major exchanges is probably over $500 trillion per year. That is $500,000 billion, $500,000,000 million or $500,000,000,000,000.

The turnover of payment systems is well over $1500 trillion per year or $1500,000,000,000,000. These systems get through world GDP every fortnight.

Flows of financial assets are much larger than flows of trade goods—maybe 100 times as much.

The outstanding stock in 2015 of listed equity shares and bonds plus syndi-cated loans was probably around $250 trillion. About 25 per cent was the market capitalisation of listed equity shares, about 45 per cent were bonds (most of which were government and bank bonds) and about 30 per cent were bank loans.

The corporate assets of the world's biggest bankruptcy was about $530 billion (Lehman, 2008). The previous record was $100 billion (Worldcom, July 2002). The assets of Enron (bankrupt 2002) exceeded $60 billion. The Argentina insolvency in 2002 involved over 80 bond issues totalling perhaps $132 billion. The Greek bankruptcy in 2012 involved around €530 billion.

The largest securities settlement system in the world holds securities worth over $37 trillion, that is, around half world GDP. It is called the Depositary Trust Corporation and the actual nominal holder of the securities legally is Cede & Co.

Euroclear (a securities settlement system in Brussels) holds securities worth around one-and-a-half times the GDP of the entire EU 27. Settlement systems are effectively trusts.

The great religions never contemplated anything like this. These figures go some way to explaining why even apparently technical areas such as payment systems (which are governed by a body of laws of great sophistication), are extremely important, leading to cataclysmic results if they go wrong. If these institutions or their companions fail, our urban societies would, for example, quickly find there is no food on the table.

# Introduction to the Tour of Law

The hierarchy of legal needs lists the main branches of the law. It is worth now walking quickly through some of the subjects, but only looking at a few of the main sites, not every room in every house in every street of the law. The purpose of this tour is to show the depth and range of secular law so as to demonstrate how wide the gap is between secular and religious law.

# Criminal Law: The Test of Civilisation

Criminal law is morality at its most intense—merciless, implacable, ferocious in its determination to protect and save us, our future. It is at the heart of the rule of law which liberates us.

Most people have a rough idea of what crime is—for example, murder, assault, rape, sexual assault, bigamy, riot, perjury, theft, robbery, burglary, handling stolen goods, racial aggravation, harassment, extortion, blackmail, deception, fraud, arson, intentional damage to property, conspiracies to do these things or aiding and abetting them. Most people have a rough idea that crimes are distinguished by the seriousness and gravity of the harm they do—death or injury to people, damage to or loss of property, disgraceful offences to feelings such as racial insults, even harm to oneself (seat belts, suicide). Most people roughly know that crimes are considered to be so serious that it is the state itself, not just the victim or his or her family, that seeks redress and the state itself which imposes a punishment, not just compensation to the victim, as was the case in ancient times. In the case of the civil non-criminal law; such as breach of contract or negligence causing injury, it is the victim not the state who must pursue the remedies and who is awarded compensation.

There are all sorts of theories about punishment—whether it satisfies the desire for revenge and retribution, whether it results from a need to protect the public, whether it is a form of deterrence or whether it is designed to reform and rehabilitate the criminal. Once punishments were symmetrical—an eye for an eye. Some states preserve this proposition for murder. There is a great diversity as to whether to protect the victim or the criminal.

The abolition of the death penalty in most countries and, in most of those which retain capital punishment, the restriction of the death penalty to very serious offences, such as aggravated murder, is a modern development. Even in the 19th century, a large number of non-homicidal offences attracted execution. The death penalty was abolished in England in 1965, in France in 1977. The last beheading in Britain was in 1747. The last hanging was in 1968.

Not everybody knows how many criminal offences there are and indeed probably nobody knows since there is such a vast number of them. Every statute, whether to do with road traffic, or regulation, or corporations, sets out offences and the penalties. Thousands upon thousands of them, hundreds of thousands. The criminal law is expanding at a fearsome rate. Many of the offences are minor and only attract a fine—the equivalent of a parking offence, such as not filing corporate accounts on time. The criminal law can be abused by being over used.

Let us start with murder.

**The sinking of *The Mignonette*** The case which first excited me to go into the law was the famous English decision of *The Queen v Dudley and Stephens*, decided in 1884.

Four sailors were employed to sail a small yacht to Australia from England to deliver it to a buyer in Sydney. This was a distance of over 14,000 miles. Normally it would then take about 110 days, nearly three months.

The boat was called the *Mignonette*—'Little darling'. They were caught in a storm in the South Atlantic, hundreds of miles from anywhere, somewhere in the middle of this turbulent ocean between southern Africa and South America. The yacht sank. They got into a small dinghy just over 13 feet long. At its widest beam it was four feet. It was only 20 inches deep, about the height of the seat of your chair. They kept afloat in the huge waves by turning the boat with their oars so that it always faced into the wave.

They survived for three weeks before they were picked up by a German trading ship sailing from Chile to Hamburg. They had by then travelled over 1000 miles in this tiny boat but were still nearly 1000 miles from Rio de Janeiro. In the meantime they had to eat something. They had only two tins of turnips on board and no fresh water. In the three weeks out there, they caught only one turtle. So three of the sailors ate the fourth who was the cabin boy. The cabin boy was only 17, an illiterate orphan. He was lying sick and weak at the bottom of the boat when he was killed. 'What me?' he said.

Their position was bad. A huge sea had smashed into the yacht. Quite possibly some underwater planks on the yacht sprang open because of the impact. This would explain why the boat sank in about five minutes—far too short a time for them to get the dinghy in the water and get some provisions into the dinghy as well. Their suffering was immense—raging hunger and thirst, burns from the sun, swollen bodies covered with sores, desperation and despair, madness from drinking seawater.

The sailors themselves admitted everything with complete candour when they got back to England. They said it was the custom of the sea, it was necessary that one should die to save the rest; they were surprised to learn later that this might be murder. The skipper (who had once been a ship's cook) cut the cabin boy's throat with a penknife. He pierced the boy's jugular on the left-hand side. The knife had a two-inch blade, a very small knife. As his blood spurted out, they caught it in the case of the chronometer they had saved from the yacht and drank the blood. They said the cabin boy was dying anyway. They said they needed the blood nice and fresh. The pick-up by the German ship was about five days later by which time they would otherwise certainly have all died, but for the fact that they had consumed by then most of the cabin boy.

Two of them were convicted for murder when they got back to England—the other sailor was not implicated in the killing. It was a big moral issue, whether you could kill and eat one to save the others in a situation when it looked like otherwise everybody would die.

You can imagine the terrors out in that stormy sea, the shocking temptations, the horrible deed and the iron discipline of the law in enforcing the moral discipline, a rule so tough that hardly anybody can keep to it. If the law is a survival code, a moral survival code that everybody can believe in, some of it is beyond us, we can't keep to it. The fact is, if we don't keep to it, the blind charioteer will come out from the dark forest on his foaming horses, and that's the end of us on this planet. That is why this foundational case, this statement of civilisation, is so incredibly potent and moving.

The accused were sentenced to be taken to a place of execution and there hung by the neck until they be dead. But, as the court probably expected, they were pardoned by Queen Victoria and served only six months in jail. The court had made the point.

All English law students know about this case. Dudley was the skipper, Stephens was his mate. Tom Dudley subsequently emigrated to Sydney where he died in an outbreak of the bubonic plague which hit Australia in 1900. He was 46.

One issue was whether the men on that little dinghy drew lots to decide who should be executioner and who should be executed, as the custom of the sea demanded. It seemed that they did not; they just picked the youngest and weakest.

Above is an old photograph of the dinghy in which the cabin boy Richard Parker was killed. The dinghy was exhibited in September 1884 in the hall of the Royal Cornwall Polytechnic Society in Falmouth. This photograph came from AW Brian Simpson, *Cannibalism and the Common Law* (University of Chicago Press, 1984), by far the best work on this case.

One of the most poignant aspects of this case was the inscription on Richard Parker's gravestone laid over the unmarked grave of his mother in the churchyard in Pear Tree Green, Southampton. It read: 'Lord, lay not this sin to their charge'.

**Killing one to save the others** There was a similar case in the United States in 1842. The US case was called *US v Holmes*. A ship carrying Irish emigrants struck an iceberg 300 miles off the coast of Newfoundland, like the Titanic.

About 42 of the 83 people on board got on to a longboat which was far too small for that number. Some others got in another boat, leaving about 31 people on board. They went down with the ship amid the ice floes. After a while the crew of the longboat, including the accused Holmes, began to throw some of the passengers overboard to lighten the load. They seized some hapless passengers and shoved them into the icy sea where they perished within minutes.

Same issue. Sacrifice some to save the others. The issue has been discussed for centuries. The Roman senator Cicero debated what should be done when two men are holding on to a plank in the sea when the plank will only hold one. There is the Russian story of the insatiably hungry wolves chasing the sled and eating first the horses and then the occupants one by one. So who should be thrown to the wolves? We know of the tales of cutting the rope on the mountain so that one man falls to his death to preserve the others.

In the US case the Pennsylvanian jury convicted Holmes. Obviously. The passengers thrown overboard did not consent, they had no say.

**Crime and civilisation** So this is the real test of courage and morality—when people are faced with death, how they behave then. That is when we find out whether we are altruistic or whether we are cruel beasts and monsters. The criminal law is a test of civilisation and involves an exquisite balance.

The result in *Dudley and Stephens* is contrary to what most people think should be the rule. In Marc Hauser's book, *Moral Minds* (Ecco, 2006), the author posits the case where a runaway truck is racing down the railway line where five people are tied to the line and will be run over and killed. Luckily there is a siding with some points with a guard standing there. The only problem is that there is also a person tied to the line in the siding who will surely be killed if the points are thrown.

In this situation, according to the author, 90 per cent of people think it is permissible for the guard to throw the points. The killing of one is better than the killing of five. But if the facts are changed and, instead of the siding, the diversionary track is a side loop which rejoins the main track before it reaches the five people tied to the line. There is a very fat man near the loop who would stop the truck if he got pushed on the line. Should the guard throw the points and push the fat man in front of the runaway truck? In this situation most people apparently think it would not be morally permissible because the fat man is being used to rescue the five. It would be as if a doctor went into the waiting room to pick up a patient and killed him so as to use his organs to save five patients who otherwise would have died. We are told that 97 per cent of people think that this would not be permissible.

In both cases what is really happening is that one person is killed to save the other five, or, to put it another way, it is permissible if five of you are starving in an open boat out in the sea to kill the cabin boy and eat him. The fact that most people think that this is ok in the artificial case of the runaway truck shows how poor is the judgement of most people about fundamental morality. Their judgement is driven by expediency, not by moral absolutes.

**Conclusion** I relate the story of the *Mignonette* and the related situations at length because they are symbolic of the intensity of the moral conflicts involved in the criminal law—morality pushed to its limits, on the edge of the cliff. That tale also invites the question of whether we are on the raft and, if so, how we will behave.

Judges have to make these moral decisions in the here and now. The morality requires a punishment in this world, not the next. Unlike religions, the rewards and punishments of the law are real in life, not something postponed until after your death.

# Family Law and Sex

Cultural attitudes around the world to family law and sex are visceral, primitive and emotional, mixed with completely opposing views of economic and rational objectives. You could hardly find an area of law where people differ so profoundly and so passionately.

The law of many countries on these subjects is transient and ephemeral, so that what is vice today is virtue tomorrow, what is repulsive and immoral in one year is perfectly acceptable and indeed a mark of forward-looking and progressive liberality in the next year.

**Sex and the family** Family law and the law relating to sex have historically and up to the present time been driven almost exclusively by the attitude to family and marriage. In former times, the only legal and morally acceptable method of permitting sex and child-rearing was by marriage. When there was no contraceptive pill and abortion was prohibited, sex would almost inevitably result in the birth of children and the prevailing wisdom was that the children should have two parents. The reasons for this were partly emotional and partly economic. From the emotional point of view, it was considered that children needed both a senior male and senior female to bring them up so as to be able to cope with life. One economic reason was the division of economic responsibility between the parents, that is, the wife stayed at home and looked after the children while the husband initially gathered food and nowadays had a job to earn money for the whole family. In addition, the pattern was that when parents were old they were assured that they would be looked after by their children who were under an obligation to support them. For all these reasons, which one can readily see were based on the needs of children, divorce was difficult in most countries.

All that has now utterly changed in most Western countries, or has at least been brought into question. The main reasons for this appear to be (1) the desire of women for equality, (2) the recognition that children have rights, including rights against their parents, (3) the growth of the welfare state which fulfils roles previously belonging to the family, such as support of the elderly, and (4) secularisation which resulted in the religious taboos on family and sexual subjects being fatally weakened.

It followed that divorce became much easier and no longer depended on marital fault, such as adultery. In most Western states, divorce is in substance available on demand by one partner, although there are still severe financial consequences for both parties. Most spouses are not able to afford to maintain two families.

In Western countries, cohabitation is now widely accepted so there are fewer marriages and therefore fewer divorces. For example, in a recent year 40 per cent of births in France were to unmarried mothers. The view taken by many women is that the burdens of marriage outweigh the advantages. The advantages of cohabitation sometimes include the fact that women often do not accept the role division between parents and they also aim at freedom from male dominance in the marriage. In many countries the tax system may be weighted in favour of marriage.

The questions for the law now are whether marital-like obligations should be imposed on unmarried partners, such as division of assets on a breakup, who looks after the children and how you prove sufficient marital-like status if there has been no formal ceremony.

The equality of women, although begun in the 19th century, was mainly a late-20th century phenomenon in the West. One can grade the degrees of female subordination, all of which are still found in one or other part of the world. At the most shocking are infanticide of female children, acceptance of rape, death or cruel punishments for adultery or unmarried sex, female genital mutilation, atrocities aimed at women by soldiers, and the transfer of female children to settle tribal disputes.

Other instruments of subjection include the inability to own property, enter into contracts, have a personal bank account or inherit. They include exclusion from jobs (teachers, doctors, priests), lower pay and discrimination in jobs, inferiority in education, arranged marriages, necessity for father's or brother's consent to marry, and a duty to carry out the orders of a patriarchal father. They include denial of a second marriage, payment for marriage by dowries, very low pre-puberty age of consent, unequal divorce rights, unequal rights to the house and family property, exclusion or disregard of evidence in legal proceedings, exclusive burden of child-rearing, lack of redress for domestic violence, and rape in marriage and sexual harassment. They include exclusion from voting or sitting on juries, subordinate status at church, temple or mosque, unequal rights to custody of children, polygamy by men, and the need for the husband's permission to travel away from home or to issue legal proceedings. They include denial of abortion, contraception, in vitro fertilisation or surrogate motherhood, non-recognition of lesbianism, covering up of the face and body by black robes, and no maternity rights. They include debasement by pornography and prostitution, and inability to drive a car without male escort.

Progress on ameliorating the above has been rapid in some countries, beginning mainly in the 19th century and accelerating from the 1960s onwards. But the equalisation of women is very uneven around the world.

Homosexuality was legalised in Britain only in 1967. Set out below is a map showing countries where homosexuality is legal or illegal. Red indicates countries where homosexuality attracts the death penalty and yellow countries are where violations attract imprisonment or some other similar penalty.

Countries in blue are where homosexuality is legal (usually if above a certain age). Those countries in white have not been investigated.

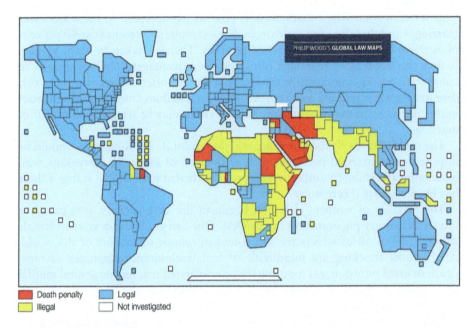

**Legend:**
- Death penalty
- Illegal
- Legal
- Not investigated

**Legality of homosexuality**

Similar patterns would be shown by a map on the legal endorsement of gay marriages.

One consequence of the above examples is that morality changes, sometimes very swiftly. Does that mean that morality is ephemeral and depends on the time and the country, the era and the region? Are there any areas of morality which are permanent, unchangeable, not subject to human fashions and fads, not subject to the spirit of the age or to the culture of the local inhabitants?

The answer to that is complicated. Yet you could compile a list of what is subject to change and what is not. To some, the rules of morality relating to sex and the family are changeable and ephemeral. The rules relating to the social structure of society—such as caste versus equality—seem to be fickle. But some things are absolute, such as the prohibitions on murder, robbery, fraud and the like.

Another consequence is that the breathtaking pace of change on issues such as those identified above where one group of countries shifts its moral culture but others do not, is a major source of conflict and violence. On a great many of these issues, the West is poles apart from Islamic countries, most African countries and India. We therefore observe deep schisms, chasms, between regions on issues which provoke profound emotions, as if the interlocked continental plates of world moral culture were shuddering and buckling and then jolting violently apart.

**Plunge in birthrate** Most unexpectedly, the birthrate has plunged in most rich countries and is well below the minimum replacement rate of 2.1 children per woman. This figure results from the fact that there have to be two children to match the two parents and the remaining 0.1 results from mortality rates for children. The plunge of the birthrate was unexpected because in the 1970s a forecast population explosion was seen as one of the greatest challenges facing the planet.

In many countries, ranging from Japan to Italy, the birthrate is well below this, for example, 1.4, and in some places such as Hong Kong it is around 1.1. So the human race is dying out. Thus it has been forecast that in a few decades the population of Japan, currently 126 million, will sink to 90 million. There is forecast to be a similar huge decline in the population of Russia, which is now 148 million. Maybe one day some countries will have only two humans left. They will have to be put in a special cage, like the pandas, in the hope that they will mate.

At the same time, there are forecasts of massive increases in the population in some Muslim and African countries. Thus the World Bank in 2014 forecast that the population of Nigeria (currently around 167 million) will be over 700 million in 2100, and that the population of Tanzania (currently 48 million) will be 306 million in 2100.

The mixture of the lack of children and an ageing population in many countries puts in question the survival of the welfare system, such as pensions, healthcare and unemployment benefit, because the pyramid idea behind the welfare state is threatened; there are not enough young workers to maintain the aged. This factor could not just challenge social welfare but could threaten the sustainability of Western civilisation. That is because societies which can no longer pay for themselves are likely to be dominated and subordinated by others who do not have the same welfare culture. The problems of the vanishing of the pyramid could only be solved by (1) much higher rates of productivity by the younger workers, (2) immigration, or (3) people working until they are much older—if the jobs are available. See the excellent essay by Harry D Krause, chapter 34 in Reimann and Zimmermann *The Oxford Companion to Comparative Law* (Oxford University Press, 2006).

Christianity, Islam and Hinduism all put great emphasis on the importance of the family, although with considerable erosion at the edges.

# Inheritance Laws: Free or Not Free?

The purpose of inheritance laws is to ensure predictability in the devolution of assets on death and to forestall family skirmishes harmful to society.

One of the most ancient principles of inheritance was that assets should go to the next head of the family, usually the eldest son, so as to avoid the splitting of the assets of the patriarchal family, especially the land needed for subsistence. In modern times it is almost universally the case that, if a deceased does not make a will, the assets pass to the nearest family members, for example, spouse and children, and that, if the deceased does make a will, there is relative freedom of disposition.

The main exception to freedom of gift is that in many countries, particularly those based on the French Napoleonic system, a part of the assets is compulsorily reserved to close family members, notably spouses and children—'forced heirship'. Another international difference is the availability of the right to put assets in trust so as to tie up the assets in the family forever: the next generation only has rights for life over the property and does not own it. This was prevented in civil law countries by the non-recognition of the trust and was curtailed in common law countries by limiting the duration of these generation-skipping trusts so as to ensure that assets, especially land, are marketable. In practice few people nowadays, except those owning vast landed estates, want to tie up their property in this way.

The principal threat to inheritance is taxation on the assets of the dead, presumably in the name of rectifying economic inequality.

## Constitutional Law and Democracy

Constitutional law is primarily concerned with the freedoms and protections of the individual and the rule of law. The most pervasive issue is the degree of representative democracy enabling the citizens to elect the government periodically.

Most countries have written constitutions setting out the establishment and powers of the supreme legislator, the head of state, their executive, the major departments of government and the judiciary plus emergency powers and plus, sometimes, human rights. In a few countries such as the United Kingdom, the constitution is spread out over a vast number of different laws of different dates and judicial decisions. The US Constitution is quite short but many others cannot be said to have prioritised brevity. Written constitutions first appeared in the West in the 18th century—a Swedish Constitution in 1772, then the US Constitution of 1787 and the French revolutionary Constitution of 1793, all innovations born out of conflict.

The United States has had six constitutions since independence, whereas the Dominican Republic has had 32. In some countries the constitutions choose not to underpin the rule of law but to corrupt it.

It is also remarkable how very few countries granted full voting rights to all adults both male and female before the 20th century. After the Greek experiments with democracy, democracy virtually disappeared from the West for two thousand years until the American and French revolutions. Even then the Founding Fathers in the new United States tended to use democracy as a term of abuse, not far from mob rule. In 1941 there were only 11 democracies left in the world—Spain, Portugal, Germany and Italy were autocratic countries. All Americans were enfranchised only as late as 1965. In 1780 in England only 3 per cent of the population was entitled to vote. In the first democracy—Athens—voting was limited to adult males over 20, excluding slaves and foreigners.

Few countries have full democracies. The Economist Intelligence Unit recently treated only 25 countries out of nearly 200 as being full democracies. All the rest were flawed democracies or hybrid democracies or authoritarian dictatorships. Other organisations have recognised around 85 to 120 countries as being democracies of a sort. Whatever the figures or the criteria, this is a shocking reminder of the realities of the world. It remains a riddle that so many people live under despots.

Female suffrage is recent as this table shows:

| | |
|---|---|
| New Zealand | 1893 |
| Australia | 1902 |
| Finland | 1906 |
| Norway | 1913 |
| United States | 1920 |
| Britain | 1928 |
| France | 1945 |
| Belgium | 1946 |
| Switzerland | 1971 |

Many attempts have been made to justify democracy on the ground that it is economically the most efficient form of government since, for example, freedom and the absence of arbitrary governmental power enhance enterprise and prosperity. History has many examples. Compare for example North and South Korea, East and West Germany, South America and the United States, Hong Kong and Manila, the USSR and Western Europe. Simon Bolivar, the patriotic independence leader of the 19th century in South America, failed to create a United States of South America in contrast to George Washington.

Nevertheless the arguments in favour of democracy supporting economic prosperity are not absolute since there are many examples of countries which achieved economic success without democracy. For example, the generals in South Korea up to 1987 who steered the country through its industrial revolution and Lee Kuan Yew in Singapore were all essentially absolutist even if enlightened. Monopoly parties ruled in Taiwan and Japan in the second half of the 20th century. Hong Kong was ruled as a British colony until 1997. In all of these cases, democracy followed economic success and did not precede it. But there is no question that communistic dictatorship or other forms of absolutism were disastrous economically in countries such as Cuba, Vietnam, Angola and Ethiopia, as well as Russia.

As Niall Ferguson remarked in his book *Civilization* (Penguin, 2012), perhaps the greatest mystery of the entire Cold War is why the Workers' Paradise did not manage to produce a decent pair of jeans.

There are other reasons for democracy which are nothing to do with functional economic success. One is that democracies, for all their inefficiencies, are to protect the individual against oppression which usually, but not always, accompanies authoritarian rule, in other words to protect the moral system and its expression through the rule of law. The preservation of the moral system is fundamental to survival and is the most utilitarian and functional of all ideologies. For those who have never lived in an authoritarian country, it is hard to imagine how arbitrary despotism affects every aspect of one's daily life. It induces fear, saps energy and removes incentives. You even fear that the attendant in the loo or the waiter in the restaurant is a spy.

Democracies are a legal creation: they are enshrined in law. They are one of the most crucial inventions of the law. Effectively when the law establishes the rule of law, the people are empowered.

Even democracies have to be protected by entrenched laws designed to prevent, for example, the tyranny of the majority over the minority. This role is performed by the rule of law—constitutional provisions sometimes called human rights, the most basic of all constitutional principles. These are enshrined either in separate conventions, as in Europe, or in the constitution itself as in the United States, or in both.

The principles typically include such things as the right to life, the right to a fair trial and the protection of private property.

## Tort or Delict: The Limits of Liability

Civil law is different from the criminal law. The courts order somebody who causes harm or injury to another or their property to pay compensation to the victim for a breach of the civil law, not punishment. The compensation is only the loss which the victim has suffered, whereas punishments can exceed the loss suffered and are calibrated according to the culture of the country and the severity of the offence. Criminal fines are payable to the state, whereas civil compensation is payable to the victim. A crime requires a deliberate intent to commit it, whereas a civil wrong can be just negligent or even without any kind of recklessness or intention. An example is killing somebody by negligent driving as opposed to murdering them by deliberately running them over.

Apart from breach of contract, the main civil wrongs are called torts (called 'delicts' in civil law countries). A tort is considered less serious than a crime. Accordingly the victim and not the state is left to enforce the wrong and extract a remedy.

The rationale of the law of torts is similar to that of the criminal law—the protection of the people and indirectly their survival because they are compensated for injury. The law therefore has a moral base. The tolerance or vindictiveness of a society is revealed by what acts they shift over the boundary into the criminal law which attracts the stigma of crime and the potent punishments of the state. You do not go to jail for commission of a tort, nor are you executed

They include such things as product liability, negligence resulting in death or injury, negligent accidents, killing or injuring the breadwinner, trespassing on somebody else's land, libel, assault, interfering in somebody's property, false imprisonment, infringement of privacy, pollution, procuring a breach of contract, wrongful deceit or misrepresentation (lies or negligent fibs)—anything which harms your life, body, health, property, reputation and privacy, or otherwise causes you injury or loss. Some torts, such as assault, are also crimes. Most cases involve liability for negligence, such as motor accidents. An accident can ruin the person who caused it unless they have insurance. In the 19th century the Napoleonic codes took the view that you could sum up all the torts in just a couple of lines and indeed the Napoleonic liability in tort is based on one article in the French Civil Code, article 1382, which succinctly provides 'Any act whatever done by a man, which causes damage to another, obliges him by whose fault the damage was caused to repair it'.

The number of cases where manufacturers are sued for defective products is stupendous, especially in the United States. In England product liability is based on the case of *Donoghue v Stevenson* (1932) where one lady bought her friend a bottle of ginger beer in a cafe which her friend drank, only to find a decomposed snail at the bottom of the bottle. The court decided that the manufacturer was liable. The corresponding foundation decision in the United States involved the Buick Motor Co in 1916.

The law of torts has had a more complicated career than contract or crime and sits uneasily in the middle. One of the most basic questions has been the degree of liability, that is, the degree of risk that people should take towards others and the extent to which potential victims should look after themselves, for example, by taking out insurance. The fear of judges has often been that individuals could by some trivial accident incur unlimited liabilities to an unlimited number of people, for example, by striking the match which burns the house which lights the fuel in the tanks which burns the city, whose flames scorch rescuers who rush to help and whose destruction cuts off light and power in surrounding towns which interrupts their businesses which damages buyers in other countries who can't deliver to their buyers which ... These are ricochet cases. At some point you have to cut the chain of liability, the chain of causation. Unlike contract, in tort it is not practicably feasible to limit your liability to third parties since you do not know who they are and have no contract with them. You can't walk around holding up a placard proclaiming that your liability is limited. In any event, exclusions of liability are often invalidated, especially in the case of consumers.

The other defect of tort is fine-trigger liability, where a householder or a doctor or a municipality is liable, even though they were not really negligent or the injured should really have taken more care not to slip on the mat.

In some countries, especially the United States, tort law is virtually out of control (and often criminalised by the award of punitive or treble damages), while in others, even those in the same tradition, such as England, the courts are alive to limiting the scope of the risk in the public interest, to avoid concentration of liability on single people flowing through to insurance companies, and to advance the cause of stability.

## Contract: The Peak of Legal Freedom

Contract is the ultimate legal freedom. One of the greatest triumphs of the law is that, subject to some very basic restraints, you can agree what you like with whom you like and the state will enforce it. In most countries you can freely decide that the law of another country will apply to the contract and freely choose the courts of another country to enforce the contract. You don't even have to go to a court; most countries allow you to insert an arbitration clause and then the courts will in most states enforce a private arbitration award, even (under a New York international convention of 1958) an award made by an arbitrator in another country. The law therefore favours freedom, subject to some fundamental rules to preserve basic fairness. The religious moral codes rarely favoured freedom—it is just not a value which they considered worth aspiring to.

A remarkable aspect of the freedom of contract is that the law is not a restriction, it is a power, a facility, something you can do but only if you want to. You are empowered. But once you have entered into a contract, yes, the law has rules about the contract and it is binding on you. The courts will enforce it. You don't have to go through the door but once you do the lights are on.

This restriction, but liberation, is the essence of the institution of contract. We would make few advances in prosperity or wellbeing or survival unless there was a means of keeping people to their commercial promises.

Contract is king. The variety of contracts is stunning. They include contracts of sale (of goods, oil and gas, electricity, companies, foreign exchange, groceries, toys, land, investments), construction contracts, the latter being surrounded by satellite contracts with architects, engineers and the like, insurance contracts, employment contracts, contracts with labour unions, contracts to make loans, ranging from the mighty syndicated bank credits to the humble working capital bank loan to a family business, all kinds of credit contracts, agreements for the issue and sale of bonds and shares in the capital markets, contracts to transfer money in payment systems, charters and other transportation contracts, contracts for the lease or hire of a car or a ship or a plane or an apartment or an office, derivatives contracts, contracts to lend investments, custodianship contracts for the safekeeping of investments, contracts to manage investments, licences of intellectual property, franchises and distributorship agreements, guarantees, bank bonds and agency contracts—all these are subsets of contract. A mighty network of rights and obligations spanning the world.

Contract is everywhere. There are so many contracts made continuously that they are as evanescent as ephemeral shimmering ripples of a lake in the yellow evening sun. Every time somebody goes into a supermarket and buys a can of beans or a piece of fish, there is a contract. The result is that many billions of contracts are concluded every day.

Internationally, the law of contract is a done deal. There are so many different types of contract that the law books groan with the colossal accumulation of experience and rules—explaining the difference between a legal contract and asking somebody out to dinner, how you make a contract in terms of offer and acceptance, whether the contract has to be in writing, what happens if there is a mistake or you are induced into a contract by a fib or a lie, whether there are any implied terms such as warranties about the suitability of a product, what happens if some force majeure event intervenes, how you terminate a contract and the level of damages if a party fails to comply, how you sell a contract, what happens to a contract if one party is bankrupt.

The differences in contract law between the major legal systems (as opposed to insolvency or property law) are not as great as may be imagined—at any rate in the areas which really matter. It is unusual for contract law to impose insuperable problems defeating legitimate expectations.

**Limitations on freedom of contract** I said earlier that contract is free. That is not quite true. For example, you cannot usually provide that a breach of the contract by the other party will attract some massive penalty in excess of the actual damages you are likely to suffer. More importantly, many countries have limited the ability of a contracting party to exclude liability for non-performance of the contract, for example, liability for defective goods sold. There are limitations created by employment law, by consumer credit laws, by financial regulation—a long list of clamps on contract. These are primarily consumer protections. The consumer is made god by the statute-makers and strolls around the park, humming a tune, clothed with an invisible armour. At the time theorists clamoured that this was the death of contract, but this proved not to be the case. It just meant that business expenses increased and had to be built into prices.

Apart from consumers, one of the major issues in contract is the extent to which a party can exclude liability as between business parties who are sophisticated enough to know what they are doing and the extent to which the law requires that parties act towards each other in good faith. The issue is one of predictability.

The hard-edged English approach to predictability in contracts between business parties of equal bargaining power was dramatically shown in a ship charterparty case.

In *The Laconia* (1977) a shipowner chartered a ship to a charterer. The charterparty provided that the charterer had to pay the hire in advance and, if the charterer did not pay on the due date, then the shipowner could cancel the charterparty and forfeit the ship. The contract also provided that time was of the essence, ie, there were no grace periods. After the charterparty was entered into, the market rate for hiring ships of the type concerned went up, so it was obviously to the advantage of the shipowner to get the ship back and to charter it out again to somebody else at a higher rate. So the shipowner lay in wait ready to pounce if the charterer made a mistake.

The chance soon came. A payment of hire due from the charterer fell due on a Sunday. Somebody in the charterer's office thought that this must mean that the charterer had to pay on Monday since the banks were not open on a Sunday. So the charterer transferred the money on the Monday. The shipowner sent it back and cancelled the charterparty. The House of Lords held that the shipowner was entitled to do this. Since the hire fell due on a Sunday and since it had to be paid in advance, this meant that it had to be paid on the previous Friday, not the following Monday. Since the charterparty said expressly that, if the hire was not paid on the due date, the shipowner could withdraw the vessel and that time was of the essence, the shipowner was entitled to forfeit the vessel. This was commercially abusive behaviour by the shipowner, but that is what the contract said.

The courts either enforce the contract as written (the approach of the English courts) or they amend the contract. But if they amend the contract, is the grace period to be 24 hours, three days, one week or one month? If the creditor fails to divine in advance the view of the courts, then a creditor taking possession of security or repossessing a ship could he liable for very substantial damages for interfering with the ship. The view of the English courts is that, if a contracting party wants a grace period, then it must agree it in the contract and indeed this is commonly done. These are not situations of an overweening disparity of bargaining power or unconscionability. The predictability approach to the enforcement of contract as negotiated in business situations is a major factor in the international goodwill of a legal system. That means that the legal system must tolerate the occasional abuse and unreasonable conduct. Some other jurisdictions have a completely different approach.

I mention this case in detail to show how nuanced and sophisticated the law can be in balancing the interests of the parties and the competing ethical policies—a sophistication far beyond the broad-brush attitudes of a religious ethical code.

# Conflict of Laws: Whose Law Applies?

In a globalised world, there are bound to be questions about whose law applies. For example, is a marriage or divorce recognised if it is performed in another country contrary to the rules of the country where the spouses are now living? What are the inheritance rules for assets located abroad? Whose law applies in the case of a crime or tort which has international connections? Can you enforce a judgment obtained in one country against a corporation located in another country? Is the bankruptcy of an international corporation recognised in another country where it has assets? These questions are the field of conflict of laws or private international law. Again religious codes contain only rudimentary rules on this topic, if they touch on it at all.

In effect the collision of different criminal and civil laws is subjected to an orderly set of rules and method of enforcement in the interests of peace. These rules require sovereign courts to exercise restraint and tolerance and to comply with the principles established to resolve conflicts of law. It is to the credit of the courts round the world that in the main they do respect the rule of law in this important area. In practice, the most important questions concern international contracts as opposed to torts. This is because of the enormous number and ubiquity of contracts and the amounts involved, especially in financial contracts.

**Governing law** Every legal issue under a contract must be determined in accordance with a system of law. An aspect of a contract cannot exist in a legal vacuum.

In England and in most developed countries the parties to a contract may normally choose the governing law of the contract which will govern many of its aspects. In syndicated bank credits or bond issues, this law may, for example, be the law of the borrower's country, the law of the creditor's country, the law of the market, such as English law for the London market or the market in which the bonds are issued, or a neutral system of law.

Factors which influence the choice of law for a financial contract include non-legal preferences, such as patriotism, tradition, familiarity and convenience, avoidance by the parties of a detailed investigation into an unfamiliar system of law, commercial orientation, stability and predictability of the chosen legal system, and similar factors. Insulation of the loan contract from legal changes in the borrower's country defeating the contract (such as exchange controls) is one of the most important reasons for the choice of an external system of law which the legislature of the borrower's country cannot change.

This point is dramatically illustrated by the case of *Helbert Wagg & Co Ltd* (1956) which stunned me by its beauty when I first read it as a student. In this case a British bank made a loan in pounds sterling to a German borrower in the 1920s. During the whole of the 1920s and 1930s, Germany's finances were in a parlous state. There had been a runaway inflation in the early 1920s and Germany had to pay huge reparations to the victorious Allies under the peace treaties agreed at the end of the First World War. These reparations were beyond the capacity of Germany to pay. In 1933 Adolf Hitler came to power. At around that time, Germany passed a law which provided that all foreign currency loans had to be paid to a custodian in Berlin in German currency. So the British bank never got paid.

After the Second World War, the British lender brought an action in the English courts claiming payment. The English court held that the loan agreement was governed by German law. That meant German law as it was from time to time, including subsequent laws, so that if you contracted under the governing law of the borrower's country, then you took a risk that those laws might be changed. As the 1933 decree was a German decree, it therefore bound the parties to the loan contract and so the British lender was not entitled to enforce payment.

This startling result, whereby the British lender was in effect expropriated, was made even more startling by the fact that the case was decided only ten years after the end of a particularly savage and existential war. You would have thought that the court would have leant over backwards to try and find a reason not to decide the case that way. But the fact is that previous cases had already decided that, if you contracted under one system of law, you must inevitably accept any transformations of that law, for better or for worse. You can't freeze the law by contract, just as you cannot stop time by contract.

If the lender had contracted under, say, English law, then the result would have been completely different. A German decree could not change an English law agreement so that lenders did have a safe harbour if they wanted. So the most astonishing feature of this case was the iron determination of the English court to cling to an essential principle, which was entirely rational and logical, notwithstanding that the merits were the other way. In a case like this, the law transcends rage. That is why the purity of the morality is beautiful.

Another case decided a couple of years later proved the point.

*National Bank of Greece and Athens SA v Metliss* (1958) was also a case born out of the financial disruptions of the Second World War. A Greek bank had issued bonds to international bondholders. The bonds were expressly governed by English law. Because of the dislocation of Greek post-war finances, the Greeks passed a decree which reduced the interest rate on the bonds from 5 per cent to 3 per cent. One of the bondholders sued the bank for the full 5 per cent. The highest English court, then the House of Lords, decided that the Greek decree could not change an English law contract and therefore the borrower was liable to pay arrears of interest at 5 per cent. The effect is that the English governing law insulated the contract from changes in Greek law. The principle was quite clear that lenders who wanted to protect their loans could choose an external governing law and in that way get the protection they wanted.

This principle of insulation by an external governing law is a principle endorsed to a greater or lesser extent by courts of most Western jurisdictions and is one of the reasons why in major international loan contracts, and indeed in many other classes of contracts, parties choose English or New York law. The result is that in England the foreign lender can, by choice of external law, have complete certainty in knowing that the borrower's country cannot unilaterally alter the obligations by a change of local law, for example, by exchange controls or a moratorium. The piece of paper, at least, is inviolate and retains its bargaining power. The piece of paper—whether a credit agreement or bond or whatever—is all the creditor has to represent the money and plainly the creditor's position is somewhat unhappy if that, too, is destroyed.

**Near monopoly of English and New York law** Anecdotal evidence suggests that English and New York law enjoy a dominant position as the governing law of major international financial contracts. These are international syndicated bank loans, international bond issues and derivatives transactions—all of which involve colossal amounts. These legal systems are international public utilities.

The reasons for this dominance are partly historical. In the 19th century Britain was the world's largest economic power, and the United States was and is the world's largest economic power, a mantle which it assumed around 1900. Financial institutions tend to prefer their home law and so it was inevitable that countries which gave birth to these banks and very deep capital markets would see a tendency for those banks and markets to choose their own law with which they were familiar.

Once a legal system views itself as international and as being used in major foreign commercial and financial transactions, then courts, judges and legislators tend to see it as their job to ensure that the legal system meets the requirements of its users. Markets cannot be bothered with a proliferation of choices: they are content with even a single option, provided that the chosen option reasonably meets their needs.

It is too complicated for markets to investigate a different legal system on each occasion and so they tend to gravitate towards legal systems which they are used to and which they can trust. So that legal system acquires a virtual monopoly.

**Long arm of court jurisdiction** Most of the non-criminal court battles in private international law are about which court in which country has jurisdiction over a case, ie, in the power to hear the case. Unless the parties actually have a place of business or live locally, the exercise of jurisdiction may be on the basis of more fleeting connections with the forum—often called the long-arm, or extended, or exorbitant, or excessive jurisdictions. Almost invariably in the case of the long-arm jurisdiction courts have a discretion as to whether or not they will accept jurisdiction so that jurisdiction is not automatic. This jurisdiction is generally exercised on the basis of whether the courts concerned are the most convenient forum. In many parts of the world, the courts are quite slow to refuse jurisdiction if technically they have it, even though the real centre of the action is elsewhere. This is particularly the case in plaintiff-orientated jurisdictions if the court considers that the plaintiff will have a better result in their courts than elsewhere, for example, in terms of large damages awards. The result is a great deal of forum-shopping.

The main heads of long-arm jurisdiction internationally include transient presence locally of an individual debtor and local assets of the defendant, however small, such as a bank account—the 'toothbrush' jurisdiction. There are other long-arm rules in particular jurisdictions, for example (in England) a contract is to be performed locally or (in France) the plaintiff is French.

In England and many English-based countries, jurisdiction is primarily based on the presence of the defendant within the forum state. The presence may be purely temporary. The court has jurisdiction over an individual if the claim form is served on the defendant while the defendant is physically present in England even though the defendant is merely passing through England, and whatever the defendant's nationality or residence—the 'Heathrow writ'. Thus in the case of *Maharanee of Baroda v Wildenstein* (1972) (a case involving a painting sold in Paris alleged to be erroneously attributed to Boucher) the Maharanee secured the jurisdiction of the English courts by serving the writ on the Parisian Mr Wildenstein while he was at Ascot Races for the day. Transient presence was taken to its ultimate conclusion in the US case of *Grace v MacArthur* (1959) where the writ was served on the defendant in an aeroplane while flying over the judicial district.

A famous example of the 'toothbrush' or 'umbrella' jurisdiction involved a magnificent 1970s sportsman from France. He was subjected to the jurisdiction of the Austrian courts in a patrimony suit on the basis of a pair of boxer shorts which he left behind in an Austrian hotel.

# Public International Law

Public international law is a system of law governing the relations between sovereign states in the main. The issues covered by this area of law include such matters as when does a state exist (especially if it is a breakaway state or there is a coup—the law of state recognition), how do citizens acquire nationality, and what you do with stateless people. They include the extradition of criminals from other countries and rights of asylum, how one decides how everybody can use the sea and space and the extent to which land territories own these commons, and the degree to which sovereign states are responsible for crimes and wrongs. They include what happens if sovereign states break up or unite, for example, who is liable for the public debt and who owns the property of the state (this speciality is called state succession), and the immunity of states from judicial actions and enforcement over their assets in the courts of other countries. They include the law relating to treaties (which are really just contracts between sovereign states), the judicial settlement of international disputes, the laws of war and neutrality, the law relating to nuclear proliferation and weapons of mass destruction, and a great many other subjects.

Public international law proves a point—that it is possible to have law without the sanction of enforcement, but it also proves the point that if a law does not have some means of enforcement, then the law ends up by being unpredictable and those who are supposed to be bound by it often take no notice of their obligations. It is regrettable that the principles of public international law which are so important to our survival, especially the law of war, should be the least enforceable of our legal regimes and that our societies do not appear to notice that conduct permitted between states internationally would immediately, if committed by an ordinary individual, result in the perpetrator being pounced on by many men in uniform and incarcerated in chains. This is because of the sacredness of the principle of non-interference in sovereign states by other states.

One of most controversial issues in the field is the extent to which nation states are prepared to delegate authority to an international body. The European Union, the United Nations and the IMF are examples of the tensions.

The law has been built up over centuries out of customs between states and treaties as well as quite a few judicial decisions. Many countries incorporate public international law into their own legal systems, although it is often hard to know what it is.

Although there are some limited courts, such as the International Criminal Court at the Hague, the tribunal of the World Trade Organization (WTO) and the International Court of Justice, the fact is that often the only sanctions against sovereign states which do not comply with the law are ostracism, disapproval, an exclusion from invites to parties at the United Nations, trade embargos, and in extreme cases armed attack. The WTO is an exception: the dispute settlement division of the WTO is astonishing as regards the speed with which it reaches decisions. It has a remarkable compliance rate of 95 per cent.

Nevertheless around the turn of the third millennium there was an astounding development which completely transformed public international law. For many years nations had been entering into bilateral investment treaties, usually between a developed country and an emerging country, whereby each party reciprocally agreed not to expropriate the investments of nationals of the other party, to accord those investments fair and equitable treatment, to give those investments full protection and security, not to subject investments to discriminatory treatment, and among other things to give investors a direct right to submit disputes under the treaty to international arbitration.

The purpose of these treaties was to encourage investments by investors from developed countries in emerging countries. There are about 4000 of them. To the consternation of the developing countries, arbitral tribunals took the treaties at their word and held that they were prepared to enforce these treaties at the suit of investors against violation, for example, expropriations. So for once an international treaty had real bite and public international law came of age.

Well, to a degree. The reality is that sovereign states are still above the law. Although they may and often do waive their immunity from legal proceedings in contracts and treaties, in virtually all countries the domestic assets of the state are immune from seizure by creditors, and foreign assets, which might be de-immunised by the contract waivers and therefore exposed to seizure by creditors, are generally held by their central banks or state-owned enterprises which are separate corporations which are not therefore liable for the obligations under the treaty or contract. The sovereign is the debtor, not the state-owned corporation. So sovereign states are still specially privileged in a way that ordinary mortals, ordinary corporations, are not. It would seem hard to change this state of affairs but it does mean that states have a licence to behave without the sanctions of the law as privileged creatures. They are above the law.

# Bankruptcy Law

The objects of bankruptcy law are to ensure that, once an individual or corporation is unable to pay their debts as they fall due, individual grabs of the assets by creditors are frozen and the debtor is relieved from creditor harassments and possibly able to be rescued and start again. An insolvency administrator sells the assets and distributes the proceeds to creditors or else proposes a plan to rescue the debtor which creditors vote on. In practice probably more than 90 per cent of financial difficulties are dealt with out of court. In that case the law is the shape behind the curtain with an axe if the parties fail to agree.

Insolvency law is the root of commercial and financial law because it obliges the law to choose. There is not enough money to go round and so the law must choose who to pay. The choice cannot be avoided, compromised or fudged. In bankruptcy, commercial law is at its most ruthless. It must decide who is to bear the risk so that there is always a winner and a loser, a victor and a victim. That is why bankruptcy is the most crucial indicator of the moral attitudes of a legal system in its commercial aspects.

Bankruptcy has a profound effect on normal legal relationships. Bankrupts and their creditors are disqualified from working. Property is seized and sequestrated. Assets are expropriated without compensation. Contracts are shattered and their terms interfered with or negated. Security interests are frozen or avoided or debased. The cost of credit is increased or credit—the lifeblood of modern economies—is withdrawn. People lose their jobs and their pensions. The collapse of banks and insurance companies destroys other banks and corporations and destroys the savings of the citizen. The economy of the state itself may be sapped. No wonder bankruptcy causes such passion and rage.

Bankruptcy is the great driver of legal change. If a large corporation like Enron becomes bankrupt—which it did in 2001—the reaction is to tighten up on corporate governance codes and legal duties regarding financial statements. If banking systems become bankrupt, as they did in 2007–08, the reaction of the legislature is to introduce more laws, law in profusion.

You can trace bankruptcy laws back to ancient times but there is no question that they took off in the 19th century and by the end of the 20th century were one of most rapidly expanding areas of law with some countries amending their bankruptcy laws every few years. Apart from episodic statutes in the 19th century the United States did not have a bankruptcy law until 1898— provoked mainly by railroad collapses.

If the bankruptcy law protects one set of creditors of a debtor, then other sets of creditors are prejudiced. The twin competing policies of bankruptcy law are the protection of creditors and the protection of debtors. Insolvency law is preoccupied with the collision of these interests and who to protect. Jurisdictions occupy all positions of the clock on this.

One of the most fundamental sources of legal risk in relation to bankruptcies is the ladder of priorities. The proposition that bankruptcy involves the pari passu or pro rata or equal payment of creditors, each proportionately out of the pool of the bankruptcy state according to his debt pro rata, is not true. Even the most cursory examination of bankruptcy internationally shows that this pari passu rule is nowhere honoured. On the contrary, creditors are paid according to a scale or hierarchy or ladder of priority. Nowhere is there a flat field, but rather an intricate series of steps as creditors scramble for a higher position, gasping for more air. Everywhere there is a ferocious fight to survive, to escape drowning in the dark swirling tides of rising debt, to breathe in the squeezed bubble of oxygen at the top.

So important are the priority steps that in most insolvencies the pari passu creditors get little or nothing and it is only the priority creditors who get paid. For example, if an employee's wages are paid first, or if a bank has a mortgage over the assets, then those creditors are paid in priority.

The bias of the bankruptcy law of a jurisdiction can be broadly assessed by using key indicators. An example is a security interest which is a generic term for mortgages, charges, pledges and the like, such as a home mortgage or a charge given by a company over all its assets to a bank to secure an overdraft or line of credit. If the customer becomes bankrupt, the bank can sell the collateral and hence get paid ahead of other creditors: the bank is on the first rung of the priority ladder. Security interests are therefore a protection of creditors against bankruptcy, and the wider and more easily enforceable the security, the more is the protection afforded to the secured creditor.

It follows that if a jurisdiction has a wide and easily enforceable security interest, then that jurisdiction is creditor-friendly on this point. If it does not have this, then it is debtor-friendly. Whether a jurisdiction should support the providers of money—typically banks—or should support the corporations who borrow the money is highly contentious. The argument in favour of protecting the bank is that, in substance, the bank is using other people's money to lend, namely, ultimately that of the citizen who deposits his or her cash with the bank. So the real creditor is not the bank, but the citizen who might argue that the law should be tilted in his or her favour, rather than in favour of the typical unsecured creditor, short-term trade suppliers, as compared with banks as suppliers of large amounts of medium-term credit to finance enterprise. Those in favour of pro-debtor policies propose opposite policies.

**Sovereign insolvency** Nearly half the sovereign states of the world became bankrupt, in the sense that they were unable to pay their debts as they fell due, during the 25-year period between 1980 and 2005: see the map below. Nearly all of them were emerging countries. Since then a number of other states have been bankrupt, including Greece in 2012. The reason that states become bankrupt is not invariably mismanagement. Sometimes it is bad luck or an external event such as an economic depression in other countries. But it usually results from negligence by governments, often ruled by unaccountable despots.

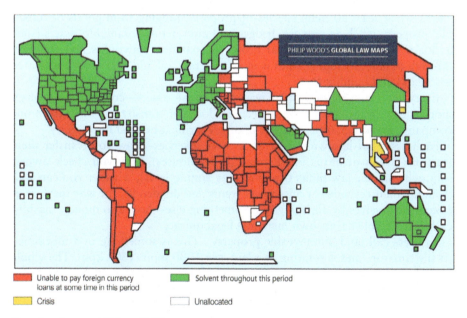

| | Unable to pay foreign currency loans at some time in this period | | Solvent throughout this period |
| | Crisis | | Unallocated |

**State insolvency 1980 to 2005**

The bankruptcy of a state can have a hugely adverse effect on the legal risks experienced by those with businesses in the country or those with financial or trading links with the country. Sovereign bankruptcy often leads to the bankruptcy of local banks and corporations, a precipitous decline in the value of the currency, and large losses to the population.

State insolvency poses a major philosophical or jurisprudential problem for lawyers. In the case of the ordinary bankruptcy of a corporation, the law takes over in a highly prescriptive manner. A bankruptcy law requires a petition to the court, a stay or freeze on creditor individual attachments of assets, the appointment of a liquidator, the sale of assets and the distribution of the proceeds among creditors, or else a rescue plan voted upon by creditors and a ladder of priorities according to which of the creditors are paid.

In the case of sovereign states, none of these laws applies. Yet the process works—it works even though there is no targeted bankruptcy law for sovereign states, only free contract. In practice, state bankruptcies are concluded a great deal more quickly than the ordinary bankruptcy of corporations, which can drag on for even more years than a sovereign bankruptcy. Typically more than 90 per cent of sovereign creditors agree to a rescue plan. So should the principle be that there should be no law, only free contract?

# Property Law

There are at least 50 main species of property, ranging from goods or 'tangible' property (such as oranges, fridges and aircraft) to 'intangible' assets (such as loans, shares and intellectual property—patents, copyrights and the like) through to land, including what is in it (minerals, oil and gas) and on it (water, woodland and buildings).

Every day lawyers deal with nearly all these assets—creating a universal mortgage or charge over them to secure a loan, or transferring them from one company to another, or leasing them, or preparing a bequest of property.

Each asset has its own character, its own essences—how you transfer them (easy for a can of beans but lugubrious for houses), how you check ownership, whether the law limits their use (like zoning laws), whether you can split them up, their revenue-earning power (rents and dividends), the way they are as ephemeral as elves by changing into something else—honey to money, mash to cash. Each foible has its own matching legal quirk.

Lawyers call land 'immoveable property'. This is something of a misnomer. At the equator, land is rotating at a leisurely 1000 mph (1600 kph). The whole package is moving around the sun at a comfortable 67,000 mph (107,000 kph). Our sun in this suburb of the Milky Way is speeding round the galaxy at an impressive 483,000 mph (792,000 kph). And the Milky Way is ... ok, you have got the picture. (Actually it is 1,300,000 mph or 2,100,000 kph towards the Great Attractor, so check that the kids are under adult supervision.)

The main legal issues with land, portentously latinised into 'real property', are whether you can record ownership in a public register also showing mortgages, tenancies and rights of way (yes in Europe, no in most of the United States—which relies on title insurance—and fitfully in emerging countries so that the ability to raise money on the land as collateral is poor) and whether you can own it at all. In such countries as China and Nigeria, you only have rights of occupancy for a limited period, and in Nigeria you cannot sell, lease, mortgage or bequeath these rights without government permit—a legacy of a military dictatorship in 1978. In many more territories, including Saskatchewan, aliens can't own land.

It has been calculated that land and buildings may account for three-quarters of the wealth of some countries.

Altogether there are about 148 million square kilometres of land on the planet. Without this land and all the beauteous things on it, we would be in trouble. The legal modes of dealing with property are one of the most artistic and aesthetic activities in the legal firmament, although also sometimes archaic.

Just about everybody knows that you transfer goods by handing them over. It can get more complicated when the goods are a slippery share of oil in a tanker ploughing the oceans. Most people in countries with any sort of formal land system know that investigating transferring the title to land is quite a complicated process.

But few people realise the massive legal structures which have been erected in order to transfer shares or bonds which are listed on a stock exchange. These financial assets used to be wrapped up in a piece of paper so as to give them tangibility and personal individuality, such as a share certificate with a number on it or a bond, also having a number and looking for all the world like a large and very impressive banknote. But nowadays, all the paper has been ripped off leaving a nude asset, completely naked. However there is nothing to see because the asset is invisible. In the jargon, it is dematerialised. These assets cannot be simply handed over (how would you grab a handful of air?) The identity of what is transferred can only be described in words or by numbers, and possession can only be virtual—you cannot slip a handful of nothing into your briefcase. The ownership of the shares is recorded in an account, like a bank account.

When one foreign share broker on behalf of a client agrees to sell some shares listed on the New York Stock Exchange to another foreign broker on behalf of a client, a huge machinery clanks into action. You don't get on your bike with your share certificates, ride across town to the buyer and then ride back with the cash in your satchel. First the shares race up one side of an upside down V like the profile of a pyramid by a series of debits to accounts. The selling broker debits the client's account with the amount of shares, the US broker debits his account kept for the foreign broker, the bank which is a member of the stock exchange debits the US broker's account, the clearing company debits the account of the member bank, followed by a series of credits to accounts down the other side of the inverted V, all the way down to the account kept by the foreign broker of the buying client.

Since the shares or bonds have to be paid for, you get a parallel system of debits on the buyer's side through several steps up the pyramid from foreign bank to US correspondent bank, to money centre US settlement bank, to the Federal Reserve as the central bank, and then down the other side through corresponding participants to the seller's bank.

At the same time, and most ingenious of all, when the two foreign brokers first do the deal, the contract between them is smashed into two contracts—one from the selling broker to a central counterparty owned by the members of the stock exchange, and the other a mirror contract from the central counterparty to the buying foreign broker. The effect is that all market contracts by all market participants with this particular foreign buying broker are now contracts between the central counterparty and that broker and therefore mutual. If this buying foreign broker becomes bankrupt, the central counterparty can cancel all of these contracts and net the gains and losses out across the whole lot. The result is a quite fantastic reduction of exposures—up to 95 per cent—in some cases—which would not be available without the use of a central counterparty. This is called 'netting'. If you can't talk about netting at dinner parties, you need to get back to stamp collecting.

In addition, if the foreign buyer has to buy US dollars for the transaction, then this foreign exchange contract will be routed ultimately through CLS Bank located in New York. The job of CLS Bank, which many people will not have heard of, but just happens to handle perhaps the most colossal volumes of any bank in the world (because it is involved in most wholesale foreign exchange contracts) is to ensure that the exchange of currencies is simultaneous. This is called the *Herstatt risk* after the name of a small German bank which failed in the 1970s early in the afternoon when the sellers of Japanese yen had already paid their yen to the bank earlier in the day, but Herstatt had not paid the dollars because the New York payment settlement had not yet taken place. More netting.

Although the above classic transactions don't always happen that way, all of these institutions are fundamentally important to the market. The number of transactions and the amounts involved are so huge that it would not be feasible to have a market without these structures—even the paperwork would be mountainous. The contracts which set up these institutions and the protocols are a legal speciality of their own at quite another level. If we did not have them, life would come to a halt.

If property is to have value and be of benefit to us, it must be marketable, transferable. Why should our assets, the product of our work, be frozen so that we cannot realise their value? The above description demonstrates the lengths to which the law will go to ensure marketability and its efficiency.

# Conclusion

There are other legal arenas, including subsets—intellectual property monopolies, such as patents and copyrights, maritime law, insurance law, taxation, for example. I come later to yet more topics.

The conclusion I draw so far is that the assertion that without religion there is no morality and no law is not correct. The moral systems of religion have been overtaken by secular law. Secular law has now become the main pillar of the moral framework necessary for our survival.

# 10

# *Money, Banks and Corporations*

## Money, Banks and Financial Law

The scope of law and why it has advanced far beyond the scope of religions can be demonstrated by the role in our societies of money, banks and corporations. These legal creations have frequently been the object of distrust, not just by the great religions. Yet they are marvellous inventions of our legal imagination and essential to our prosperity. It is worth examining what they do and what they are for. These are the fields of financial and corporate law.

## What does Money Do?

Chapter 3 has shown that the history of some of our greatest inventions is comparatively recent, only a few hundred years, most of them since 1800.

Long before these modern inventions there was another great invention. This was the invention of money. Without this money, these tokens, even buying a loaf of bread would not be practical, especially if you were in a hurry. You could not barter eggs or a sardine or a knitted sock each time. Without money, there would be no trade.

Money is not just a medium of exchange, not just used for buying things. Money connects us to other people who live abroad. It enables people to export and import so that the produce and manufactures of the world can be shared. It forms a vital link between different peoples and societies. It binds us together.

Money also connects us to our future, once it is transformed into financial assets such as bank deposits, bonds and shares in our pensions and savings pots. These financial assets are the ultimate store of our work and labour, the fruits of our efforts, which we can keep for our future, especially when we are old.

It is therefore clear that money is a public utility of enormous importance in people's lives. It is the commons. Because of the importance of money, it engages the rule of law, the rules for survival.

# What Do Banks Do?

Once money was invented it was necessary to have somewhere safe to put it. Hence the founding of banks. Once there is a means of exchange, then there have to be banks. It is much easier and safer to transfer money from bank account to bank account than to hand over a sackful of notes.

Banks in turn were an ingenious invention. The banks soon found that they could use other people's money by lending it to borrowers. When one switches on the light, the light comes on. It comes on because there is a power station. The power station has often been built out of bank money. The bank money derives from the savings of the depositors, that is, the citizens. So it is the citizens' money which makes it possible to switch on the light.

When you are young, you could live in a tent on the mud flats by the river. You could have your dinner by the river, you could wash in the river, and the kids could play in the mud. When you had saved up enough money and were in the autumn of your life, you could buy a chateau on the hill and go and live there instead, for a happy retirement away from the mud.

Alternatively, you could right at the beginning borrow somebody else's money from the bank and buy the chateau on the hill right away. Of course you have to pay back this money because it is somebody else's. But at least you do not have to live in a tent in the mud.

So it is with hospitals, schools, roads, ships, cars, factories, offices, palaces, and all the other creations we have. Credit produces them now rather than later.

The main vehicle of international bank lending is the syndicated bank credit agreement. Under this agreement between a borrower and a group of banks, ranging from three of them to a hundred, the banks agree to lend the borrower a loan according to their separate commitments. These epic contracts routinely carry more money than practically any other single agreement. Yet despite their complexity, you could hardly imagine a simpler agreement in concept. The banks agree to lend the money; the borrower agrees to pay it back with interest. There are clauses whereby the borrower undertakes not to create security to another lender ranking ahead of the banks (the loans are typically unsecured), to comply with financial ratios testing financial condition and the like and events of default, such as non-payment and insolvency, on the occurrence of which the banks can call in the loans. In practice these agreements run to over 100 pages—much more in the case of project finance for power stations, pipelines and the like. They are intricate in their detail, for example, syndicate democracy (whereby banks can vote for changes to the agreement) and sharing or recoveries between the banks, the impact of withholding taxes and how the banks transfer loans if they want to. The total amount of a syndicated bank credit is typically above one billion US dollars and some are for $50 billion or more.

Banks are not the only suppliers of credit. The other main form of credit is the bond issue where the lenders are insurance companies, pension funds and mutual funds. Bond issues are also loans but documented in a bond which is much shorter and simpler than a syndicated loan agreement. Each bond for, say,

$10,000, is listed on a stock exchange and is easily transferable. In most countries most medium-term credit comes from banks—more than 90 per cent in some countries. In a few countries the debt capital markets provide more credit than the banks, for example, the United States. The largest issuers of bonds are sovereign states, banks and other corporations—typically each about one-third of the total.

Finally, there are issues of shares by companies—called equity issues—which also raise money for the company. The amount of equity issues is a small proportion of bank loans and issues of debt in capital markets.

Banks and capital markets are therefore like lakes that gather up the droplets of peoples' savings and their stores of value. They use the water to irrigate the land. Much water is wasted. But then many people waste their lives and this is not unreasonable.

If one strips away all the veils of incorporation and all the creative figments of the legal imagination, the real creditor is ultimately the individual who places his or her savings with the banks as a depositor, or who pays insurance premiums or pension contributions. There is an ultimate see-through to the individual. In the end it is the individual savers who are the lenders to the power station and to the dwellers in the chateau on the hill.

In addition, it is the money of the people created out of their labour and which finds its way into banks and taxes which funds the promotion of science which is one of the main beacons of our survival hopes.

There is no question that this arrangement is ultimately beneficial. The idea that creditors should share their savings with debtors is a good idea. For one thing it gets a roof over our heads. Karl Marx totally misunderstood the role of capitalism. One of the main features of capitalism is a system for sharing the money of the people in an efficient and useful way which is also just: somebody who borrows other people's money should repay it plus interest. Communism was a system for expropriation by despots.

One of the biggest regulatory questions regarding banks is whether they should be allowed to carry on other activities through the same bank, such as trading in securities for themselves as opposed to trading on behalf of clients, and whether there should be complete separation between the lending arm of the bank and its investment banking business.

To some people, banks and capital markets are peopled by Draculas that eat children and drink blood. In fact, in my experience many of those who work in banking and capital markets are quite ordinary people, although I do not know what they do at night.

## Securitisations and Derivatives

It is worth noting two transactions which received much criticism after the financial crisis in 2008—securitisations and derivatives—so that at least we know what they are.

**Securitisations** A securitisation is simply the sale of receivables by a creditor, that is, debts or amounts owing by a debtor, such as home loans, to banks, insurance companies and other lenders in capital markets. The idea originated in the Italian Renaissance when merchants piled up IOUs from the buyers of their goods. The merchants would then sell the IOUs to a bank, such as the Medicis, so that the merchant would get paid for sure and be able to continue financing their trade. The Medici bank would take the risk that the IOUs were not paid and so would only buy them at a discount, ie, after a deduction from their face value, to reflect the risk and interest costs. This transaction, known as the factoring or discounting of receivables, became very common in the 19th century and afterwards as a way of raising finance without all the bother of creating a pledge over the receivables (then as now, pledges and security interests are a legal mess in many jurisdictions, especially in the case of receivables) and without having to get entangled in the views of the Roman Catholic Church about usury—the transaction was a sale and not a loan.

In the 1980s there was a huge demand in the United States for home loans and so banks which made these loans had to be able to sell the loans they had already made so that they could make more loans without having to issue more expensive equity capital to maintain their legally required ratio of equity to loans—the buffer to prevent banks from becoming insolvent if their loans are not repaid. It was impracticable to transfer all these existing home loans to a mass of individual bondholders so the banks developed the ingenious but wholly mechanical idea of transferring the home loans to a newly formed company. The bondholders would then make a loan to this company represented by bonds and the company would use the proceeds to pay the purchase price for the home loans. If the homeowners did not repay their loans, then that was a bondholder risk. Since the historical track record for home loan repayments was good, the risk did not seem particularly great and often the senior tranche of the bonds—which was paid first—was rated triple A by the rating agencies. The technique was expanded to other receivables such as commercial bank loans and car loans, but the biggest sector by far was home loans.

A very elementary transaction. The assets were simple—home loans, vastly simpler than the assets of an ordinary industrial group. All you had to know was the likely value of home loans. Unhappily, prior to 2008 there was a bubble in house prices, something which every taxi driver on 52nd Avenue in New York knew, but not apparently the rest of the population, let alone the people in charge. It turned out everybody was, after all, not getting rich by doing nothing, so the people, after previously cheering on the show, now denounced securitisations, so innocent in their simplicity and ancient in their ancestry, as arcane, exotic, and designed to confuse and mislead. A home loan which put a roof over your head was 'toxic' and people who so wickedly dealt in these things were 'socially useless'.

**Derivatives** These transactions too are simple in the idea, though complex in their detail.

Derivatives are a way of insuring your financial assets. Most people these days are on one end or the other of financial assets. For example, they may have a home loan or contribute to a pension managed by an insurance company. They may have shares in mutual funds holding their savings. They may have a business which exports goods for a price in a foreign currency.

Just as you can insure your car against a crash and your home against a fire, so you can insure a loan against interest rates going sky-high like smoke and the value of your bonds in your pension pot from crumbling in a crash. For technical reasons the deals are not insurance in law, but they have that effect in substance. Thus if your company takes out a bank loan, you can arrange for a bank to pay you if the interest on your loan goes over a certain amount. If your company has sold goods abroad in a foreign currency, a bank will be prepared to insure you against the risk that the foreign currency will not depreciate in value. For this you have to pay a fee, like an insurance premium. In that way you can fix your risk—in the jargon you can 'hedge' it. Derivatives are risky for those who deal in them, but then so is insurance—they both involve bets about the future. They are called derivatives because they are contracts which are derived from an underlying asset, such as a share or bond.

Derivatives go back to ancient times and were well developed in grain markets in the 19th century. Their application to financial assets dates mainly from the 1980s because of the volatility of interest rates, currencies, bonds and commodities, stemming partly from the collapse of the fixed currency parity of the dollar and gold with other major currencies in 1971 and the removal of exchange controls in advanced countries. So everything floated in value. They are usually documented on the basis of a standard form master agreement prepared by the main association of dealers, the International Swaps and Derivatives Association. The amounts concerned are enormous. The largest class by far insure interest rates.

Derivatives too came in for reprimand after the financial crisis. These insurances were characterised as casino products and again socially useless, an odd reaction towards insurance and more consistent with the 13th century than the 21st. Ancient sharia law also disapproves of insurance.

## Banks and Disasters

Like many useful inventions, banks have their dangers. Debt itself can be dangerous to those who over-borrow. The biggest danger is that in the worst case the collapse of a bank can lead to catastrophic collapses of the whole banking system. That annihilates the savings of creditors and it annihilates the debtors who rely on savings to finance their enterprises. Few countries have escaped the failures of their banks en masse over recent decades.

Historically many systemic bank collapses were caused by the insolvency of the sovereign state, or by the imprudent political direction of bank loans by governments, or by disastrous macroeconomic policies leading to inflation, currency collapses, gyrations in interest rates and money supply, excessive borrowing by governments and the build-up of bubbles which the central bank should have stopped. In other words, most of them were caused by bad government, defective politics and populist or imprudent monetary policy. For example, nearly half the world's states have been insolvent at some time over the last 35 years—an event which usually bankrupts the banking system.

In a few cases the flames were fanned by the banks and irresponsible banking (and borrowing). Some of the most cataclysmic banking disasters have been caused by pure bubbles, especially land and securities, where both banks and borrowers (and often much of the rest of the population) think that prices can only go up which they duly do, until reality dawns. In these cases, if you want to know who is at fault, just look in the mirror. Serious collapses caused by deliberate bank fraud have been minimal over the past 35 years.

In just about all of the situations, the crisis emphasised the basic design defect at the heart of the idea of a bank. This is that their deposits are short-term or on demand while most of their loans are medium-term or liquid and so cannot be sold quickly enough to satisfy a run on the bank. At the core of the structure of the bank there is this fault, this fatal instability in the foundation.

In any event the bankruptcy of banks invariably led to an intensification of the regulation of banks, an intensification of the law, and hence an increase in the amount of law.

## What are Financial Assets?

Financial assets are things like corporate shares, bank loans and bonds. It is sometimes said that lawyers who deal in financial assets are involved with something which is intangible, invisible and therefore sterile and remote. You cannot have a picnic on a financial asset or race it down the motorway. But unlike other classes of asset, such as land or goods, financial assets do not exist without two people, for example, a lender and a borrower, a bank and a depositor, a shareholder and a company, a seller and a buyer. The asset does not exist without the people at either end, circling each other with a mixture of suspicion and admiration, shackled together by contract and law. The result is that the passions, hopes and fears of the counterparties are built into the asset and it is those emotions which are the source of the fascination and excitement, the romance of the job. One is not dealing with an asset, but with the two people at either end.

## Corporate Law

Although corporations were heard of long before the 19th century and go back perhaps even to Roman times, it was only in the 19th century that the corporate form became generally available to the public and generally used as a vehicle for business.

A corporation is a figment of the legal imagination. It is a mark in a registrar's book, a creature without a physical being or substance. You cannot taste, feel or smell a corporation. It is a ghost, a phantasm.

A corporation is an idea. But the idea is a simple and beneficial one. The idea is that a business should be carried on in such a way that those who provide the capital for the business by way of shares or bonds or loans are not liable for the debts of the corporation—otherwise the investors would never invest in the corporation because of the risks which they could not manage or control—and the corporation itself is the only person legally responsible for claims against it. The corporation also owns all the assets of the business in its own name: the assets do not belong to the shareholders or creditors. If they did, it would be impossible to get consent from everybody to sell or mortgage the assets, it would be impossible to deal with the situation if one of the shareholders or lenders became bankrupt so that its share had to be realised. It would be completely unrealistic for the shareholders and investors themselves to deal with the assets and accompanying liabilities.

The twin ideas of the limited liability of investors and the ownership by the legal corporation of its assets and liabilities were crucial to the development of enterprise and prosperity, and hence to survival.

Corporate law is intricate and often unexpected. The reason is that key indicators of corporate law are not just based on a straight line between debtors and creditors (as is the case with financial law) but involve a triangle of three main interests whose aspirations collide.

These three main interests are (1) creditors, (2) shareholders, and (3) management in the form of directors. Most aspects of corporate law result from the attitudes of the jurisdiction as to which of these three the legal regime supports in a particular contest. It is possible to use technical key indicators (maybe seven of them) to track which of the trio the jurisdiction tends to back. If you apply these key indicators, you will discover that the corporate law of Delaware (where most corporations listed on the New York Stock Exchange are incorporated) is favourable to management. Traditional English jurisdictions (somewhat altered in advanced English law countries), plus to a lesser extent the Napoleonic and Roman-Germanic jurisdictions, are favourable to creditors (for example, the shareholder claims must be kept subordinated to creditors). The Napoleonic jurisdictions broadly tend to be more favourable to shareholders and less favourable to management so that, for example, in some members of this group it is much easier than in the others to find directors responsible for deepening an insolvency.

Some people believe that companies owe special duties to the public in the nature of altruism or charity beyond those owed by ordinary individuals.

Ordinary corporations do everything. They manufacture goods, from chocolate to cars. They operate mines. They produce oil and gas and refine the oil. They carry out construction. They run hotels and offices. They have shops. They operate aircraft and trains. They produce chemicals and medicines. They produce food and healthcare equipment and services. They offer tours and leisure travel. They run newspapers or publish books. They own land. They run telecommunication networks and produce computers. They run water or gas companies. They are banks or insurance companies.

Except for very small businesses, such as the corner family shop, corporations are the main vehicles of our entire economies.

Large companies and banks have huge organisational ability. They have gigantic teams which can design, build and deliver cars in their millions, manage the bank accounts of millions of customers, buy in, collect and sell vast quantities of fresh fruit and vegetables from all over the world every day. Although to those working in them, everything seems a shambles, the fact is that their powers of management and execution of massively complicated tasks are colossal. Even the bees and the ants with their social drills formed by evolution are nowhere near the precision and masterful execution of the great corporations.

The same applies to modern governments, to the municipal government of large cities, to the military. Some of the religions were well organised but nothing like the scale of corporations or modern societies in general. The small cities of old were like chaotic villages in comparison. It is this skilful organisation which produces inventions, new medicines, space probes, fast communications. It produces the advances of science. Individuals on their own don't do this. Corporations, public or private, do it. They are at the forefront of the effort to survive.

There are now millions of corporations in the world—silent invisible dreamlike fantasies of the intellect. Most are small businesses owned by families. Others are piled high in groups of companies—some large firms have thousands of companies in common ownership. Most large enterprise projects—power stations, mines, office blocks, pipelines—are owned by single-purpose companies owned by several sponsors. The object is for the sponsors to insulate themselves from the bankruptcy of the project and also to insulate the project from the failure of a sponsor. Can you imagine running a power station when one of the direct owners is going through an insolvency proceeding—how would you sell part of a power station? The single-purpose company is at the heart of project finance around the world in whatever continent. A simple idea has become extraordinarily useful, productive.

However, as with banks, corporations also became bankrupt, for example, because the market for their products failed, or because they borrowed too much, or because they were badly managed, or because they were hit by a domino bankruptcy of some other corporation.

Hence these bankruptcies in turn led to an increase in the volume of law and regulation mainly intended to reduce the risk of bankruptcy and hence of a loss to individuals and other corporations and ultimately significant losses to whole economies if the corporation was large enough.

If a major corporation fails, as with banks, the reaction of legislators is to wave the legal wand. Typical of the areas of law which are conjured into motion are bankruptcy law generally, the regulation of prospectuses offering securities to the public, the regulation of financial statements, the listing rules of stock exchanges which list company securities, and the upgrading of concepts of corporate governance and the like.

Laws on companies deal with a huge range of other issues, such as how you incorporate and register companies, the powers of the company, its internal rules about the appointment and powers of directors, shareholder voting, the division into private or public listed companies, and the death of companies by liquidation or insolvency, as well as codes about mergers and acquisitions.

The corporation saw the birth of the first really important financial democracy. Apart from other major decisions, such as change in the constitution of the company, the most significant matter on which shareholders vote is the election of the directors who actually run the company. The other major financial democracies are bondholder voting on the terms of their bonds, especially if they have to be rescheduled because the issuer is in financial difficulties, and voting by creditors on reorganisation plans for a corporation which is bankrupt. The remarkable feature of these financial democracies compared with political democracies is that financial democracies are more moral, for example, the majority cannot by resolution oppress the minority, bankruptcy reorganisation plans must be approved by the court as fair and equitable and, if bondholders are in some way related to a debtor corporation they may be disenfranchised. Many jurisdictions also have very strict rules about secret payments to win bondholder votes.

The shareholder democracy of a corporation is part of a mini-constitution which each corporation has. Like political constitutions, these corporation constitutions do not always succeed in containing the despots or preventing mismanagement.

Because corporations do everything, they attract the regulation of everything, for example, product liability, health and safety rules, employee protections, antitrust and competition rules, the regulation of food and drugs, the regulation of transportation and advertising. Corporations sometimes attract the rancour and resentment felt by some indiscriminately towards those who are wealthy or who are in positions of power, often identified as banks and large corporations or big business. Corporations are therefore not only the beneficiaries of law but one of the main targets of the law.

# Conclusion on Money, Banks and Corporations

Money, banks and corporations are fundamental in modern societies. Without them we would not have a society at all. If we didn't want them, we could snuff them out with a stroke of the pen. But we don't because they are indispensable. Some complain that these institutions are wicked, gorging their greed on the rest of us. The bookshops heave with denunciations. They have defects like practically everything else we create. They are run and staffed by ordinary people who have the same fallibilities as the rest of the population and who are therefore regulated by law. They are nevertheless some of the most ingenious creations of the law and it is hard to conceive of institutions which could replace them. They empower us. They fill the plate at the table, put the roof over our heads, symbolically or actually.

It would be an unfair generalisation to allege that religions are hostile to money, banks and corporations as a matter of principle. But one can say that on the whole religious leaders are not overly enthusiastic about these things.

# 11

# *Secularisation and Religious Decline*

## Introduction

In chapter 4 the view was expressed that religions are in decline, and it is now time to consider this in more detail.

We must not forget some of the supreme objectives of the supernatural religions—not just to explain the cosmos and our role but to redeem us, save us from the darkness, grant us immortality. They were life-affirming and optimistic, they gave hope. If therefore large parts of our societies turn from religions, turn their backs on them and decide they are untrue, we are left face to face with a different reality.

The duties and the purpose of our lives then have a different focus and direction, although not fundamentally contrary to what the religions were saying. We have a duty to survive owed to future generations, we have a duty to discover the mysteries of the cosmos, to penetrate the dark enigmas, to bring them into the light. We have this duty so that we may control our fate instead of being subject to it, drifting helplessly out here in our little galaxy, accelerating into space to we know not where. In order to realise this duty we have to ward off oblivion and to do that we need a moral framework to guide us and keep us alive as long as possible. We need to survive so that our science can protect us by enabling us to meet our destiny with knowledge, and, if we no longer adhere to the moral regimes of religion, we must promote the ethics of our legal systems to defend us from nullity, the void of nothingness. We do these things knowing that the effort may be doomed and that the universe may be pitiless or just blind.

## The Meaning of Secularisation

A society secularises when its people cease to believe in supernatural religions and when these religions cease to influence the government and laws of the country and to influence the morals, the way of living and culture of the country. The two main features of secularisation are a decline in believing and practising devotees, and a decline in the influence of religion over government—numbers and governmental power, both interlocked.

There are many other indicators. For example, priests, imams and the like may cease to run schools and universities or provide hospitals for the sick or community homes for the poor. Church may be separated from state in the sense that the state does not have an official religion, is neutral on religion and does not finance religious establishments.

A further feature of secularisation is where the people stop complying with the moral regime laid down by the religion, for example, its rules on divorce, abortion or contraception, or its other requirements, such as what you eat, what you wear, how you do your hair. Religion becomes a matter of choice by individuals, not social obligation. Religions lose their authority and their power to control or influence the laws or government. The state, the government, the economy, science, the arts and learning are no longer the domain of the clerics. The laws too are freed and need no longer be based on scripture or doctrine. Max Weber called the process the 'disenchantment of the world'.

This is not just specialisation where religions do religion and governments do government. What is really at stake is control—control of minds, control of morality and control of the laws.

My overall conclusions are that the number of practising religious adherents who believe in the core tenets of a supernatural religion has declined substantially over the centuries as a proportion of the world's population and that religiosity has cooled. That decline has been accompanied by a loss of control by the religious authorities over the administration of justice, of the control of the punishment of crimes and enforcement of contracts and civil transgressions, of the power and influence of religions over government policy and the laws of most societies. As always, there are some countries where the above is not true. It is these conclusions which must now be examined.

At one time some thinkers—Auguste Comte, Emile Durkheim, Max Weber, Karl Marx and Sigmund Freud, for example—thought that religions would just fizzle out. That has not happened and is not likely to happen over the medium term. The question is the extent to which religiosity has cooled, a question which has given rise to a lively literature and many academic papers. Indeed there are claims that religions have not cooled but on the contrary are expanding and that the new religious are more fervent. Obviously the number of religious people may expand as the population expands at its current rate, but the real test is whether the number is expanding as a percentage of the world's population.

## Decline in the Number of Devotees

In around the year 1600, practically everybody went to church, mosque, temple or synagogue. In the West, societies were drenched with religion. The bells rang out religion. Even the guilds and the universities were religious institutions.

As to the position now, one may mention two symbolic sets of statistics.

In 2014 a former Archbishop of Canterbury declared that Britain is a 'post-Christian country', not a nation of believers any more. This remark was prompted by research which showed that half the population identified themselves as Christian, but less than 15 per cent identified themselves as practising Christians.

He added that Britain was a Christian country only in the sense of still being very much saturated by the Christian vision of the world and shaped by it.

The *Statesman's Yearbook* for 2015 noted that only 2 per cent of Iranians attended Friday prayers at the mosque. According to *The Economist* of 16 January 2003, it was reported that no more than 1 to 1.5 per cent attended Friday prayers and a cleric complained that 73 per cent of Iranians did not even say their daily prayers. Even if we think that these statistics seem on the low side, if one is in Kuala Lumpur or Jakarta at the time the mosque loudspeakers call the faithful to prayer five times a day, one does not see everybody rolling out their prayer mats. Instead, the interminable traffic goes on as before, the office workers continue to labour at their desks and the shoppers continue their shopping.

It is clear that there are some dramatic underlying trends. Some countries, such as China and Japan, are now almost completely secular.

## Some Statistics on Devotees

Statistics on religion come from five main sources—official censuses, polls by private pollsters, churches and religious organisations, estimates by experts and field work.

We will take first the example of Britain—a fully developed country with a history of steadiness, a strong sense of tradition and a high respect for the rule of law.

A YouGov poll in 2014 found that 77 per cent of the British population did not consider themselves religious and 40 per cent did not consider themselves religious at all. A British Social Attitudes Survey of 2014 found that the number of people in Britain who said that they had no religion at all rose from 31.4 per cent to 50.6 per cent between 1983 and 2013. Religious affiliation for young people between 15 and 24 was only 31 per cent. Only for those over 55 was the number of respondents affiliated to a religion a majority. In this survey 42 per cent of people in the UK identified themselves with Christianity compared with 50 per cent in 2008 and 65 per cent in 1983. Membership of the Church of England more than halved from 40 per cent of the population to 16 per cent in 2014. The survey found that 58 per cent of the population never attended religious services while only 13 per cent reported going to a religious service once a week or more.

The Church of England estimated that in 1968 about 1,600,000 people attended Sunday service on average. In 2002 it was just over a million and in 2012 it was 800,000. In other words, attendance had halved over 44 years, notwithstanding a large increase in population over that period.

When Christian Research carried out a census of 18,720 churches in Britain on Sunday 8 May 2005 the real rate of attendance was 6.3 per cent of the population—down 15 per cent since 1998. In the British census of 1851, which was the first time the census recorded religious attendance, 25 per cent of the population was still attending the services of the established Christian Church of England.

Prior to 1960, most marriages in England were solemnised in a church. This fell to 40 per cent in the late 1990s. In the first half of the 20th century, Anglican Easter Day communicants accounted for around 5 or 6 per cent of the population in England which then slumped to 2 per cent after 1960.

In 1910, there were 227,135 confirmations in England—a Christian ritual ceremony accepting children finally into the church at puberty. In 2007, there were 27,900, notwithstanding a very large increase in the population. This was 16 per cent lower than five years previously. Between 1960 and 1979 the confirmation rate among 12- to 20-year-olds fell by more than half and now fewer than a fifth of those baptised are confirmed. The practising Christians are mostly older people, not British youth. For discussion of some of the figures, see Niall Ferguson, *Civilisation* (Penguin, 2012) pp 266–69.

By contrast the United States, which has a similar cultural background to Britain, is a highly religious country. Yet even here there has been a slow but steady decline. University sociologists concluded that in the 1930s and 1940s the number of Americans who were religiously unaffiliated was around 5 per cent. That had risen to 8 per cent by 1990, but by 2014 it had accelerated to over 20 per cent. The Pew Research Center said in 2014 that one-third of US adults under the age of 30 did not identify with a religion. A Gallup poll in 2011 found that 40 per cent of Americans regarded themselves as very religious, down from 65 per cent in 2008. A World Values Survey of 2005–08 said that 36 per cent of Americans attended a church service once a week, although another survey in 2014 reported that 53 per cent attended church once a month or more compared with 62 per cent in 1994. On various measures of religiosity pollsters have recorded a steady decline of about half a per cent per year since 1994—not a sudden crash but relentless erosion over many years.

Nevertheless, whatever survey you look at, US Christian religiosity is higher than in other developed countries of the West. Many reasons have been advanced for this, for example, the influence of the original Puritan tradition in the Bible belt, the presence of a large black population who for most of their history were oppressed or subordinated and may therefore have sought refuge in Pentecostal and salvationist movements to assuage their misery, the arrival of large numbers of religiously conservative agricultural immigrants from Europe in the 19th and early-20th centuries, the lack of an established conformist church, thereby encouraging the competitive promotion of evangelical sects which had to support themselves by appealing to the people, the entrepreneurial spirit of Americans which led to money-making mega-churches exploiting radio and television, and the like. None of these theories seems to be a complete answer.

I have already noted in chapter 8 that the US interpretation of the English common law is markedly different from that of England and in some respects more severe, and that culture wars about sex, Darwinian evolution and the like are a more prominent feature of society in the United States. Politically, you could say that the United States is about 10 per cent to the right of England. We must be cautious about stereotypes and unfounded prejudices, but clearly there is a difference which needs explaining.

If we look elsewhere in the world, according to a World Values Survey of 2005–08—the statistics from the waves of the World Values Surveys collected over many years are particularly impressive—4 per cent of Norwegian and Swedes and 8 per cent of French and Germans attended a church service at least once a week. Yet these countries often come out at or near the top in surveys of observance of the rule of law, stability and the absence of corruption: one could hardly label the extraordinarily civilised Scandinavians as wild godless anarchists. The above figures compare with 44 per cent of Indians and 48 per cent of Brazilians—in each case less than half the population. But evidently 78 per cent of sub-Saharan Africans attended church once a week. The European figures were higher for predominantly Catholic countries such as Italy (32 per cent) and Spain (16 per cent). Religious observance is lower in Russia and Japan even than Protestant countries. In China, God is reported in this survey as being important to even fewer than in Europe—less than 5 per cent.

A survey by Gallup International in 2012 asserted that the global average decline in religiosity ('are you a religious person?') between 2005 and 2012 was 9 per cent and that some countries reported a decline of more than 20 per cent—Vietnam, Ireland, Switzerland and France.

**Commentary on the statistics** One can go on and on citing statistics, some saying this, some saying that, a cacophony of confusing numbers, each proclaiming its mathematical purity and truthfulness. What is clear however is that there is a dramatic difference of many multiples between statistics on religion, largely but not only flowing from the huge disparity between the number of people who say they are religious and the number who actually practise their religion. For example:

— As mentioned, a former head of the Church of England said in 2014 that less than 15 per cent of the people were practising Christians but that half of the population had said that they were Christians so that the nominal figure was more than three times the actual. Pew Research Center reported in 2011 that 72.6 per cent of people in the UK regarded themselves as Christian, which is nearly five times the actual figure reported as practising by the Archbishop.

— According to the figures I have cited above, 4 per cent of Norwegians go to church once a week. Yet Pew Research said in 2011 that 86.2 per cent of Norwegians regarded themselves as Christians, that is, 21 times those who actually go to church regularly.

— The same Pew report said that 90.2 per cent of Brazilians regard themselves as Christians—about three-quarters are Roman Catholics. But the Roman Catholic Church in Brazil said in 1991 that only 35 per cent of their flock regularly attended church, almost a third of the number claiming to be Catholic. WIN-Gallup International also asserted in a 2012 report that 85 per cent of Brazilians said that they were religious persons—more than twice the church's mournful report of those practising. In the late 1990s a Brazilian Conference of Bishops said that only 20 per cent of Roman Catholics in Brazil go to church regularly and participate in church activities, notwithstanding that in 2007 a local poll reported that 97 per cent of Brazilians believed in God. So Brazil with its enormous population may have the largest congregation of Catholics in the world but also the largest number of lapsed Catholics. The CIA World Factbook reported in 2014 that 92 per cent of Argentinians said they were Christian but less than 20 per cent practised the faith regularly. In Mexico, although nearly 83 per cent were reported in 2010 in a census to be Roman Catholics, the Catholic News Service, citing a senior clerical source, said in 2012 that only 10–20 per cent were committed church-goers and involved in parish life.

— A figure commonly given for the number of Shintoists in Japan is 65 million—about half the population of Japan—whereas the actual number of practising adherents is about four million at the most, so that the nominal figure is sixteen times bigger than the figure for those practising.

— The Pew figures given in a report of 2011 as to attendance by Muslims at Friday prayers at the mosque in various countries showed that 94 per cent of Pakistanis said that religion was very important to them but only 59 per cent reported that they regularly attended the mosque. Other figures comparing those in Muslim countries who said that religion was very important to them and those who actually showed this fervent piety by going to mosque once a week were: Turkey 67/44 per cent, Malaysia 93/57, Egypt 75/61 and Morocco 89/53.

— Commonly found statistics on the internet say that around 84 per cent of the world's population regards themselves as nominally religious. By way of contrast, in 2012 a Gallup International poll asserted that 59 per cent of the world thinks of themselves as religious—just over half—nearly a quarter as not religious, and 13 per cent as convinced atheists. In 2015, Gallup International reported that 63 per cent of the world says they are religious.

— There are colossal divergences between pollsters as to the religiosity of China with one pollster reporting a number which is eleven times that of another. The difference was therefore over 700 million people.

There are therefore massive discrepancies between the number of devotees who tell the pollsters they are religious and the number who actually observe their religion by practising it, and between the statistics of polling organisations as to how many report that they are religious.

The polling organisations I have cited are highly reputable and experienced; they are reporting accurately what they are told and they very properly set out in detail what their methodology is. For example, a Pew Research Center report of December 2011 on Christianity states that their definition of Christianity in that report was very broad, that their intent was sociological rather than theological, and that they are not measuring quality of the faith or the degree of practice—elements which I endeavour to assess here.

So how do we explain the mismatches? Surveys of religiosity are notoriously difficult to do. Even straightforward surveys on other topics such as election results can be wrong-footed.

The first obstacle is that the survey may be too small to be representative. It is not easy to cover the views of seven billion people.

Second there is a major issue peculiar to religious surveys. Many people are unwilling to admit they are 'atheist' or even non-religious—it is like they are confessing to being a hedonist, anarchist or devil-worshipper, a godless degenerate. They treat the question of whether they are Muslim or Christian as really a question as to whether they are moral—to which there is only one predictable answer. Surveys of this type rely completely on the accuracy of the self-reporting and the view which people have of themselves.

The framing of the question also has a big impact. For example, you get a very different result when a polling organisation asks the question 'Is religion an important part of your daily life?' compared with another which asks respondents to state whether they had 'no religion' and a researcher who confrontationally requested respondents to describe whether they were atheist or agnostic. One figure could be ten times another, and indeed the US sociologist Phil Zuckerman showed how dramatically the figures differed according to the framing of the question: see his contribution to Martin (ed) *The Cambridge Companion to Atheism* (Cambridge University Press, 2005).

Related to the above is the problem of anonymity. Some surveys are based on face-to-face interviews so there may be pressure on respondents to give responses which improve their religious credentials, especially where there are strong taboos against admitting religious indifference or even criminal liability. Thus in many Islamic countries blasphemy and apostasy are serious criminal offences sometimes punishable by beheading, or there is a marked taboo against expressing indifference to Islam, let alone atheism.

Then there is the problem of unintended bias in the selection of respondents for the sample. In countries with a stress on religious conformity, again including many Muslim countries, a respondent is unlikely to agree to participate unless the respondent will give answers which are positive about the religion. If the respondent is not religious or does not visit the mosque once a week, that respondent in a strict Muslim country might well decline to participate with the result that those participating will push up the 'yes' percentages and create a bias in the sample not intended by the pollster. If this tendency is general, the credibility of the survey, when combined with the other problems, may be called into question.

Polling organisations are of course well aware of these obstacles and endeavour to overcome them as best they can.

But by far the greatest source of the disparities lies in the definition of what is being measured when somebody says that they are 'religious'. In the minds of some, being religious could include just feeling spiritual, or that there is something out there bigger than us, or that there are ghosts in the attic. The key to this is defining specifically what it means to be religious. The strict criteria of what it is to be religious should be the core definitions used by the religions themselves as to their creeds, the most basic things that you have to do and to believe in to qualify for their label and their benefits. Many people have a very hazy idea of what they believe in and so some precision is needed to test the character of the belief. This definition typically in the great religions has three basic aspects:

1. **Immortality of the soul** First, according to the great religions you must believe that you have a soul which is immortal and lives on after death. This soul either goes to a heaven or hell forever (as in the Abrahamic religions— Judaism, Christianity and Islam) or else transmigrates to another living creature for a transient period in a cycle of birth and rebirth before coming to rest in some ultimate godhead (as in the Indian religions). If you do not believe this, you may very well believe in a commendable ideology but you do not comply with an essential belief of the supernatural religions we are mainly talking about.

2. **Personal god** Second, the great religions hold that you must believe that there is a God who personally knows your deeds and misdeeds so as to be able to judge you when you die so as to determine whether you go to heaven or hell or transmigrate up or down. It is not enough to them that you believe in some force of nature, or some god who started the universe, or an intelligent designer who is not interested in you personally. It is not enough that you think vaguely that there must be something out there in this vast universe or in some other universe, or in some much bigger show, or that you have a sense of the numinous.

   The reason for this stress by the religions on a personal god is that it is of the essence of religious creeds that there is an immortal soul and that there is a god, and it follows that you must also believe that this god records your good and bad conduct so as to judge what happens to your soul after death. Both these requirements of the main creeds insist that to be religious involves a belief in the supernatural, not just in some philosophy of life such as humanism or a political philosophy or a way of living which is ethical. It is quite true that some sects of Hinduism and Buddhism do not require a belief in a personal god or in the immortality of the soul. To the extent they do not, they are not supernatural religions but rather humanist philosophies of life, like Confucianism.

   A religion must have some coherent moral beliefs, some distinct view about the role of the supernatural and immortality, and not merely be a jumble of terrors and fearful superstitions about the evil eye, witches, magic, sorcery, spells, faith healing, telepathy, divination, possession by spirits or voodoo or exorcism or speaking in tongues, or be just an emotional spiritualising of otherwise innocent mountains, lakes, trees and rocks. We are not measuring superstitions of that kind.

   And a belief which does not have a supernatural element at all ceases to be a religion at all as commonly understood. Nationalism, communism, socialism, science, folk culture and the like are not religions.

3. **Ritual practice once a week** Third, the great religions require that you must practise your religion by some active outward sign which demonstrates commitment to their God or gods. For the purposes of measurement of religiosity, the minimum practice should be the performance of some

significant approved ritual at least once a week, such as attending a church service or mosque prayers or performance of some equivalent ritual, rather than the full rituals prescribed by the scriptures. Most of the great religions place great emphasis on these rituals and regard them as an essential part of the faith. Many of the mismatches in the statistics mentioned earlier are accounted for by the fact that there is a big difference between those who say they believe and those who actually practise. Careful independent audits are unusual outside some Western countries. Some religions emphasise private prayer and private meditation, especially Buddhism, but the fact that these are more difficult to measure accurately should not affect the assessment in a major way.

Strictly, to be even more statistically robust, you should score your supernatural beliefs on a scale of one to ten, with ten being absolute unshakeable belief and zero being absolutely no belief.

My formulation of the three requirements laid down by the great religions is much less prescriptive than those required by the various scriptures themselves. They are the minimum for the purposes of measurement. They do not require adherence to the detail of the religion, other than the two fundamental tenets about a personal god and the immortality of the soul. They do not require belief in the mass of other theological propositions. They do not require observance of all the other rituals, such as the Islamic giving of alms or the observance of Ramadan. All that is required if you say you are a tennis player is to hit the ball over the net in accordance with the basic principle of tennis. If you instead hit the ball against the wall, or throw it over the net, or throw it into a basket, or kick it into a goal, or hit it away as far as possible with a bat or fall over a line with it, it is not tennis.

The strict three-pronged definition defines the religiosity we are trying to measure. I am seeking to assess the number of people who practise their religion and believe in the supernatural tenets of their religion as required by the books to test whether there has been a decline compared with the universal belief and practice which was the case a few centuries ago; that is, we should be testing the intensity and quality of faith over the years.

Thus, if people claim to belong to the Christian flock but do not believe in the resurrection of the dead and the immortality of the soul in either heaven or hell, they would need to justify why they qualify as a Christian in the sense of the scriptures. This is because the resurrection of the dead and the immortality of the soul are core beliefs of Christians, set out in their creeds and fervently repeated in their prayers and hymns and liturgies. A person may still believe in a Christian morality or way of life or in the philosophy of loving kindness to all, but this does not make that person a believing Christian in the strict sense required by the gospels and holy fathers.

A tennis player hits the ball over the net. If the aim is to kick the ball into a goal, then this is football, but not tennis.

Just about everybody believes in a moral system, at least nominally, and of course if we asked people whether they believed in morality or whether people should be good, they would normally say yes.

Both tennis and football are excellent sports but it would be strange if we reported that 84 per cent of the people of the world had played with a ball and therefore 84 per cent of the world population were tennis players.

The reality is that many people think of themselves as being, say, Christian, because they live in a Christian country, or were baptised as Christians, or their parents are Christians, or because they celebrate Christmas and Easter, or because they vaguely identify with a morality associated with Christianity, without going to church weekly or indeed ever and without believing in a personal god and the resurrection of the dead. They consider themselves culturally Christian or brought up in a milieu of a customary morality which is Christian. They may consider that Christianity is part of their national identity, an incident of their patriotism. They are affiliated to Christianity without practising the religion.

## Summary of Religious Adherence

In around 1600 we can safely surmise that there were no serious challenges in the minds of the people to the central supernatural tenets of their religions and that the churches, mosques and temples teemed with the faithful. Now is very different. Using the three requirements of religiosity discussed above, I estimate very roughly that now only between 28 and 42 per cent of the world's population satisfy the criteria stipulated by their religions, criteria which practically everybody fulfilled a few hundreds years ago, so that we are comparing like with like. These figures are well below those often found, for example, that more than 80 per cent of the world is religious.

My methodology was brutally broad-brush, order of magnitude, chainsaw. I took the 53 most populous countries which between them had about 90 per cent of the world's population as my sample—countries from China to Madagascar, all having populations of 22 million or more and assumed that the remaining 10 per cent representing 150 countries were the same (subject to an adjustment to reflect that the remaining 10 per cent had more nominal Christians than the 53 countries). In each country I surmised the percentage of the population who were practising and believing devotees of their religion on the basis of the cruel statistics above and other statistical sources, ie, that the number of practising and believing devotees was typically a fraction of the nominal amount who said they were religious. In the case of countries with significant splits between religions, such as Nigeria, I had to take a decision from among differing authorities as to what the split was. I treated the resulting numbers as the minimum and introduced a much higher number to recognise a very substantial margin of error and to avoid getting into pointless arguments when we all know that figures on this subject are going to be pretty wobbly whatever you do. I rounded the figures. The population figures come from an *Economist* publication of 2015 and were for a past year.

On this basis I estimate that the total practising and believing religious population of the world is on my criteria somewhere between 1970 million and

2960 million people, ie, between 28 per cent and 42 (roughly a quarter and two-fifths) per cent out of a total population of 7050 million—slightly less than the ever-climbing actual as of now. The number of people who are not practising and believing in a religion on this basis is between 4090 and 5080, ie, between 58 and 72 per cent.

Hence the table below. The table shows my tentative estimates of the percentage of world population and the gross numbers, based on the requirements of practising and fully believing criteria, followed in each case by the nominal numbers which are sometimes cited. These are the numbers of people who say that they are 'affiliated' to or belong to a particular religion or are religious. The nominal numbers do not test whether the respondents actually practise the religion and actually believe in the core supernatural creeds of the religion. There is no way we can have certainty that these figures are correct and they can hardly be more than reasonably informed guesses.

| Table of world religious populations | | |
|---|---|---|
| Practicing and believing devotees (number and percentage of world population) | | Typical nominal adherents |
| Christianity | 640m (9%)–850m (12%) | 2200m (31.2%) |
| Islam | 630m (9%)–990m (14%) | 1600m (23%) |
| Hinduism | 420m (6%)–700m (10%) | 1100m (15.6%) |
| Buddhism | 140m (2%)–210m (3%) | 350m (5%) |
| Other | 140m (2%)–210m (3%) | 650m (9.2%) |
| Total religious | 1970m (28%)–2960m (42%) | 5900m (84%) |
| Total non-religious | 5080m (72%)–4090m (58%) | 1100m (16%) |

My table shows that Christianity may be slightly ahead of Islam and I later explain why this seems to be so. Hinduism's high figures come from the fact that India is the second most populous country in the world with a population of about 1300 million. Buddhism and other religions are small by comparison to the giants.

I prefer the lower figures which I have marked in bold which points to just over a quarter of the world's population being practising and believing devotees. In any event, if a quarter to two-fifths of the world's population is religious, then that is still a substantial amount. But it is much less than was the case and the present trend is downwards.

As to Christianity, most developed Christian countries are highly secular. The European region of origin seems to have grown bored with one of its most vibrant and creative inventions, almost as if they were tired of the fact that there were no more splendid wars to fight between themselves on sectarian issues. In Europe, Canada and Australia, examples of the ranges of percentages of the Christian practising and believing proportion of the entire populations including minorities are: UK and Australia, 8–12 per cent of the entire population; Germany 8–10 per cent; France 6–10 per cent; Italy 15–30 per cent; Spain and

Canada 10–15 per cent; and Poland 30–60 per cent. Apart from Poland, these countries are probably representative of the other European countries whose populations are too low to appear in the sample. The percentages in Scandinavia and the Czech Republic are thought to be below the above spreads.

The United States with a population of 316 million is much more religious than Europe and I propose that 25–45 per cent of the entire population including minorities satisfy the three criteria for Christianity. The American Christians continue to wage the theological wars which the Europeans had given up out of exhaustion, though luckily now a war of words rather than weapons. A higher figure of 50 per cent would indicate that 158 million Americans go to a Christian church regularly every Sunday—half the population. The American National Election Survey and the US General Social Survey both indicate that church attendance in the United States hovers around 25 per cent.

The above figures seem reasonably well documented as regards the number of practising adherents.

On the other hand 70 years of communism seem to have done their work in Russia (population 143 million), which was once the stalwart of the Eastern Orthodox Church: my estimate is between 8 and 10 per cent of the population are Christians satisfying the criteria. The same applies to Ukraine. The expectation of some that the ideological vacuum left by the fall of communism would be filled by religion does not seem to have transpired.

The Latin American countries in the table (which does not extend to small countries) plus the Philippines are entered as being between the United States and Europe in their piety: these include populous countries such as Brazil (just under 200 million on a recent count), Mexico (116 million) and the Philippines (97 million). The populations are mainly Roman Catholic and my typical spreads are as follows, calculated on the entire population including minorities: Brazil, 20–35 per cent satisfying the criteria; Philippines, 30–50 per cent; and Colombia, Argentina, Venezuela and Peru, 20–30 per cent. These percentages seem in line with the statistics recorded above. There is a largish nominal Christian evangelical and Pentecostal population in Brazil and your view about that country depends on whether the beliefs satisfy the criteria. I account for some ecstatic religions under 'Other religions' below. The other countries in the region are below the threshold on population.

There are significant Christian populations in sub-Saharan Africa but in some of them you have to divide the population between Christian, Islamic and indigenous religion, for example, Nigeria. Most polls indicate higher levels of religiosity in this region than in, say, Latin America or Europe. I mark the Christian slice of these countries entered in the table as having the following spreads satisfying the criteria: Nigeria, 50–70 per cent; Kenya, Uganda, Ghana and Mozambique, 40–60 per cent; South Africa, 30–60 per cent (of the entire population); Tanzania and Madagascar, 30–50 per cent; and Congo-Kinshasa, 20–40 per cent. Some of the beliefs may be a meld of Christianity and local indigenous beliefs, raising the question of whether they qualify as Christian or rather as 'Other religions', or whether they qualify as a religion at all.

The statistics for sub-Saharan Africa are not as plentiful as those in the developed countries and there is much room for disagreement. On the other hand it would take big errors to make much difference to the overall for Christianity because you need 70 million more adherents for every 1 per cent increase in the overall. An error of ten percentage points up or down in the sub-Saharan figures would make a difference of less than one-half per cent to the Christian numbers and so the change to the overall Christianity figures would be marginal, even if the commentators who think that there is a massive growth in Pentecostalism in Africa are right. The African populations are growing at a huge rate and so if the religions keep pace there could be growth for both Islam and Christianity in Africa, depending of course on trends up or down. If the population growth is accompanied by a growth in wealth, then this may result in a decline in religiosity over the medium term, as it did in the West.

Do not forget that these figures are based on practising and fully believing devotees.

In the final result I suggest that between 640 million and 850 million people in the world are practising and believing Christians fulfilling the criteria, that is, between 9 and 12 per cent of the world. The number often cited for those who identify themselves as nominally Christian is around 2200 million or just over 31 per cent so my figures are around a quarter to a third of the nominal figure.

We may as well deal here with China and Japan, both of which have large populations. The reports seem to justify the view that both these countries are secular. I suggest that between 6 and 9 per cent of the Chinese population of 1400 million is religious within the criteria, so that between 84 and 126 million people in China are religious as defined, split between Christianity, Islam, Buddhism and folk religions. A low percentage seems consistent with the history of the culture because, apart from ancient ancestor worship, China adopted Confucianism which is a way of life but not a religion (Confucianism does not have a belief in the supernatural), because Buddhism faded there and because the communists completed the decimation of the faithful. People often dump huge numbers of Chinese in the folk religion basket but for the reasons given below one would need more evidence that this easy solution is legitimate for the large numbers often quoted. A Gallup International poll of 2015 reported that China was the least religious country in the world, a view also taken by a World Values Survey of 2005–08 (less than 5 per cent religious). Despite some assertions to the contrary, Christianity seems to have a very small hold on China, again not surprising in light of the historical reaction of the country to foreign religious systems. There is a Muslim minority in the western provinces.

You can get much higher estimates of the religious in China but the definition of religion seems much looser than mine. Thus in 2008 Pew reported that the proportion of Chinese people who deemed religion as important was 56 per cent so that there is a difference of 700 million people between Pew and the other pollsters mentioned above. A great many of the respondents in that survey reportedly had problems in naming their religion. In my view Confucianism is not a qualifying religion, nor is ancestor worship, and Chinese Taoism and Buddhism are only marginally so, if at all, depending on the sect.

Japan seems to have largely given up on traditional supernatural religions, after their flirtation with Buddhism in medieval times. Like China, the Japanese have typically been more interested in philosophies of life, in which they excel, than worshipping unseen gods. Even Shintoism is doubtfully a religion and in any case the number of practising adherents is small. I mark Japan as being 7 per cent religious for all qualifying religions, that is, nine million out of a population of 127 million: some Shintoists, some Buddhists. In 2015 Gallup International reported that Japan was the third least religious country in the world after China and Hong Kong.

Taiwan and Vietnam are considered largely secular, although there are small Christian and Buddhist minorities in both countries. There are larger minorities of these religions in South Korea. North Korea is considered secular.

Hinduism is substantially the national religion of India and therefore one can expect Indians to perform the customary rituals and enjoy the national festivals just as Christians celebrate Christmas without necessarily being pious devotees. Possibly belief in the transmigration of souls will wane as India grows richer and the collection of gods might soon appear increasingly implausible to Indians. Some sects explicitly reject the supernatural. One suspects that many Indians nominally cling on to the belief as part of their identity with India, but without commitment to its supernatural beliefs.

Since India has such a massive population, an error in the numbers of Hindus can have a large distorting effect on the overall numbers of religious people in the world. Out of the population of 1300 million one has to deduct other religions, including quite a large Muslim population. Jains are only about 0.5 per cent of the overall. The Sikhs are somewhat larger at just under 2 per cent. There seem to be about 26 million nominal Christians—2 per cent. Zoroastrians in the form of Parsees number only a few thousand. Buddhism is virtually non-existent. Nepal is 80 per cent Hindu and there is a diaspora of Indians. One then has to deduct those whose religiosity does not satisfy the criteria and is rather a way of life or set of moral customs than a religion. There are thought to be just over 1000 million nominal Hindus in the world.

I enter Hinduism as being between 6 and 10 per cent of the world, that is, between 420 million and 700 million satisfying the strict criteria (about 40–70 per cent of nominal Hindus). But even these enormous spreads may not reflect the reality up or down. There are just too many imponderables in terms of the supernatural beliefs, as well as problems of measurement, and hence these figures could be seriously astray either way.

If you think that almost all of the 1000 million nominally Hindu Indians satisfy the criteria of belief and practice, then Hinduism is a contender for the title of the world's largest religion.

It is astonishing that India is so religious and China so secular—a fact which cries out for an explanation—if indeed my surmise is true.

Buddhism is contracting as a universal mass religion. Though born in India, it was almost completely obliterated by Hinduism in the medieval period and it met with a similar fate in China. In Japan Buddhism was treated as a foreign import and shunted aside by Shintoism at the time of the Meiji restoration in 1867 which was a nationalistic response to this alien interloper.

Some commentators have put the upper figure of Buddhists at 1500 million but this seems very implausible on the criteria. A figure of between 140 and 210 million practising and believing Buddhists seems closer to the mark—between 2 and 3 per cent. Burma (Myanmar) is still quite solidly Buddhist, entered at 60–80 per cent of the relevant slice as Buddhist satisfying the criteria. I enter Thailand as 40–70 per cent Buddhist within the criteria. I do not include Buddhists who do not believe in a supernatural god and in the transmigration of souls: these concepts are not central to the Theravada sect which predominates in Sri Lanka, Myanmar and Thailand. This is because I do not count philosophies of life, such as Confucianism, as religions by reason of the fact that they do not adhere to a belief in the supernatural.

If we exclude the alleged multitude of Buddhists in China, Japan and Vietnam—although there are some millions in those countries—we struggle to make up the numbers. Buddhism is a doleful example of the destiny of a religion which for some reason lost its universal appeal.

As to other religions, Judaism has a few million devotees but for some Jews in developing countries the religion may be more a mark of national identity and customary culture than something they actually practise with any degree of regularity. Gallup International reported in 2015 that 65 per cent of Israelis said that they were either not religious or convinced atheists. The total number of Jews in the world is about 14.5 million so the numbers of those satisfying the criteria will be very small in world terms.

Sikhism may have 15 to 20 million adherents—this is an ethnic religion of the Punjabis. Zoroastrianism has only about 200,000 remaining believers. Taoism is probably too vague to count as a religion any longer, even if it ever did. The number of Taoists is thought to be tiny nowadays. The same goes for the ecstatic trance religious movements favoured by hippies in the 1960s.

My qualifying criteria—especially the non-acceptance of unstructured animistic beliefs—probably excludes many folk religionists which is why my figure for 'Other religions' is lower than the usual. On the other hand a range of between 140 and 210 million (2–3 per cent) seems to give ample scope for animist or hot religions in Africa and Latin America, and folk religions in China in those few cases where the beliefs satisfy the criteria.

That leaves Islam. My analysis suggests that this giant religion is just behind Christianity in terms of numbers, but not in terms of geographical spread: Christianity has a much larger territorial empire. My estimates based on the criteria are that there are between 630 and 990 million Muslims which amount to between 9 and 14 per cent of the world. Both religions are established in very populous countries. Indonesia, the biggest Muslim nation, has (or had) a population of 245 million, Pakistan 180 million, Bangladesh 152 million, Egypt 84 million, Iran 76 million and Turkey 75 million, although in each country there are minority religions as well. Christianity also has some very populous nations, as mentioned—the United States (316 million), Brazil (198 million), Russia (143 million), Mexico (116 million), the Philippines (97 million) and Germany (82 million). Christianity and Islam are now the only two contenders in terms of Big Religion.

I assess practising and believing Muslims in most countries at three to five times or more of the percentage I assess secularised Christian countries. The reason for this uplift is that pollsters typically report higher percentages of people saying they are religious in Muslim countries than in most Christian countries.

Since in many countries women are discouraged from attending the mosque my assessments for ritual performance are based on a mix of mosque attendance and the saying of prayers several times a day.

I enter Saudi Arabia as between 70 and 90 per cent of the entire population as being practising and believing Muslims satisfying the criteria, Afghanistan as between 70 and 85 per cent of the population and Yemen as between 60 and 80 per cent. Illustrative figures for other countries include 50–80 per cent for the Muslim slice of Nigeria, 50–70 per cent for the Muslim slice of Indonesia, 40–70 per cent for Algeria, 40–60 per cent for Pakistan (which swings between political secularism and fervent religiosity) and the Islamic slice of Egypt, 30–60 per cent for the Islamic slice of Bangladesh and 10–30 per cent for Uzbekistan (slice). Iran and Turkey are comparatively secularised according to various reports. In 2012 a survey by Gallup International reported that only 23 per cent of Turks regarded themselves as religious persons. I mark the two countries as between 20 to 50 per cent of the entire population. The very large spreads for Muslims between minimum and maximum reflect the uncertainties of the process.

There are rapidly expanding populations in most Muslim countries but this does not necessarily mean that adherence to Islam will keep pace. Experience shows that many other factors come into play in the future of a religion in today's world.

Some surveys do show remarkably high global belief in Islamic supernatural doctrines and in sharia law and attest to high attendance at Friday prayers. These surveys are generally face to face and may suffer from the other problems inherent in surveys of countries where there are very high degrees of religiosity and hence possible distortions in the results as described above, for example, fears about anonymity, pressures to conform and the tendency of disbelievers to drop out of the survey, thereby loading the weight of the believers. Further, some reports of low figures for attendance at Friday prayers in such countries as Turkey and Iran indicate caution in assuming that in Muslim countries nearly everyone is a practising Muslim. In those countries where the population can vote, the support for secular parties and Islamic parties is often more or less evenly matched or tilted in favour of secular parties.

In the end the statistics for Muslim countries are not as abundant as those for most Christian countries. If therefore you believe that the number of practising and believing adherents in Muslim countries is in the upper 80 to the upper 90 percentages as some surveys have suggested, then Islam will be considerably larger than Christianity and you would move up the world percentages of practising believers by 1 per cent per 70 million additional devotees. In effect an overall error of 10 percentage points in the number of Muslim devotees would move the Islam numbers by around 2 per cent of the world population.

If on the other hand you believe that the number of Muslims is overesti-mated and that secularisation or religious scepticism in the big Muslim coun-tries, in particular Indonesia, Pakistan, Bangladesh, Iran and Turkey, is much greater than is reported, then the reverse is true: you would move the Muslim overall result down 2 per cent of the world population for an overall error of 10 percentage points in the Muslim devotees.

There seems to be a high correlation between the degree of development of a country and the degree of adherence to religion. Most Muslim countries are emerging countries (if we ignore oil wealth) with very conservative populations, many of whom are engaged in traditional agriculture or pastoralism.

There are some factors which may cause Muslims to be less religious in the future than they are now:

— The subordination of women is less likely to appeal to half the religious population (women), especially in view of the fact that it tends to be the women who have most influence over their children, at least in early years.
— The system of sharia law belongs to an ancient pre-commercial era. Fun-damentalist sharia criminal law is inconsistent with modern views on punishment.
— Many Islamic states have not been an economic success in the way that Christianity was the religion of economically very advanced states. Although it does not follow that religion determines economic progress, there is a cor-relation which is high enough for Muslims to question whether the religion meets their economic expectations.
— The religion in some parts of the world is conservative and slow to adapt.
— The fanatical terrorist wing which has caused so much mayhem poten-tially brings the religion and hence the reputation of ordinary Muslims into disrepute.
— Sectarianism is rife. The experience of Christianity is that societies eventu-ally tire of the constant violence between warring sects.
— Freedom and democracy are weak in many Muslim countries and this is often associated with religion, leading to anti-clericalism.
— There is a correlation between economic development and decline in religious observance. This may affect the rapidly developing countries with very large Muslim populations such as Indonesia.
— A dogmatic theocratic education may cease to appeal to parents who are ambitious for their children.
— Young people tend to be less religious than older people. The youth of such countries as Iran may give less respect to the religious restrictions imposed by elderly ayatollahs.

**Conclusion on numbers of devotees** It seems inescapable that, apart perhaps from Islam, the number of practising religious adherents proportionate to popu-lation has declined substantially around the world and that the intense ardour of many who still describe themselves as religious in name has cooled. Far more people class themselves as religious than those who actually show a commitment by practising the religion. There must be few priests and their counterparts who do not bemoan the godlessness of our age.

The trend seems to be that, as countries grow richer, the populations and especially the youth become less interested in religions. Religions seem to have a greater hold on rural and poor populations than on urbanised and well-educated city dwellers, although there are exceptions to this. One of the most glaring exceptions is China. To succeed, religions would have to appeal to the richer sector which is the one most likely to grow over the longer term. In the end we are speculating about long-term trends—not just a hundred years from now, but a thousand years, more, many more. So we must not get too engrossed in the present.

I consider later the question as to whether religions have lost influence over the morality and laws of our societies. But first we must discuss some of the possible reasons for the decline in religiosity.

# 12

# *Reasons for the Decline of Religiosity*

## Introduction

The main attacks on religion came from three principal sources—the advances in science, the growth of rationalism and the growth of state power over law-making which displaced the power of the priests. I set out below some of the reasons advanced by doubters to justify their doubts, and then the replies of the theologians.

I ought to say that I do not regard all the arguments against religion as necessarily valid: I am merely listing some of the reasons that may have influenced people into questioning religious belief and endeavouring to work out why this happened. Further, one could say that the degree of plausibility varies from religion to religion.

## The Erosion of Religion by Science

For many people, science brought into question a fundamental of religions—the belief in the supernatural. To them, once that fundamental pillar is toppled, then the whole structure collapses. To doubters the supernatural beliefs of religion seemed increasingly implausible for no other reason than they appeared impossible to prove and strained credibility in principle. To them, science triumphed over superstition, light over darkness. Science and religion are not explicitly at war but there seems little doubt that science has been one of the prime drivers of religious doubt.

It does not follow that the erosion of belief in the supernatural should inevitably result in a fading of a belief in the moral systems and the ethics of living promoted by religions. But in practice in many people's minds, the ethical codes, especially those governing sexual conduct, are so entwined in the supernatural faiths that, once the supernatural is questioned, then the ethics go with it, leaving a vacuum to be filled.

Galileo showed in the 16th century that we are not the centre of the solar system and therefore we may not be the central object of divine interest. Later it became clear from Hubble's observations in the late 1920s that we are extremely tiny in a small part of a very big universe where galaxies are receding from each other at a fearsome speed. We were reduced from everything to just about nothing. That begged the question as to why God should be especially interested in the creatures on this minuscule planet in a galaxy which is one of billions upon billions.

Newton declared in 1687 that the solar system was held together not by God but rather by an impersonal force—gravity. According to Newton, God just started the clock and then took a non-interventionist role.

Darwin announced to a shocked world in 1859 that we were not divinely created but are descended from apes. He postulated that variations in our genes are heritable so that changes can be passed on by mating and that advantageous variations gave the progeny a greater chance of surviving so that they could produce progeny of their own who would incorporate the favourable variations. These variations would become more common in succeeding generations. This was natural selection—an enhanced fitness to stay alive so as to reproduce. This astounding announcement flew in the face of the religious ideology that all living things are the product of a Grand Design invented by the Great Designer in one go. Instead the process of evolution took aeons and happened by chance.

When Christian creationists responded that something like the eye was far too complex to be created by evolution, the Darwinians showed that vision has evolved independently at least half-a-dozen times and that on each occasion sight, however limited, gave the creature such immense advantages in gathering food or hiding from predators that its chances of survival were immeasurably improved so that its chances of reproducing sight with tweaks each time leapt forward apace.

Scientists suggested that ultimately the source of life was not God who created us but rather a chemical reaction or a collision of molecules which started off a process of replications or something like that. Those doubtful of the role of the Great Designer were prepared to accept that; even though we do not know precisely how this happened, there are enough theories around to show how it could have happened. To them we do not need to propose a less credible creation story when more credible versions seem to be within reach.

The failure of the scientists to explain or reproduce the origin of life in the laboratory does not seem to worry the sceptics. Maybe they assume in their broad-brush way that a stroke of lightning struck the mixture of chemicals in the primeval soup and, hey presto! the chemicals began to combine, reproduce and manufacture DNA. After all, people have been subjected to rather more incredible creation stories in their religions.

Quantum mechanics showed that things can happen by chance contrary to what Einstein said—that 'God doesn't play dice'. Everything is ultimately uncertain and therefore the idea of a God who could know everything was doubtful.

In the 1960s, the contraceptive pill, invented in 1951 in a laboratory in Mexico and approved for use in 1960, enabled women to take their destiny into their own hands. Sex became a matter of pleasure and was not restricted to marriage. Sexual morals broke down under the sheer power of the pleasure of sex, once unlinked from the risk of children which brought commitment and responsibilities. Rubber condoms had been invented around 1916 but the pill meant that women did not have to implore men to put on a condom and run the risk of upsetting them. They could run the show themselves. Sex became uncoupled from procreation and became a source of recreational pleasure.

The relaxation of sexual morals dealt another blow to religion because it caused people to turn away from one of the major areas of law within the jurisdiction of religion, that is, sexual conduct. So religion was forced more and more into a corner, seeming less relevant to modern people. Religious restrictions on sex were widely thought to encourage people to fear their passions and to alienate people from their sexuality, to fetter love, desire and emotional freedom. Religions were seen as life-denying.

Secular minds point out that we have not found the abode of God or the location of heaven or hell. We now see billions of miles through our telescopes—to the furthest reaches of the universe—but nowhere do we find the fabled paradise. These sceptics also note that, even with all our exquisite recording equipment and antennae, we have never picked up a recordable message from God which can be subject to scientific scrutiny. They admit that there have been many reports through the ages of visions, of appearances of God on mountains or in caves, and direct communications with favoured recipients and mystics. But notwithstanding the fact that millions of people pray devoutly to God and implore God to help them, that they do this every day and have been doing so for many centuries, according to those of scientific inclination, God never replies, not even one single crackle of the cosmic voice which can be authenticated.

The sceptics do not give special supernatural credence to the fact that planet earth is in the special zone which is friendly to life. It has liquid water. The temperatures are right and do not vary much because of the earth's near circular orbit (only a slight ellipse). Jupiter has a huge gravity field which deflects dangerous asteroids. The moon stabilises the earth's axis of rotation. Our atmosphere has not been sucked away as with Mars. The constants of the universe, such as the size of the strong nuclear force, are friendly to us. If they had been different, even different by a tiny amount, the universe might have been hostile to the formation of life. To sceptics even these favourable conditions do not lead inevitably to belief in a designer god who created the favourable conditions especially for us. Instead, the favourable conditions were coincidental and just happened to favour the development of human beings.

## Rational Attacks on Religion

The pell-mell discoveries of science coincided with the scientific approach which sowed doubts about the supernatural—gods, a heaven, a hell, or a soul or the transfer of souls to snakes or ants next time round. The whole structure of the supernatural seemed to be implausible, improbable and therefore a myth, a superstition.

The rational attacks on religion began in the West in the 1700s, quite recently. Independently of science, this spirit of rationalism led to doubts about the claims of religion. The fact that religions often stood in the way of scientific discoveries tended to cause people to regard religion as backward and out of date.

The way of rational, scientific thinking proposed by the 18th century Enlightenment and before requires that truth depends on actual observation, repeatable experiment and independent data, not belief or faith or opinions. One of its earliest exponents was the lawyer and philosopher Francis Bacon (1561–1626) whose book *Novum organum scientiarum* had far-reaching influence in its emphasis on inductive reasoning. The Enlightenment thinkers had a profound mistrust of authority and orthodoxy: they were sceptical free-thinkers. In this light the beliefs of the religious were implausible. For example, Christianity claimed that Christ was born of a virgin, that he was God, that he rose from the dead three days after his crucifixion and that he did this to save the world. To many people, the story strained ordinary common sense credibility.

It was Martin Luther who said, 'Reason should be destroyed in all Christians', ie, that reason was the enemy of religion. He was right that reason and rationality would, as he feared, bring religion and spiritual things into question.

Doubters lost conviction in the various proofs of the existence of God put forward by theologians and philosophers. Thus Thomas Aquinas in the 13th century sought to prove the existence of God by five proofs. These in summary added up to the argument that there must have been a first cause and therefore that this must have been God, that we can only judge goodness by a maximum goodness, which must be God, and that there must have been a designer of creation. These arguments seemed questionable. For example, there would have to be a creator of God and this creator of God would have to be even more omniscient and all-powerful to dream up a being who was omniscient and all-powerful and could fabricate a rather large universe from nothing. And so on backwards infinitum.

The portrayal of God as omniscient and all-powerful also raised problems. If God is omniscient and knows everything, he must know the future and so it seems odd that he should put us through moral tests. It would mean that everything is predestined and we have no free choice, no free will. Our lives are pre-programmed, known in advance. This seemed to many to be illogical and elude rational explanation.

If we take further the proposition that God is all-powerful and can do anything, to those who are suffering it seems inexplicable that God should allow misery, death and disease. To many it seems inexplicable that the good should also suffer.

For rational thinkers, it was not credible that there is an all-seeing all-hearing God who tunes into our emotions and knows everything we do and say, all seven billion of us, and then evaluates our lives. To some it seemed importunate of us, a conceit, to propose that there is a being who is that interested in us when there is so little hard evidence.

The argument that, if there is something we do not understand, there must be a God to explain it—'God in the gaps'—ceased to find favour. The reason is that there are many things in the past which we had not been able to explain, which were a mystery and which we had subsequently decoded. Thus the strange movements of the planets were explained by the fact that we are all travelling around the sun. We no longer feel it necessary to put God in the gaps of our knowledge. Rather we prefer to explore the question rationally and, until we find a solution, to suspend a firm view one way or the other. If we took the view that all unanswered questions are really God at work and therefore outside nature, we would never discover anything. The big questions about the origin of the universe are considered by rationalists to be matters for science, not the creation legends of the religions, however advanced and convincing they were when first proposed.

An example of a metaphysical puzzle is the central Christian doctrine that Christ died on a cross to atone for the sins of humans. For many people, this assertion raises complicated questions. It seemed obscure to establish how the grisly death of God's son could redeem the sins of mortals. The idea that Christ was a symbolic scapegoat, that is, an innocent who dies for the guilty in a terrible sacrifice, and did so to redeem transgressions of mortals is a concept elusive to the understanding. If all this was just symbolic, it seems odd that an all-powerful God—who could presumably forgive sins without this procedure—thought it suitable to allow his son to be executed merely to engender a symbol. So even a doctrine that had huge emotional appeal to early converts to Christianity ceased to make sense to the modern rationalist mind.

And if a God sends you off to burn in hell forever, screaming from pain, the rationalist asks how this God can say he loves you. The punishment seems disproportionate to the offence.

In the minds of the secular there are issues about the religious moral codes. The moral systems propounded by many holy books, particularly those of Judaism, Christianity and Islam, are in parts barbaric, for example, the Old Testament of the Jews prescribes the death penalty for adultery and picking up sticks on Sunday. If it is claimed that the scriptures are the unchangeable world of God, then it would not seem right to go along with these repugnant ideas about criminal punishment. If on the other hand we can ignore some bits—which is the most logical way out of the impasse—then that raises the question of which bits are true and which untrue. The result is that the validity of the whole text is brought into question—which is why fundamentalists are forced into insisting that every word still has force and is not open to reinterpretation.

Biblical scholarship, commencing mainly in the 19th century, showed that there were historical inconsistencies in Christian versions of the life of Christ in the New Testament which led to a loss of confidence in the accuracy of the Bible. The timing of creation in the creation stories was disproved by geology and carbon dating. The legendary stories of early gods in Hinduism were clearly myths. The authors of authentic scriptures paid little attention to historical fact and were unreliable: it was apparent that they were writing long after the events they were describing. It involved a suspension of disbelief to have confidence in the historical accuracy of even the most revered texts. They were revered because they were the most ancient texts but the most ancient texts seemed in fact to be the least credible.

Following the European voyages of discovery and improved communications, it became abundantly clear that there are many more religions in the world than people in the West thought. Their adherents typically claim that their God is the one true God, their scriptures were spoken directly by their God and that theirs is the only true religion. Either one religion is right and everybody else is wrong or the whole lot are wrong. It seemed hard to dismiss other religions out of hand and claim sole truth. They stand or fall together.

## Other Reasons for the Decline in Belief

There were other reasons for the weakening of the hold of religions over people's lives and we can mention some of them.

When patriarchal authority and obedience by children to seniors faded in the West in the late 1960s, young people no longer accepted the opinions of their elders as accepted truth. They were inclined to reject the beliefs of their elders for no reason other than that they were the beliefs of elders.

Some people have been put off by the fact that religion has played a part in numerous atrocities throughout history, including witch hunts, the Crusades, anti-Jewish pogroms, burnings by the Inquisition, the sectarian brutality during the Thirty Years War (1618–48), the massacres during the Yugoslav war in the late 1900s, the atrocities during the partition of India and Pakistan in 1947, those in Northern Ireland in the last quarter of the 20th century, and the savagery of Islamic jihadists in the 21st century. It is hard to tell whether religion or tribalism was the main impulse behind these horrors.

In practice many of those who committed these atrocities were not motivated by some religious doctrine—whether the doctrine of transubstantiation or the command to say prayers five times a day. More likely they were motivated by some vendetta stemming from tribalism, past injustices, a past family insult, the taking of land, exclusion from jobs or political positions, views about the role of females or the father, or a desire for adventure, greed or something else quite non-spiritual. Nevertheless religion seemed to promote the identity of the warring group and give them a banner and a label under which to fight, to bind them under a common name of ancient and respectable vintage, immorality and wickedness under the banner of morality and holiness. In that way atrocities have tainted and poisoned religion in the minds of many.

It has not helped that blasphemy is still a capital crime in some fundamentalist countries. In 2001 a doctor was sentenced to death in Pakistan for blasphemy. In 1992 a man was beheaded in Saudi Arabia for apostasy and blasphemy. In 2006 a man was sentenced to death in Afghanistan for converting to Christianity.

For many people, the issue is not decided one way or the other. They take the view that as yet the evidence is insufficient, too thin. They are agnostic but not atheist.

Most advanced states took over the responsibility for education, healthcare and looking after the poor via the welfare state. Religions accordingly lost a role which formerly attracted the admiration and affections of the people. These roles were secularised. The sick now go to medical doctors, not priests. The mentally ill are advised by psychiatrists, not shamans.

There is a high correlation between the wealth of a country and its decline in religiosity. On the whole poor countries are often more religious. This may be because religion provides reassurance and meaning for those who are extremely insecure and under threat—from starvation, famines, disease, early death, tribal gangs and rapacious governments: see Pippa Norris and Ronald Inglehart, *Sacred and Secular: Religion and Politics Worldwide* (Cambridge University Press 2nd edition, 2011)—a work which has a lot of interesting things to say about secularisation generally. The United States is an exception as a rich country which is much more religious than others at the same stage of development. Another exception as a poor(ish) country is China. If this explanation is correct, then the comforts of money replace the comforts of religion.

We shall see later that secular authorities in almost all countries elbowed out religions and the clerics from playing any role in government.

# Defences of the Theologians

Theologians have answers to these and other doubts. They point out that it is quite possible to be religious and to accept the major advances of science, in particular, the diminished place of the earth in the universe, the theory of evolution and the Big Bang. Physics, chemistry and biology are not waging a nuclear war on religion, nor is mathematics. It is not cataclysmic to recognise that creation stories were the state of the art at the time, even though now plainly legendary.

If it is hard for theologians to explain what came before God; they riposte that scientists have the same problem explaining what came before the Big Bang and that the solutions of the scientists—multiple universes, wormholes, etc—are just as improbable as the concept of a God who exists in a plane which has no time, which exists forever in an infinity and which we don't understand. They mention that the creation story of Genesis whereby God created light and the world in six days out of nothing may be discredited but as a scientific theory it was not too far off the modern explanation that the universe and light were created out of a 'singularity' in a big bang.

They may say that we are programmed to assume that time always goes forward in a sequence and therefore is infinitely long backwards, although in a different realm time may not be a sequence and therefore it may not be necessary to show that there has to be something before God to create God and something before that to create the God who created God and then something before, etc.

Nor is the departure from the accuracy of historical facts a show-stopper, they say. The authors of scripture were relating moral allegories where the accurate recital of actual events was not a priority.

On the moral side most religious people accept that the criminal punishments recommended in some of the sacred books are barbaric now and that the rejection of these sanctions does not injure the central message of the religions for reasonable people. Reformed theologians concede that some of the religious principles about sex can be reviewed without sending the religion spinning out of control down the mountainside into the abyss.

**Conclusion on reasons for the decline in belief** The tit for tat goes on interminably. One has to admit that many of the arguments advanced one way or the other are about peripheral matters or issues which could be accommodated within the framework of religions without completely shattering them.

Still, we are left with the unchangeable foundations of religions—a supernatural personal god and the immortality of the soul. These are the underpinnings. Once we rip out the essential planks, the sea pours in and the boat sinks.

Then we are left with various moral regimes left hanging in the ruins to take us forward. My view is that the law is by far the most developed and mature of our moral orders, leagues ahead of anything else.

In the end the contest in relation to the supernatural is between the rationalists who rely on reason and the believers who rely on faith. One of the purposes of our existence is to resolve this question so that we can at least make some progress on the issue. In order for that to happen, we have a duty to survive.

# 13

# *Secularisation of Government*

## Political Secularism: The Erosion of Religion by State Power

The object here is to analyse whether, apart from the decline in the number of the faithful, there has been a decline in the influence of religions and their leaders in terms of government power and decision-making. The literature debating this question is as copious as it is disputatious. We have already demonstrated that the law is fundamental to our societies. We shall see later that lawyers play a large part in government and that through the judicial arm lawyers are indeed part of government, an essential part. What of the priests and the religions?

The comparison is not strictly between priests and lawyers but rather between religions and the law. Nevertheless the role of priests and lawyers needs to be considered.

We shall see that over the last two thousand years, at least, there are very few cases where priests did control government. Yet, in former times the priests or their equivalents sometimes did play a significant role in government. Often they were the only people who could read or write. The Chancellor to King Henry II of England was a priest—Thomas à Becket (1118–70). He subsequently became Archbishop of Canterbury and quarrelled with Henry II, a quarrel that led Henry II to exclaim in anger, who will rid me of 'this turbulent priest?' This provoked four knights to murder Becket in Canterbury Cathedral. At the time of the Reformation in Europe priests were commonly ministers in the government. For example, Henry VIII's principal adviser was Cardinal Wolsey (1475–1530).

It was typical for the state to have a state religion, for example, Zoroastrianism in ancient Persia, Christianity in the Roman Empire and the various states of Europe after the Thirty Years War (1618–48). The emperor might be venerated as the chief priest, as in the case of Julius Caesar and Emperor Hirohito in Japan. St Augustine's City of God contemplated both a City of God and an earthly city.

In the Middle Ages, although the pope did not act as ruler of foreign countries, he had powers of excommunication and interdiction (a ban on attending church rites) and also claimed power to appoint bishops. In addition, the pope claimed the right to depose Catholic kings in Western Europe. He won at Canossa in the Investiture Conflict over the right to invest ecclesiastics in 1122 but lost to Henry VIII of England in 1530 when the pope declined to annul Henry's marriage to Catherine of Aragon.

All this was part of the struggle for dominance between popes and kings. Innocent III excommunicated King John of England in 1213. In 1302 Pope Boniface VIII issued a decree *Unam Sanctam* which declared the universal lordship of Christ, and here on earth, of his vicar the pope. But a decade later the then pope retreated somewhat in the face of increasingly autonomous secular states. The relocation of the papacy to Avignon in France under the thumb of French kings for about 70 years until 1377 did not help, nor did the subsequent appointment of rival popes.

There had been peasant uprisings in the 14th century in England and France, probably precipitated by the Black Death and also having a strong anti-clerical flavour. The corruption of clerics was acidly criticised by the reformer John Wycliffe (c 1330 to c 1384) in England and Jan Hus (c 1372 to c 1415) in Bohemia who both denounced the pope as Anti-Christ.

The next steps in political secularisation in Western Europe came with the Renaissance and Reformation. First kings became nationalistic, jealous of their power and unwilling to cede political authority to the pope. These included the English monarchs Henry VIII and Elizabeth I, the French kings Louis XI and Francis I, and the Spanish king Philip II, all of the 16th century.

Secondly a feature of the Renaissance was a rediscovery of and fascination with ancient Greece and Rome, pagan peoples. This led to a spirit of humanism, exemplified by Erasmus of Rotterdam (c 1469 to c 1536), which emphasised intellectual enquiry, intellectual freedom and independent judgement, values which challenged the medieval authority of the Church which insisted on unquestioning obedience to its doctrines.

Third the Reformation, led mainly by Martin Luther (1483–1546) and John Calvin (1509–64), rejected papal authority and rejected the necessity for priests to act as intermediaries between God and the lay people.

It was the horrors of the Thirty Years War in Europe which finally ended the question of who was in charge. It was kings and rulers who exclusively determined the religion of their subjects. The national sovereign state ruled by secular sovereigns had come of age.

# Theocracies

True theocracies have been quite rare throughout history, at least after ancient primitive times. Leaders were taken from the warrior class and advised by members of the aristocracy who were initially warriors. A true theocracy arises where a priest makes the laws, controls the army, declares war and appoints the judges.

While kings and rulers may have had priestly advisers or ministers, one has to search hard to find rulers who are also priests. This was generally not so of the rulers of Egypt or of classical Athens or Sparta, or of the Roman or Chinese emperors, or of the Persian emperors of ancient times, or of the sultans of India or of the Ottoman Empire, or of European monarchs, or Russian tsars, let alone US presidents or British prime ministers. It seems to follow that, although rulers were often deified as gods, true priest-kings appeared only in very primitive societies in most cases, long before the founding of the great religions.

In the strict sense of theocracy, there are few true samples. Mecca was a theocracy under Muhammad and the first four caliphs. One might include the medieval Papal States, technically lasting through to the 19th century, and possibly some medieval prince-bishoprics. In 1356 for example there were archbishoprics of Mainz, Cologne and Trier and on the eve of the Protestant Reformation, there were 53 ecclesiastical principalities, mainly in Germany, which finally were dissolved on the dissolution of the Holy Roman Empire in 1806. And you could possibly say that Tibet was ruled by the theocratic Dalai Lama, now in exile. Some would say that the Geneva of John Calvin was a theocracy but in fact the city council restricted his powers and had the last word. The Massachusetts Bay Colony of the early Puritans was ruled on religious principles. There was a brief reign of the Dominican priest Girolamo Savonarola over Florence from 1494 to 1498. Possibly pre-colonial Burma had strong theocratic influence.

The initial rulers of the Muslims were caliphs but after a couple of centuries or even less the caliphs became merely ceremonial heads of state and the real rulers were the secular sultans.

The deal between the secular and religious authorities was often that the secular authority would support the priests on the understanding that the priests then legitimised the secular rulers.

There have been a number of Islamic theocracies—for example, in West Africa and in the Yemen between roughly 1000 and 1962. Hindu or Buddhist theocracies appear to have been unusual.

In the modern era, theocratic states are a tiny minority. The Vatican is theoretically a separate state where the pope has legislative, executive and traditional powers: he is elected by cardinals. This is a very special case and is the subject of a treaty with Italy. Modern Iran has a religious leadership which has control over officials, over important government posts, which can control government candidates and which can veto legislation.

Nowadays, the process of the elimination of clerics from government is a fact in most states round the world. It is rare to find clerics as government ministers, let alone heads of state having executive capacity. The fact that there are Lords Spiritual (bishops) sitting in the House of Lords in Britain is exceptional and the powers of the House of Lords are small. Even in strict Islamic states the secular authorities are in charge. The imams do not rule in Saudi Arabia or Pakistan or Kuwait. The country is ruled by the king or an emir or by a chief minister, in each case with his ministers, the chief of whom are not usually clerics.

In some traditional monarchies, such as the United Kingdom, Spain, the Netherlands, Denmark and even Thailand, the monarch may be both head of the church and also head of the government but the post is titular.

# Influence of Religions on Policy

It is difficult and probably impossible to measure the influence of the religious establishment and religious morality on policy, that is, to unravel and disentangle what is religion and what is common morality or ethics. My view however is that the religious influence is now small in most countries as regards most of the legal terrain. There are several reasons for this (I am speaking here of most countries, not the exceptions, such as fundamentalist Islamic countries):

— On the whole, religions are no longer in the mainstream of modern law and no longer intervene to any significant degree. The religious authorities do not in general participate in debates about the law of corporations or banks or bankruptcy or contract or the tort or taxation or the welfare state or other topics which dominate modern law. They do not generally become involved in debates about the rule of law or the institution of democracy. As commentators have said, Demos replaces Eros. This is because secular law took off in the 19th century when religions had already settled their legal and moral scope and saw no reason to change. Their codes were settled in a simple agricultural or pastoral world long before industrialisation and long before the scientific revolution.

— In addition, the religious authorities were not interested perhaps because they did not think that they had the competence, because they regarded the issues as technical or because their flocks were not particularly interested either (since the lay people felt that the areas of law concerned did not really affect them).

— The secular authorities did not and still do not in most countries welcome clerical intervention.

— As religiosity declines, so does the preoccupation of the population with religious morality.

— Although the religious authorities continue to be interested in the law relating to sex and the family, even this is declining. One reason is that many people regard the religions as too restrictive or an infringement of personal freedom. Another is that the secular authorities have taken control of even these arenas.

— The founders of the great religions and subsequent holy scriptures did not express a view on many major modern issues in the law. For example, even a subject like the rule of law deserved little more than assertions that kings and judges should be just and merciful. Anything not in the ancient scriptures did not qualify as serious.

— When religious leaders do express a view on matters of state, it is often generic, for example, that societies have a duty to protect the poor or to mitigate economic inequality or that people should be good. This is of little assistance to politicians endeavouring, for example, to match intricate taxation, sovereign borrowing and the budget to the no less intricate needs of a welfare state.

— It is a matter of common sense that morality is not a religious preserve. Therefore when it is claimed that this or that policy is required by, say, Christian moral principles, it is also typically required by moral principles generally which happen to overlap with a religious principle. Morality is not a creation of religion and is not exclusive to religion. Religions do not monopolise morality.

The religious authorities lost control of the administration of justice to the secular authorities—control of the courts, control of criminal punishment and the enforcement of the civil law by court orders for compensation and execution over assets.

In the case of Islam, the imams are unlike Christian priests. Sunni imams are appointed by their communities as especially qualified by their learning and they officiate at Friday prayers at the mosque. Almost invariably the secular authorities are dominant.

The Buddhist influence came mainly from monasteries which were and are not citadels of political power over law-making.

There are no formally trained and ordained priests in Hinduism. Instead there are numerous holy men who perform rituals, conduct rites of passage and officiate at the temples—at least 15 main groups. The pujari conduct worship (*puja*) at temples or a shrine. It seems unlikely that as a group they have their hands on the levers of the law. In the Hindu caste system, which still has great force in India, the caste of the rulers and warriors—the nobles—is separated from the priestly class of brahmins so that the separation of religion from secular leadership was institutionalised.

In the 19th century political parties were set up in Europe intended to import Christian principles into government. These were often called Christian Democrat parties. In continental Europe these parties are still very much a force and tend to be mildly right-wing. In Latin America their counterparts are typically mildly left-wing. Again, it seems most doubtful that these nominally Christian parties still refer to the Bible or the Christian gospels in considering policy in their legislatures or display campaign posters declaring that they will bring in original Christian laws as promoted by Christ and his apostles.

The position is different in some Islamic countries where there is a constant battle going on between secularist and Muslim parties for control of the laws. In fundamentalist Islamic countries the battle is between modern legal systems and the ancient sharia law. In these states, the scope of religious influence is widened to include the main tenets of sharia law, such as the prohibition on interest and insurance, the stoning of adulterers, the cutting off of the hands of thieves, and floggings for various other offences.

We have already seen in the chapter on families of law that non-fundamentalist Islamic states have ordinary Western-style legal systems, not sharia law, for example, Indonesia, Malaysia, Turkey, Pakistan, Egypt and Morocco, although sometimes, as in Pakistan, with a sharia flavouring in the personal law. Their banks lend the citizen ordinary interest bearing loans. The reality is that it is difficult to run a modern state on the basis solely of sharia law especially with its ban on interest. This is so notwithstanding the presence in many non-fundamentalist

Islamic states of Muslim political parties which occasionally are in power. These examples underline that the facts of religious political influence diverge from the myths.

It is sometimes claimed that in the United States religion dominates politics. This does not seem to be the case outside the usual domains of cultural wars over sex and the family which are a very small corner of the overall law in the United States, as elsewhere. The impression that it is so may be attributable to a large and noisy fundamentalist Christian right wing. US policies towards the USSR in the Cold War and towards Islamic jihadists were and are not primarily driven by religion but by straightforward defence against military or terrorist threats. US policy on the rule of law or the law relating to money or bankruptcy or democracy are not based on what Jesus said in the Bible (he had little to say about politics or law) but on the civilised moral values of that country, quite independently of Christianity.

Apart from the activities of fundamentalist jihadists, some of the most important modern national rivalries are not driven by religion. The rivalry between the United States and China, between Japan and China, between Russia and Europe are rivalries based on hegemony and threat, not holy books. Even the hostility between Israel and the Palestinians and between India and Pakistan, although sometimes legitimised and exacerbated by religious differences, are fundamentally not inspired by religions. Thus the Palestinians are inflamed more by loss of land than by scriptures.

It seems highly unlikely that welfare states and redistributive handouts were the consequence of religious admonitions to care for the poor and weak. They were the consequence of democratic majorities wanting more protections and getting it through redistributive taxation and, in despotic states, of the desire of populist tyrants to stay in power by gratifying the multitude.

The participants in protests, for example, against capitalism or the rich or the banks and corporations, do not seem in the first place to be fired by religious zealotry. The things which inflame them are many but they do not appear to include theological metaphysics.

# Separation of Church and State

From very early times secular leaders of states sought to diminish the powers of the priesthood to govern and to curb the powers of the priests. There was a struggle for power between the politicians, originally warriors, and the priests who were not members of the military caste and often claimed superiority over the military caste and the politicians. In some countries, for example, Turkey and Morocco, religions are subject to explicit government control to ensure that religious leaders do not interfere in politics. Hence the rise of political secularism.

There are various versions of the separation of church and state. These variants comprise an amalgam of the following for example: the state does not have an official religion, it allows religious freedom especially in modern secular democracies, and does not require that judges or other office holders profess a particular religion. The state forbids the use of public money to finance religious institutions such as schools or care homes or the provision of educational litera-ture, does not pay for the building of churches and temples or pay the salaries and pensions of clergy. The state bans the exhibition of religion in public admin-istrative offices by the wearing of icons, clothes or hairstyles of a religion, or the display of religious pictures or of scriptural passages in public buildings, takes over education and welfare to the exclusion of religions, and does not defer to the religious ethical codes or the views of the clerics in passing laws. The state does not require rites of passage such as marriages or funerals to be performed in religious churches or temples, ceases to involve religion in its ceremonies such as the opening of courts or its legislature, and does not permit public holidays based on religious festivals. It is irrelevant that the state may have a religious symbol in its national flag—a cross or a crescent moon and star. For a care-ful discussion, see Jonathan Fox, *A World Summary of Religion and the State* (Cambridge University Press, 2008).

The philosopher John Locke is often credited as being the chief thinker on the subject of the separation of church and state. According to him, govern-ments should not interfere with individual conscience: individuals would not cede control of conscience to governments. Religious liberty must be protected from government authority. Complete religious freedom was adopted in the US Bill of Rights in 1791, preceded by the French Declaration of the Rights of Man and of the Citizen in 1789.

The most important secularist movements were born out of grand revolutions or national independence movements. Prominent examples are American inde-pendence in 1776, the French Revolution of 1789 which heralded the famous French laicity, the atheistic Russian Revolution of 1917 led by Lenin and the ushering in of atheistic communism in the USSR and elsewhere, the secular Turkish Revolution led by Kemal Attaturk in the 1920s, the independence of India in 1947 led by Nehru, who was an atheist, the atheistic Chinese Revolu-tion led by Mao in 1949 and adopted by other countries in the region, and the seizure of power by secular despots or military dictatorships in the Middle East and North Africa—Algeria, Egypt, Iraq and Syria, for example. Latin American dictators of the 20th century attacked the Catholic Church in the name of pro-gress, for example, in Mexico and Argentina.

The assortment of communists, socialist and populist despots expropriated the land of the religious houses, closed churches and temples, shut seminar-ies and purged clerics. In numerous developing countries modernisation was accompanied by secularisation.

The political motives included anti-clericalism, a desire to promote national unity by promoting freedom of religion, and a desire to stifle and squeeze out another power in the land which could be a threat, an opposition. The clerics were often seen as anti-modernist, venal, opposed to progress and out of date in their views. They were seen as intolerant, anachronistic, superstitious. To them, God disapproved of wealth creation, inventions and enterprise. They were also a cost, a heavy charge on tax revenues.

Some of the US founding fathers had mixed views about religion and politics. The original US Constitution and the original state charters made no mention of biblical texts. Thomas Jefferson observed that 'Christianity is the most perverted system that ever shone on man'. James Madison remarked, 'During almost fifteen centuries has the legal establishment of Christianity been on trial. What has been its fruits? ... superstition, bigotry and persecution'. He thought that Christianity was 'the most bloody religion that ever existed'. Even Benjamin Franklin weighed in by adding, 'Lighthouses are more useful than churches'.

After the French Revolution, on 10 November 1793 the revolutionaries prohibited the worship of God and instituted the realm of reason. This was one of the first political religions of modern times and it came fully equipped with icons and rites. It soon had its martyrs too.

King Frederick the Great of Russia remarked that Christianity was 'stuffed with miracles, contradictions and absurdities, was spawned in the fevered imaginations of the Orient and then spread to our Europe, where some fanatics espoused it, some intriguers pretended to be convinced by it and some imbeciles actually believed it': Christopher Clark, *Iron Kingdom* (Allen Lane, 2006) p 187. Frederick the Great was saying directly what other Enlightenment figures were saying less confrontationally—Voltaire, David Hume and the historian Edward Gibbon. The latter thought that Christianity was one of the causes of the fall of the Roman Empire because it emasculated the republican spirit. Nehru, who was an atheist, said, 'The spectacle of what is called religion, in India and elsewhere, has filled me with horror ... Almost always it seemed to stand for blind belief and reaction, dogma and bigotry, superstition, exploitation and the preservation of vested interests'. See Richard Dawkins, *The God Delusion* (Bantam Books, 2006) pp 63–68.

The separation of church and state is now widespread and reveals the drift away from state religion and the subordination of the clerics to the secular rulers.

## Examples of the Separation of Church and State

In the United States the First Amendment to the Constitution provides that Congress shall make no law respecting an establishment of religion, or prohibiting the free exercise thereof. There are however many ceremonial signs of religion. The US dollar carries the motto 'In God we Trust', the pledge of allegiance contains the phrase 'one nation, under God'. But some ceremonial displays have been held unconstitutional such as the posting of the Ten Commandments in court rooms or Christian nativity displays on public land.

Articles 20 and 89 of the Japanese Constitution, influenced by US occupying forces, protects freedom of religion and prevents the government from compelling religious observance or using public money to benefit religious institutions. Article 16.3 of the Spanish Constitution states that 'No religion shall have a state character', but allows appropriate cooperation with the Catholic Church and other confessions. Swedish separation was achieved in 2000. In Australia section 116 of the Constitution prevents the Commonwealth from establishing any religion or requiring a religious test for any office. Brazil's Constitution since 1891 has separated church and state. In France laicity was ultimately formalised in a 1905 law designed to protect politicians from the influence of religion. Ireland has no state religion. Turkey is officially secular but there are some entanglements. For example, the state pays the imams' wages and supports Sunni religious education in public schools. There is a Department of Religious Affairs which for example controls what can be mentioned in sermons given in mosques. Mexico and South Korea are secular.

The United Kingdom has an unusual mix. For historical reasons the sovereign cannot be a Roman Catholic but since 2013 can marry a Roman Catholic. The House of Lords contains 26 bishops, but their powers are extremely limited. The parish churches have a duty to baptise, marry and bury anybody who comes along, regardless of religion. You belong without believing. But the state does not pay the wages or pensions of clerics or pay for the upkeep of their churches and other buildings except for lottery donations. Schools may have tax-exempt status as charities. Religious education is allowed in state schools but parents can opt out, as in Germany. There is a high degree of religious pomp and ceremony in the openings of Parliament and the courts, in Remembrance Day services, and in university graduations and royal anniversaries. The offence of blasphemy was abolished in 2008.

The general pattern then in developed countries is the separation of church and state and freedom of religion. Generally the state does not pay the clerics or pay for the building or upkeep of their churches unless they are heritage. The effect therefore is to place great financial loads on the churches and to make it difficult for them to survive.

The principles of church/state separation have given rise to many courtroom battles, especially in the United States, on the public funding of religious schools including payment for books or bussing, the content of the school curriculum and the right of parents to opt out of religious instruction if it is allowed at all, the wearing of religious symbols such as crosses or Sikh daggers, the conflict between savagely satirical religious caricature and provocation to violence, and the wearing of religious dress such as the Muslim veil (Britain, allowed; France, not allowed in some cases). In Britain Sikhs can wear their turbans on motorbikes and do not have to wear the usual protective helmets. In both Finland and Germany the state levies religious taxes on behalf of the churches.

On the whole the aim of these secularised states is not to drive religion off the streets or out of the workplace. But these attempts at state neutrality have not prevented outbursts of violence such as the violence over the publication in 2005 by a Danish newspaper of cartoons said to be an insult to the Prophet and the killing of 17 people during terrorist attacks stemming from satires of Islam publicised by the French magazine *Charlie Hebdo* in January 2015.

In tolerant multicultural states, the legal system is generally unified, that is, there are no separate rules for marriage, divorce and inheritance according to religious belief. There are exceptions such as India and there has been some experimentation with private arbitration in Britain. On the other hand the private international law of most developed countries recognises laws governing marriage, divorce and inheritance where the events take place abroad, subject to qualifications.

On the other hand some states profess a state religion. Afghanistan, not unexpectedly, proclaims in its Constitution that Islam is the state religion but allows other religions. Bangladesh is similar. Buddhism is the state religion of Cambodia but other religions are allowed. In China the Constitution allows religious freedom but in practice the government insists on sanctioning religions. In Indonesia there is freedom of religion but 'the nation is based upon belief in one supreme God'. The government only recognises six religions. In Iran the government recognises Islam, Zoroastrianism, Judaism and Christianity—in theory at least. In Malaysia the Constitution provides that Islam is the state religion but there is freedom of other religions. In Russia the Constitution provides for religious freedom but in 1997 a law was passed restricting the activities of religious groups in Russia. In Saudi Arabia Islam is the official religion. All Saudi citizens must be Muslims. There can be no public practise of non-Muslim religions. In Vietnam the Constitution formally allows religious freedom but in practice religions are severely restricted.

# Conclusion on Political Influence

The conclusion is that, in addition to a decrease in devotees, religions now have little law-making influence and power compared with the secular authorities in most states. Sometimes the retreat has been voluntary (monastic Buddhism, for example), sometimes forced upon them. A few Islamic states are exceptions. It may well be that the exclusion of the sacred from the secular is not a modern phenomenon but goes back to ancient times.

# Future Moral Role of Religions

Notwithstanding the decline of the pious, the religious establishments have a major role to play in the project of human survival, the defiance of the foul fiend, the silencing of the tolling of the final knell of the human race. The major religions will be a feature of the world's cultures for a long time to come.

Religions possess an enormous amount of goodwill on earth. Their overall record has been on the side of the good. They still enjoy the active approbation of a quarter to two-fifths of the population of the planet and the endorsement of a great many more of those who are not active practitioners. They have a massive infrastructure of churches, temples, synagogues, mosques and shrines and a huge corpus of philosophy and thinking, scriptures and liturgies, music and art. They have colossal experience in human nature.

Some principles are essential to our future and should be supported by religions. They include the promotion of the rule of law. They include allegiance to the common interest of human beings, a principle which is senior to nationalism or patriotism or group identity or indeed religious identity. They include support for scientific progress. These are principles which I develop later and which have high moral and survival content.

The religions should fill the gaps which the law cannot fill, in particular the moralising of people's private emotions of hate and anger and cruel conduct towards others which is below the threshold of legal redress. They should vigorously promote loving kindness and love.

Religion should be a force for the good against the violence which is born of cultural differences and which scars our societies. They should make it clear that those who wreak unlawful violence under the banner of a religion are acting contrary to universal morality.

# Overall Conclusion on Secularisation

One can argue whether the decline in committed devotees and the decline in influence were caused by science or rationalism, or power grabs by rulers, or by the welfare state, or a desire for freedom, or preoccupation with the business of life, or any other number of influences. It is always unsafe to prophesy whether these trends will continue but it would certainly seem that there would have to be major changes in either religion or in human cultures for the trends to change direction.

To some, the secularisation of the world is to be welcomed as the banishment of old superstitions. To others, the secularised are godless people without morals. What matters is where we will be on this question of religions in a hundred years from now, two hundred years, a thousand years or a hundred thousand years and what weight would then be thrown upon our legal systems and their codes of morality. It may well be that humankind will decide that it can do without religion but humankind cannot do without law.

One cannot help feeling a sense of sadness and loss that the religious experiment, begun in ancient times with such excitement and with such high hopes for salvation, should now be brought into question.

# 14

# *The Rise of the Lawyers*

## The Growth in the Number of Lawyers and Law

A dramatic symbol of the rise of the lawyers in the modern world is the number of lawyers who occupy or have occupied leadership positions in government. By lawyer, I mean trained as a lawyer or one who practised.

According to the American Bar Association, in 2006 about 53 per cent of the US Senate and 36 per cent of Congress were lawyers. More than half of American presidents have been lawyers—25 out of 44. They include John Adams, Thomas Jefferson, James Monroe, Abraham Lincoln, Woodrow Wilson, Calvin Coolidge, Franklin Roosevelt, Richard Nixon, Gerald Ford, Bill Clinton and Barack Obama. Hillary Clinton was a lawyer.

A number of British prime ministers have been lawyers—Canning, Disraeli, Asquith, Lloyd George, Attlee and Tony Blair. Two of the last four Dutch prime ministers were lawyers. When President Sarkozy of France formed his first cabinet on election in 2007, nine out of the 16 members were trained as lawyers. Konrad Adenauer and Gerard Schroeder of Germany were lawyers. Aldo Moro, then the longest serving post-war prime minister of Italy, was a professor of law. He was murdered in 1978 by the Red Brigade.

In Spain the first elected prime minster after Franco—Suarez—was a lawyer. The longest serving prime minister, Gonzalez, was a lawyer and was followed by two more—Aznar and Zapatero.

In Russia in 2012 the President Vladimir Putin and the Prime Minister Dimitry Medvedev were lawyers. The founding fathers of both India and Pakistan were lawyers—Nehru and Jinnah. Mahatma Gandhi was a lawyer and practised in Durban in South Africa. The longest serving prime minister of Pakistan, Liaquiat Ali Khan, was a lawyer. Fidel Castro was a lawyer.

In China the current leaders Xi Jinping and Li Keqiang were lawyers or trained as lawyers, although Xi Jinping only just qualifies. Lee Kuan Yew, the Prime Minster of Singapore and architect of its success, was a lawyer. Nelson Mandela, President of South Africa, was a lawyer.

Even in Japan, where lawyers are considered to be contrary to the non-confrontational culture, at least three post-war prime ministers have been lawyers—Tetsu Katayama in the late 1940s, Takeo Fukuda in the late 1970s and Naoto Kan more recently—although he was strictly a patent attorney.

Robert Menzies, the longest serving prime minister in Australia, was a lawyer. Two recent examples of Australian lawyer prime ministers are John Howard and Julia Gillard. The managing director of the IMF and a former French minister of finance, Christine Lagarde, is a former managing partner of an international law firm.

These leaders are an allegory of the importance of law in the contemporary world. Lawyers are not like priests—they do not, for example, guide the morality of their flocks, or perform communal rituals. But, because of the role that law plays, lawyers have duties to our societies beyond the normal.

# Reasons for the Growth of Law

I have already charted the historical reasons behind the fantastic growth of law after around 1830. This was when the population of the world, after having been in the doldrums for quite some time, crossed the one billion threshold, when scientific discovery took off and when wealth increased astronomically, especially in the West. These and other factors led to the need for new laws to govern the creatures of industrialisation and credit—corporations, intellectual property, banking, insurance, money, complicated products, astonishing means of transport from the automobile to jet aircraft, new markets and fields of regulation such as antitrust and securities regulation, new hazards from chemicals factories and machinery. And a new class of industrial worker.

These revolutions also led to the expansion of the rules for democracy and the refinement and codification of the rule of law. Even the old topics of contract and tort were seized upon for massive augmentation and complication to meet the upheavals which turned the ancient agricultural world upside down.

There are a number of other reasons for the huge growth of law and hence the numbers of lawyers.

— **Number of jurisdictions** First, there is the sheer number of jurisdictions involved.

Altogether there are about 320 jurisdictions. Even though the number of jurisdictions now is tiny compared with the Middle Ages where a single country could have numerous cities, municipalities and villages or provinces, each having their own customs and laws, the realities of modern interconnectedness between jurisdictions means that the amount of law and intensity of legal risk has increased.

Large banks and ordinary corporations often sell their products or have customers in virtually all of the jurisdictions in the world and indeed often have branches or representative offices in one-third or one-half of them. So they have to take into account the laws of all of the jurisdictions in which they do business. Until fairly recently most business was conducted between a much smaller number of jurisdictions. Big countries such as the USSR and China were effectively hermetically closed economies with minimal direct contact with other countries other than through their state-owned banks and state-owned entities. Large regions in the rest of the planet were excluded because of their poverty and also their closed economies, for example, many countries in Africa, Asia and Latin America.

But now practically every country has opened its economy to a degree, practically every country is now part of the world economy, from Abu Dhabi and Albania through to Yemen and Zambia. Almost all countries now participate in world markets. Even Sao Tomé, even Chad, even Kyrgyzstan, are interested in advancing their economies and are no longer cut-off from the rest of the world. Even Cambodia has a stock exchange. Only a tiny handful of countries stand loftily apart, either resentfully, such as North Korea, or because they are not really interested, for example, Bhutan. This is globalisation in action.

— **Internal tiering of the law** The second factor which increases the size of the law is the tiering of domestic legal systems. The legal systems in developed countries are like slicing through the crust of the earth to reveal layers of sand, chalk, granite and gravel.

For example, English law has about eight classes of security interest in the sense of core mortgages and charges, ranging from the regime applicable to security interests used in payment and securities settlement systems through to the security interest which individuals can give.

$8 \times 320 = 2560$.

Britain also has around 25 insolvency regimes for different classes of entity or types of corporation. It is true that some of these are fairly minor and rarely used, for example, the insolvency regime for water utilities, but the separate regimes for, say, commercial banks and investment banks are enormously important. So here the original tiering typical of most legal systems between the law applicable to individuals and that applicable to businesses has been endlessly subdivided.

$25 \times 320 = 8000$.

Some of this tiering is due to the simple increase in the number and diversity of businesses, but it is also attributable to politics. For example, in democracies there is a constant tug-of-war going on between the protection of businesses, which do not have votes, and the protection of individuals, who do. The result is that the protections for individuals or small businesses are enlarged. This means that payment systems, for example, have to be carved out and exempted from the protective tendency because of the large amounts involved and the catastrophic impact if, say, a security interest given by a commercial bank to the central bank should turn out to be invalid or difficult to enforce immediately because of a rule protecting individual borrowers or homeowners.

— **Regulatory intensification** A large part of this increase of law results from the intensification of regulatory regimes, notably in the West. These regulatory regimes, of which there are a great many, typically criminalise the ordinary law and are sometimes aggressive. I visit these in a later chapter.

— **Regulation of science** The massive increase in science and technology over the last two hundred years has increased risks and hence the need for laws to deal with the risks. For example, before the 19th century there was no need for the regulation of pharmaceuticals—apart from plants, there weren't any.

— **Extraterritorial legal risks** Apart from this internal tiering, there is the layering caused by extraterritorial laws. Because many countries, especially in the developed world, give their laws extraterritorial effect, the transactor may have to have regard not only to the laws of his or her own jurisdiction, but also to the laws of one or more other jurisdictions which have contact, often very ephemeral and slight, with the transaction. Businesses with international operations can land up in courts practically anywhere because of the wide and exorbitant long-arm jurisdictional rules of most countries.

— **Legal infrastructure** There is great diversity around the world as to how the law is actually applied and the rule of law. For example, the basic law in Congo Kinshasa and Belgium derives from the same roots but the application is very different. One therefore has to cope with a double layer—the written law, or the law on the books, and then how it is applied.

— **Rapidity of legal change** The law in many countries is mercurial and volatile. The law is much more volatile than it has ever been and changes rapidly, sometimes for no apparent reason, arbitrarily, just because somebody wants to fiddle with the law, or has a flash of anger.

In the crucial decade from 1997 to 2007, most countries made major changes to important arenas of law, such as bankruptcy and corporate law. This is attributable to underlying factors to do with the sudden growth of wealth and GDP as previously discussed.

# Complexity of the Law

It is not just the increase in the size of the law which has outstripped religion and led to an increase in law and lawyers, but also its complexity.

The law is inherently complex by reason of our uncertainty about cause and effect, disagreements about what the law should say and who it should protect, national cultural differences and histories, and disputes about how much law there should be and how intrusive it should be.

This inherent complexity of the law is shown in the figure 'Complexity of phenomena' which is based on a similar figure by the English astronomer and physicist Professor John D Barrow (who in turn based his figure on that of David Ruelle).

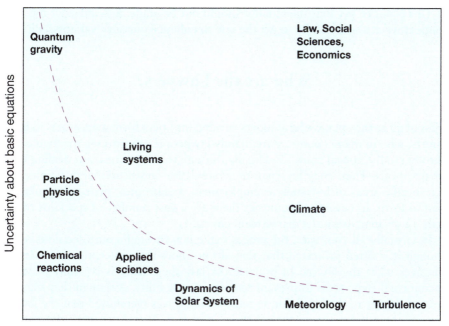

After John. D. Barrow

**Complexity of phenomena**

The vertical axis in the figure shows the complexity and uncertainty about basic equations. The horizontal axis shows the operation of the equations in the real world. For example, an equation for the speed at which a drop of water will fall is no doubt quite simple but tracking exactly what happens to a particular drop of water falling over the Victoria Falls is not. Thus in the case of turbulence the equation is simple but the practical effects defy analysis. Therefore on the vertical axis, our understanding of the equation for the speed at which a drop of water will fall is relatively simple and so the concept is low on the vertical axis. But because turbulence is extremely complex in terms of the phenomenon of a drop of water falling over the Victoria Falls, the concept of turbulence is way out along the horizontal axis towards the end.

On the other hand we have no real understanding of what quantum gravity is and what the basic equations are and so quantum gravity is very high on the vertical axis. If we did understand the basic equations, it seems that it ought to be quite simple in terms of the complexity of phenomena on the horizontal axis.

In the case of the law, the social sciences and economics, we do not understand the algebra or impact of cause on effect, how law affects conduct with any predictability. Similarly the complexity of phenomena is almost incomprehensible in its diversity and complex interrelationships. The fact is we do not really know the basic equations in law and, even if we did, the operation of the law in the real world is extremely difficult to assess scientifically and objectively.

This is not to say that the attempt should not be made, and indeed it must be made if we are successfully to get the law to enhance our survival possibilities.

# Who are the Lawyers?

First of all at the apex we have judges divided into tiers from magistrates in local courts, who in many countries are mainly lay people, up through the high court through to the appeal courts and finally through to a supreme court dealing with final appeals. There may be separate tribunals for constitutional questions and for specific areas of law such as employment, bankruptcy, financial regulation and so forth. In developed countries there are a vast number of specialist tribunals, quite apart from the mainstream courts.

In virtually all countries, the judges make law through court decisions, even though it is often protested that they do no more than interpret the codes or discover what the law is. In practice the law they make is typically in small incremental steps so as to prevent retrospective liability. Although they may on occasion defer to the legislator, in most societies it is recognised that the judiciary are the ultimate protectors of the rule of law. They often have the specific role of defending the constitution. They are the last bulwark between the people and the despots.

Arbitrators are close cousins of the judges—a kind of privatised judiciary.

Below them are many millions of licensed legal practitioners who have to qualify by passing exams and going through a period of training. They do not regard themselves as at all analogous to priests and many do not cast themselves in the role of defenders of the law, although they should.

There are about 20 very large international law firms which dominate the practice of wholesale private law. Most of them are based in England and New York but there are other locations, for example, China. These law firms specifically have many hundreds of partners and thousands of associate lawyers. The main law firms that are truly international in the sense of having numerous foreign offices are based in London and sometimes referred to as the 'magic circle' law firms. Many other firms in the United States and elsewhere have branched out into foreign parts.

The top law firms derive most of their revenues from three groups of transactions plus litigation. These transactions are (1) bank syndicated credits of all types, from project finance to acquisition finance, (2) international bond issues of all types, mainly issued by sovereign states, by banks and by ordinary corporations, and (3) mergers and acquisitions of companies, including public bids and private sales, as well as issues of equity shares. They therefore deal with the issue and sale of two forms of senior debt (bank credits and bond issues) plus the issue and sale of equity shares. Litigation is the fourth area of their practices. In addition these giant law firms have many other specialities, such as employment, tax, intellectual property, regulatory and so forth. But these specialities are the stones in the arch rather than the pillars.

Then in the mainstream middle, there is a vast population of law firms which deal with both wholesale law and also the law applicable to individuals, but all on a lesser scale.

There are 'high street' lawyers who deal with crime, family and home matters, the transfer and letting of real property, and consumer and small litigation, such as debt collecting or motor negligence.

The large law firms are nowhere near as large as the largest accountancy firms, both in terms of numbers and international spread.

In addition, there are vast numbers of in-house lawyers employed by corporations. The legal departments run into many hundreds or even thousands. In some countries such as England, barristers who appear in the higher courts are a separate profession. In civil law countries there is a separate profession of notaries who alone are entitled to notarise or authenticate or draw up certain documents, especially transfers of land.

Then there are armies of semi-lawyers, such as legal executives (paralegals) or compliance experts or those with a law degree who have gone off into other jobs, such as running companies. Finally, there is the very large number of professors and academics teaching in faculties of law in universities and in professional law schools.

In the ranks of senior judges, top lawyers in universities, partners in great law firms, and senior in-house lawyers you find some of the most potent and gifted collections of people in the world—often 0.5 per cent of the population in terms of intellectual attainment.

In the popular mind lawyers are typically associated with litigation, ie, fights through the courts. For most people litigation in the courts is a traumatic and inordinately costly experience where lawyers are at their most ferocious and partisan. Where the litigation system is abusive and the lawyers unreasonably aggressive, litigation gives lawyers a bad name.

In fact the majority of lawyers derive most of their revenues from transactions and advice, not court work. This is not true of the United States where most lawyers are litigation lawyers and the revenues of even the largest firms includes a big chunk attributable to litigation. This reflects the fact that the United States is a highly litigious society.

## Growth in Lawyer Numbers is Recent

There were probably lawyers whenever you had law, but we do not hear much of the earliest lawyers. Even in ancient Athens we do not hear the name of a single legal adviser other than court orators. The Romans had a legal profession consisting of secular lay jurists, practical in outlook and advising on deals and litigation. Thus began the rise of the lawyers in the West, to be taken up by the common lawyers of the late Middle Ages after centuries of stagnation.

There is no question that there has been a massive increase in the number of lawyers over recent decades. In 1970 few law firms in London had more than

20 partners (in fact that was the legal limit until 1967). But now many law firms have more than 500 partners and 3000 to 5000 lawyers spread around the world. The same is true of American law firms. In continental Europe, many law firms, even senior law firms, had only two or three partners operating virtually as sole practitioners whereas now they too are very large. The largest law firms in China, which were virtually non-existent 50 years ago, now have hundreds or thousands of lawyers.

From 1880 to 1973 US licensed lawyers compared with population remained steady at around one lawyer per 650 people. By 2013 it was one lawyer per 240 people—around two-and-a-half times as many. In 2013 there were about 1,270,000 licensed lawyers in the United States, compared with a population of 316 million.

# Numbers of Lawyers per Jurisdiction

The differences between jurisdictions in terms of the number of lawyers in each raise some fascinating and intriguing questions.

If we extrapolate from a sample of countries representing rich, medium-wealth and low-wealth jurisdictions, it would seem that there may be between five million and seven million licensed and active legal practitioners in the world, ie, around one per 1000. If, however, we estimate figures for particular jurisdictions, there are some quite colossal discrepancies. For example, the ratio in the United States is about one lawyer per 240 people, with Brazil close behind with one per 326. Canada is one per 390 and New Zealand is also one per 390. The usual figure for rich jurisdictions is somewhere between these ratios and one per 600 or so—Spain one lawyer per 394, UK one per 401, Italy one per 480, and Germany one per 590. But in France the ratio appears to be around one per 1000, and in Sweden the ratio seems much higher, perhaps one per 2000.

The ratios in Latin American jurisdictions are much higher than in other middle-income countries, for example, one lawyer per 550 in Argentina. This compares with around one per 1300 in Turkey, one per 1700 in Poland, and one per 2600 in Russia.

Among poor countries, one can expect one lawyer per 3000 up to one per 10,000 or so. For example, in Kenya the ratio is one per 6000, and in Nigeria one per 3700.

There seem to be around one million lawyers in India, roughly the same number in the United States, but India has nearly four times the population of the United States so the ratio is quite high at one per 1200 or so, compared with one per 240 in the United States.

By contrast, the ratio in China seems to be about one per 14,000 with a total of 110,000 lawyers (up from 200 over the last 20 years), but this may be a large underestimate.

In a country like Indonesia the ratio appears to be about one per 10,000. Compare this with Tunisia (one per 1350) and the Philippines (one per 2400).

These figures were obtained from a large number of different sources at different dates and give a general impression. Most relate only to licensed and active practitioners. They do not cover legal executives or compliance experts or judges or academics. So the actual number of people doing a legal job may have to be increased by quite a substantial percentage.

Some of the discrepancies are easily explicable. For example, the ratio in Japan is one per 4000 or so, but this flows from the fact that in Japan the situation is (or was) that less than 10 per cent of candidates pass the bar exams each year. This either means that the exams are too hard or else that Japan restricts the number of lawyers for policy reasons, for example, because the culture regards litigation as evil in the sense that disputes should be resolved amicably.

The discrepancy between ratios in other developed countries may therefore have something to do with a cultural view about the usefulness of lawyers, especially a perception that lawyers foment unnecessary litigation and strife. In the United States there are fifteen times as many lawyers per person as in Japan. This may be attributable to a legal system which encourages litigation. The United States is extremely litigious, in sharp contrast to Japan. A high proportion of members of the US legislative bodies are lawyers, much higher than in other developed countries.

The number of lawyers may be limited by a restrictive practice to benefit existing lawyers.

Apart from these cultural considerations, there is a clear correlation between the degree of economic development and the number of lawyers, that is, the richer the country, the greater is the number of lawyers. This may in turn be influenced by the fact that richer countries tend to have more complicated laws especially in the fields of regulation and the like, laws which are the product of the welfare state which tends to flow over into protective regulation, such as financial regulation, health and safety rules, or consumer credit protections. Richer countries will have more and larger banks and corporates, therefore more transactions that have to be documented and therefore more disputes.

At any rate, if there is anything in the prediction that GDP is likely to increase over coming decades, then this would seem to point to an increase in the number of lawyers worldwide as currently poor countries get richer. Every time something goes wrong, it is the population at large which clamours for more laws to punish the villains. The politicians respond to this righteous indignation by promising legal vengeance.

There are many conclusions which one might debate. One is worth mentioning here.

There are issues about the future size of law firms and of the legal and compliance departments of international banks and corporates. If we continue to inflate our legal systems as we are doing now, then this may point to the fact that international law firms and in-house legal departments are currently too small to cope with the risks, as well as the transactions. If the US/Brazil model is followed, then the wealth expansion, coupled with population growth, over the next two decades might result in an increase in the number of global lawyers from the estimated current seven million to 12 to 15 million, give or take a few million.

Countries which are now in the emerging bracket and which therefore tend to have less extensive legal systems than are found in developed countries may or may not adopt the legal policies of the West and enlarge their legal systems in the way that the West has done.

Many emerging countries still have roughly the same traditional business laws—whether common law, Napoleonic or Roman-Germanic—laws which were left by or copied from the imperialists and which they have not trans-formed. It remains to be seen whether they will pause before they accept the advice of foreign legal consultants who press for the expansion of emerging country legal systems in order to 'bring them up to date'.

As to whether legal costs, which are currently very high, will come down or go up will depend on a large number of factors, including the supply of lawyers, the width of their education, and the attitude to risk of the business community which uses legal services.

# Conclusion on the Rise of Lawyers

There is no doubt that there has been a huge increase in the law and hence the number of lawyers and that lawyers play a major role in policymaking.

One class of lawyer, the judiciary, actually makes law and in most countries the judges are the most authentic and senior voice on what the law is. The courts are at the centre of the rule of law. They provide a method of resolving disputes without resort to violence or dangerous self-help in a way which is backed by the coercive powers of the law. They bring order to unruliness which could threaten stability and survival.

As the emerging countries develop, the number of their lawyers is likely to increase. In particular there is likely to be a demand for highly competent lawyers who are internationally minded and who can put the world together. Large transactions, such as takeover of a company with worldwide subsidiaries, involve over a hundred jurisdictions. A large corporation may sell its products in virtually every country in the world and therefore have to comply with local laws.

I examine in the next chapter who in fact rules the world and also who should rule the world.

# 15

# *Who Rules the World: Lawyers or Economists?*

## Introduction

The law has its sects and its cults. It has heretics and fanatics. Some of its priests are of doubtful quality. But on the whole its adherents, namely the entire population of the earth, want the law to work.

Who rules the world—is it lawyers or economists or some other group of policymakers? And more to the point, who should rule the world?

## Economists as Contenders

The chief contenders to the lawyers for who rules the world are probably economists. Economists have not always been kind about lawyers. The following is a comment made about lawyers a few years ago by the distinguished economist Professor Willem Buiter:

> Except for a depressingly small minority among them, lawyers know nothing. They are incapable of logic. They don't know the difference between necessary and sufficient conditions or between type I and type II errors. Indeed, any concept of probability is alien to them. They don't understand the concepts of opportunity cost and trade off. They cannot distinguish between normative and positive statements. They are so focused on winning an argument through technicalities that they no longer would recognise the truth if it bit them in the butt. If you are very lucky, a lawyer will give you nothing but the truth. You will never get the truth, let alone the whole truth. Things have degenerated to the point that lawyers and the legal profession not only routinely undermine justice, but even the law (blogs.ft.com/maverecon/2008/11/ no-change-no-hope-obamas-transition-economic-advisory-board).

This observation is mercifully mild compared with other denunciations of lawyers. Actually I suspect that the professor had in mind a particularly ferocious set of US trial lawyers, in which case I tend to agree with him.

Set out below are two tableaux of world leaders, one in the left-hand panel and one in the right-hand panel.

Tony Blair

Fidel Castro

Maximilien de Robespierre

Bill Clinton

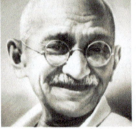

Mahatma Gandhi

Barack Obama

Christine Lagarde

Nicholas Sarkozy

Vladimir Putin

Li Keqiang

Nelson Mandela

Lee Kuan Yew

Silvio Berlusconi

Mao Tse Tung

Wen  Jiabao

George Bush

Angela Merkel

Jacob Zuma

Hugo Chávez

Joseph Stalin

Desmond Tutu

Alan Greenspan

David Cameron

Manmohan Singh

**Left-hand panel**

Tony Blair (1953–) Prime Minister of Britain
Fidel Castro (1927–) Cuban leader
Maximilien de Robespierre (1758–94) French revolutionary leader
Bill Clinton (1946–) President of the United States
Mahatma Gandhi (1869–1948) Indian nationalist leader
Barack Obama (1961–) President of the United States
Christine Lagarde (1956–) Managing Director of the International Monetary Fund
Nicolas Sarkozy (1955–) President of France
Vladimir Putin (1952–) President of Russia
Li Keqiang (1955–) President of the People's Republic of China
Nelson Mandela (1918–2013) President of South Africa
Lee Kuan Yew (1923–2015) Prime Minster of Singapore

**Right-hand panel**

Silvio Berlusconi (1936–) Prime Minister of Italy
Mao Tse Tung (1893–1976) Chairman of the Communist Party of the People's Republic of China
Wen Jiabao (1943–) Premier of the People's Republic of China
George W Bush (1946–) President of the United States
Angela Merkel (1954–) Chancellor of Germany
Jacob Zuma (1942–) President of South Africa
Hugo Chávez (1954–2013) President of Venezuela
Joseph Stalin (1878–1953) Leader of the Union of Soviet Socialist Republics
Desmond Tutu (1931–) South African social rights activist and Anglican bishop
Alan Greenspan (1926–) Chairman of the Federal Reserve Board
David Cameron (1966–) Prime Minister of Britain
Manmohan Singh (1932–) Prime Minister of India

Readers will have quickly appreciated that the leaders in the left-hand panel were all trained as lawyers, while those in the right-hand panel were not, so far as I know.

As to economists, although I have not carried out a quantitative study, it is highly likely that there is a high proportion of economists in senior policymaking posts in ministries of finance and treasuries, in central banks and in multilateral institutions, such as the International Monetary Fund, the Bank for International Settlements and the Organisation for Economic Co-operation and Development. Those policymakers who are not economists have often graduated in politics, where the economics content is large and the legal content basic.

So the issue here is: who is actually making the decisions about our lives and our future on the planet?

It would seem unfair not to mention other candidates for rulers of the world, such as scientists, medical doctors, political scientists, sociologists, accountants, management consultants, and indeed ordinary people who do straight jobs. If I were to choose the best candidates from this list, they would be scientists because they are particularly close to the ideologies and inventions that are needed for survival and are particularly well informed about what needs to be done. Also, we must not omit artists and writers who have from the beginning claimed a sacred insight into the human condition and the truth of all things. The English romantic poet Shelley claimed in *A Defence of Poetry* that 'Poets are the unacknowledged legislators of the world'.

At one time, especially in the 19th century, it was thought that high culture would rescue us from immorality. By culture the promoters of this view meant the great poets, the great artists, the great philosophers. Literature, with its depictions of punishment for the evil and reward for the good, would save us. Thinkers as far apart in time as the 3rd century-philosopher Plotinus and the 19th-century poet Keats explicitly stated that beauty was goodness—'Beauty is truth and truth beauty,—that is all ye know on earth and all ye need to know': *Ode on a Grecian Urn*. But it seems bold to expect literature or painting or music or architecture, however life-enhancing and exhilarating, to import the moral precepts of how to live, even though artists have often proclaimed that they are the guardians of truth. Many artists do not claim to be utilitarian messengers of morality; they prefer to excite the emotions, to enhance enjoyment, to awaken awareness, not to plod through an instruction manual of ethical precepts, nor to produce didactic treatises, or to write parables or allegories of morality, or to write a corporations or bankruptcy law. Nothing wrong with that. Yet in the heyday of the great religions, creative people did not hesitate to use art, music and architecture to preach their message.

There are many other philosophies of life, but most philosophy has retreated into the remote realms of scholarly sophistry. With the exception of a few outstanding contemporary philosophers, the philosophers no longer provide a large view about what we should do. Philosophy lost its way as its territory too was claimed by other intellectual fields—physics, psychology, the law, and cosmology.

You would not nowadays read Aristotle or Plato or Descartes or Kant or Hegel on the meaning of life, just as you would not read Newton on gravity or Faraday on electricity. Too much has happened since then.

Notwithstanding the very compelling claims of other illustrious classes of person who make such a huge contribution to our welfare and happiness, it seems probable that the main people in the driving seat when it comes to ordering everybody around are lawyers and economists.

# Validity of Stereotypes

One initial question must be whether there is something in the way of thinking of these two disciplines—economics and law—that might impinge on the competence and the ability to dictate to the rest of the people of the planet how they should conduct their affairs; for example, what their political institutions should be, what their law should be, the intensity of their punishments, the tax burden that they should bear, what the cost of money should be, and what intrusion the governments of the day should make into our business affairs and our private lives.

We must be careful not to assume that our jobs condition our intellects and emotions, that our work is us. As a common sense matter, the differences in attitudes and in the innermost core of the human consciousness and mind depend much more on the individual and his or her nurture and nature than on what they did at university and what their jobs are.

Further, we cannot properly lump together all economists in one distinct class and all lawyers in another.

Still, it is worth considering whether the disciplines have features that differentiate them and that might play a part, whether large or small, in the approach of their devotees to major areas of policymaking. Are there core competences, are the ways of thinking at the heart of each discipline different? We are comparing ideologies, not individuals.

In particular, it is worth at least mentioning some of the stereotypes, if only to reject them as unfounded prejudices. Some of these apparent habits of mind can be listed as follows.

**Morality** It is often said that economists are primarily interested in function, usefulness, utilitarianism, efficiency and the weighing of costs and benefits in terms of money. By contrast, it may be said that lawyers, by their training, are more inclined to consider morality, justice, individual freedom and the rule of law. Even transaction lawyers who spend their lives arguing the detail of a gas pipeline contract, of syndicated bank credits, of the terms of capital markets debt issues, of sale and purchase agreements for companies, of joint venture agreements or contracts for the sale of a home, are, however trivial the clause, constantly endeavouring to arrive at what is reasonable and fair. At this business level, you could say that the concept of reasonableness, which is a sort of justice, is embedded in their daily routine.

**Language** Economists are masters of metrics and mathematics. They are habituated to expressing their thinking quantitatively in terms of formulae, equations, graphs and models. These figures are considered absolutely and universally true, and even pure and spiritual, at least since Pythagoras. Sceptics say that sometimes the metrics denote crisp boundaries when in the real world there is a continuum or fuzzy spectrum. It is sometimes argued that economists, by virtue of the use of figures, occasionally do not distinguish between causation and correlation; that they promise a prophecy proved by holy mathematics, which, in fact, is as unsafe as all forecasts are, and that models are often too simplistic to reflect the complexity and intricacy of the real world. So their truth, on this theory, is a caricature.

That is a big discussion. Actually, synthesis and distillation are extremely important in any discipline and economists are right to aim at this. So it is not wrong that mathematical models are reductionist, so long as we know that they are.

In any event, lawyers use ordinary language, words and grammar. They have their own jargon and argot, originally no doubt designed as shortcut expressions, but sometimes used to elevate their arcane and esoteric inner knowledge above the rest of the illiterate and barbarian population.

As the philosophers of linguistics have demonstrated, whether Ludwig Wittgenstein or Jacques Derrida, language is slippery, circular, highly qualitative and often does not mean a thing.

Whether or not it does mean a thing is an interesting debate, which we must also leave for the moment, other than to note that in some probably impenetrable way the articulation of thought in either mathematical symbols or in common language may have some impact on the approach to truth.

**Emotion** It is a ritualistic platitude often bandied about that economists are unaware that people have emotions and feelings. They have never heard of sex. It is true that Keynes referred to 'animal spirits' and that Alan Greenspan referred to 'irrational exuberance', but these flashes of profundity among economists are considered rare and hence are greeted by economic cognoscenti as extraordinary words of wisdom. Over recent decades, however, economists have discovered this affective side of the human psyche, giving rise to the specialism of behavioural economics. Some economists have gone on to win Nobel prizes for their work in discovering that human beings have got emotions, which sometimes lead them to do silly things. This new discovery may in time erode the economist's approach that everybody is a rational self-maximiser. On the whole, the stereotype remains that, according to economists, or at least those who support the efficient market hypothesis, we are not stupid, never panic and never do anything out of rage, envy, lust or greed.

Lawyers, on the other hand, have from ancient times been close to emotion. From the earliest eras their codes were concerned with the family, sex, murder, theft and war. Nowadays, the business lawyer daily participates in contractual jousts in negotiating documents or in takeover battles and, when things go wrong, in a formal tournament in a court where all manner of deep emotions and egos are displayed. So they are accustomed to this primitive side of human nature. Their rules, their laws of the game and their tribunals seek to tame the wild urge to kill the competition.

**Detail** A further possible distinction, which may also be an unsubstantiated stereotype, is that lawyers are close to the real detail of life, while economists deal in grand generic movements, in large categories of actors and in soft generalised theories. Lawyers deal at the level of minute, pin-picking detail and a meticulous attention to tiny data, the milli, the micro, the nano. It is for this reason that lawyers are sometimes regarded as plodding pedants, unable to see the big picture and the real truth.

For example, lawyers can easily spend ten years and vast amounts of their clients' money in arguing a single point in litigation, which explores the virtues or evils of the little point from all possible angles, subjects it to crushing stress tests and has it debated via millions of pages of documents, until finally it is pronounced on by the highest tribunal in the land. This mighty tumult on a pinhead is then relegated to a little footnote in a great volume, a law book composed mainly of similar footnotes: something decided, done, the resolution. So truth to the lawyer is arrived at through a prodigious tininess on the basis that the accumulation of all of these minutiae over the centuries results in the grandest of edifices called the law.

This is truth by pragmatic experiment. It is legitimate to say this is a sound way to go about the discovery of truth and is scientific in method and diligence.

And the reality is that it is only by this pin-picking, this multitudinous striving to push the law just another millimetre up the sand dune, only to see it fall back again, that we achieve anything. From that perspective, it does not matter that we individually seem to be doing nothing useful. It is the combined effort which raises the law, just as it is the combined effort which raises science and learning.

## Contribution of Lawyers and Economists

While it is interesting to throw the above factors into the ring, we should perhaps not take them too seriously. We can, however, have a more serious discussion about the overall contribution of the two disciplines to the advance of the human species in its dwelling on this earth, whether long enduring or destined unfortunately to be cut off by some mishap. This mishap may be self-induced or delivered to us by an eyeless and pitiless force of fate.

It is impossible not to have enormous admiration for the achievements of economists in the pursuit of discovering what is really going on. Microeconomics has been brought to great heights of perfection. In the field of macroeconomics, economists have elucidated the role of money and the forces behind money, the factors that underlie economic growth, the features of currencies and balance of payments, and the incidents of unemployment. They initiated the measurement of productivity and they have refined demography and statistics, commencing with the great 17th-century figures of William Petty and Gregory King. In the middle of the last century, they developed the concept of gross domestic product (GDP) and its analogues. Now you can get numbers on practically anything. They have rewritten history and revolutionised our view as to what really happened through the generations and what the great drivers have been. For example, one cannot help express astonishment at the painstaking scholarship of, say, the late Professor Angus Maddison who produced the leading historical statistics on such issues as GDP and population over the past two thousand years.

The real contribution of economists is to introduce an empirical scientific method in order to test theories and to place them under the quantitative spotlight. We all know that both economics and law are not sciences in the sense of physics or chemistry, but statistics, figures, quantities and mathematics are crucial in making sensible advances in our understanding.

There is virtually no area of law that would not benefit from this approach to augment the traditional orientation. We can say that economists have brought light into areas that previously were dark.

When we come to the law, lawyers must accept that much law is essentially a form of restriction on the freedom of human conduct. The rationale of this restrictiveness is broadly that restrictions are necessary for survival, that is, if indeed we are to continue our existence residing on the earth, then we need prescriptive codes of behaviour, which limit our propensity to anarchy and savagery. So the restrictions liberate us.

Companies, banks and capital markets are artificial creatures of the legal imagination, no less fictional than dreams, but still extraordinarily potent and marvellously inventive as engines of economic growth, of technology and enterprise. They were inventions of lawyers, as were the rule of law, constitutions, the criminal law and the rest of the legal edifice. Overall, the lawyer's contribution has been fundamental in promoting the most primitive objective of preserving the species and creating ingenious structures to do it, including in the fields of productive enterprise and business.

It is remarkable to observe that, in their many fruitful debates about the underpinnings of economic growth, some economists have come round to the view that what really matters is 'institutions'. By this they appear to mean not just culture but legal institutions. Economists also vaguely refer to 'contract and property rights' as being crucial in enhancing economic potential. Lawyers have got whole libraries on contract and property rights and regard economists as being still at base camp on these issues. The knowledge of economists about human motivation, morality and the law when they propose policies often comes across as quite crude.

These comments may not be fair, but it is considered fair to say that there is a significant and unjustifiable divide between what lawyers and economists are arguing about in their specialist publications, and how they argue the points, a divide that the law and economics movement still does not bridge. Economists do not know enough about law, and lawyers do not know enough about economics.

## Illustrations of Difference of Approach

There was a discussion above about whether the nature of the job conditions the approach to policy questions and it was observed that the links are probably rather tenuous. Nevertheless another way to approach this question, which is nothing to do with conditioning but everything to do with specialisation, relates to the ability to comprehend the full range of issues and questions that have an impact on a policy choice. Specialisation prevents this.

It is clear that both economics and law have vast content. I suspect that the overall volume of law is much larger than that of economics, especially in the fields of finance, corporate law and regulatory law. These realms are now so massive that you need highly specialised experts to deal with just slivers of each topic. The same may well be true of economics, especially if the discipline is successful in its territorial grabs, for example of psychology, of history, of anthropology. I do not really know how you measure these things.

Nevertheless the specialisation and lack of tuning into the real issues can give rise to dangerous tunnel vision among economics policymakers.

For example, economists typically adduce various economic arguments in favour of the economic and utilitarian benefits of a policy of the low pricing of money. To them, it appears not to be central to the discussion that the manipulation of the price of money is a deprivation of the providers of credit, namely the citizens who have saved up their money which is then intermediated through banks and capital markets. Economists can get away with this because the public out there do not really follow the plot. To a lawyer this coercive deprivation is an obvious rule of law issue about the propriety of arbitrary governmental takings. It is not different in concept from the feudal kleptocrat who takes your land. I am not saying that low-balling interest rates can never be legitimate but that there is a rule of law issue to be counted in the balance.

To some people, this case may seem remote from everyday experience, but it is one of the hidden drivers of everyday life and affects the ordinary lives of the people. It is symbolic. Thus the low pricing of money by central banks was one of the main factors which ignited the financial crisis of 2008. In this case and others like it, it is considered that the control of lawyers is necessary to check the economists' impulse towards efficiency without regard to a much bigger picture. This is what 'institutions' are about.

These issues of morality arise in virtually all areas of our societies, whether it's economic growth or government intervention or inequality or taxation or money supply or currencies or globalisation or regulation. In proposing solutions, there is a huge hole in the thinking of economists, a basic metric missing from the equations so that the solutions are out-of-focus, bloodless. If economists do not have a figure for morality in their metrics, they should now create one.

## Heroes of Economists and Lawyers

Set out below are pictures of some of the heroes of economics, although naturally there are many others whom one could cite with conviction:

Smith

Marx

Ricardo

Keynes

Hayek

Friedman

Those delineated are:

Adam Smith (1723–90)
Karl Marx (1818–83)
David Ricardo (1722–1823)
John Maynard Keynes (1883–1946)
Friedrich Hayek (1899–1992)
Milton Friedman (1912–2006)

A notable feature of these figures is that, in historical terms, they are all quite recent: economics is a relatively new organised discipline compared with law. As a recognised scholarly field, economics is barely 250 years old, but organised law is at least 4000 years old. To put it another way, economics is about three or four lives of 70 years each laid end to end backwards from now, but law is about 56 lives.

Another notable feature is that, apart from the huge advances these economists made in improving our understanding, most of them are ranged in opposition between colliding views of society, with Adam Smith, David Ricardo, Friedrich Hayek and Milton Friedman favouring freedom, but Karl Marx and John Maynard Keynes favouring restriction and governmental intervention. In this discussion they echo a much more ancient theme which has preoccupied lawyers through the centuries—the relative weight to be given to despotism as against liberty.

If you were you ask lawyers who are the great heroes of the law, it is likely that many of them would be hard put to name the names. They do not seem to worship heroes. Instead the law has been built up quietly, methodically by multitudes of lawyers over the centuries, probably the greatest combined effort to create a universal ideology the world has ever seen. But if you think about it, the law has so many heroes that one has to give up counting.

A list of heroes could start with the boldly innovative scribes of the Mesopotamian codes of Urukagina (c 2380 BCE), of Ur-Nammu (c 2100 BCE) and Hammurabi (1732 BCE) and the scribes of the Twelve Tables of the Romans (c 450 BCE). You would include Zoroaster and the following religious leaders, among others:

Moses    Siddhartha Gautama    Jesus Christ    Muhammad

The portraits are of the following:

Moses (active around 1235 BCE) with his slate of Ten Commandments
Siddhartha Gautama or the Buddha (died c 483 BCE)
Jesus Christ (crucified around 30 CE)
Muhammad (died 632 CE) represented by the Kabah at Mecca.

These men were also among the first great lawyers. They formulated principles of moral behaviour, effectively basic rules of law, the foundation of legal systems. The achievement of the religious leaders in prescribing good conduct was massive, although often frustrated by the waywardness of human nature and often not adopted by their followers.

You would include in the list of heroes Confucius and other early Chinese laywers, and the Greek philosophers Socrates, Plato and Aristotle. You would include the Roman senator Cicero, probably one of the greatest orators ever. We would list Gaius of Rome (c 161 CE) whose textbook was one of the foundations of Roman law, Emperor Justinian of the 6th century CE whose team led by Tribonian codified Roman law in around 533 CE, the writers of Magna Carta in 1215 which set out first principles of the supremacy of the law, the medieval philosopher St Thomas Acquinas who introduced reason into theology, and the great medieval commentators Accursus (active 1250) and Bartolus (active 1350), together with the lawyers who first planted the roots of English law. You would include the philosopher John Locke of the 17th century, the towering figure of Grotius, who founded public international law and the great 18th-century English judge Lord Mansfield. You would add the leading draftsman of the French Civil Code Portalis; James Madison, one of the chief composers of the US Constitution; the 19th-century German legal thinker Savigny; the teams of determined and inspired lawyers who drafted codes for Germany, Austria, Switzerland, South American countries, Egypt and elsewhere; US judges of the early-20th century, such as Oliver Wendell Holmes and the eloquent Benjamin Cardozo; and the American lawyers who drafted the Restatements of Law and the Uniform Commercial Code. You would include the lawyers who drafted the modern codes for Russia, China and many other countries in the 20th century, those who wrote human rights codes and seminal leaders who were also lawyers, such as Gandhi. You would include jurisprudential philosophers too numerous to mention. If we brought ourselves up to date by including outstanding lawyers from the second half of the 20th century onwards, we would be spoilt for choice. An extraordinarily impressive list reaching back deep into ancient history, though many are unsung. Some of the above are portrayed on the following page.

| | | | |
|---|---|---|---|
| Hammurabi | Confucius | Socrates | Aristotle |
| Cicero | Justinian | Acquinas | Bartolus |
| Locke | Grotius | Lord Mansfield | Portalis |
| Madison | Savigny | Gandhi | Cardozo |

# Conclusion

In democracies the law is made by legislatures which express the will of the people. The law is not made by either the lawyers or the economists and it would not be right for either to usurp policy decisions which vest in elected governments. Nevertheless economists make a major contribution to policy and it is right that they should.

The focus of economists is on material wellbeing. There can be no material wellbeing, no economic prosperity, no society at all without law. Law is the most necessary, the most authentic and original ideology of our societies. But both economics and law are disciplines crucial for the making of policy and are complementary.

Lawyers have a specific responsibility to promote the wellbeing of the law. This is because they have an elite knowledge of the international legal regime, because they know how the law works in practice, their daily practice equips than to have regard to what is fair, not just what is functionally useful, they apply morality all day whether trivial or grand, they deal with ideology in flight, they are as meticulous and precise as the scientist, they have embraced metrics, the donation of the economists and because, although they may inhabit all the wings of the political spectrum, they are servants of a higher and more noble idea—the rule of law. An ideology as universal and important as the law requires the dedication of its practised devotees to ensure it is fit for its profound purposes, the purposes of survival. Lawyers should lead and set the moral agenda. It is now time for them to produce new heroes and heroines.

By the way, lawyers should not be too concerned if they do not know the difference between a type I and a type II error. It is very simple, once explained. There is nothing to worry about.

In the end, the question is: are we looking the right way about truth? Is it really about probabilities, the difference between necessary and sufficient conditions, or the concepts of opportunity cost and trade-off? The problem is that at our back we always hear some terrible chariot hurrying near, its horses whipped by a blind charioteer who cares nothing for either GDP or the rule of law. Is it the cat? No, it is not the cat. Whether lawyers or economists or anyone else, our record so far in turning full face to the charioteer is not good. But turn we have to. That is why this debate about the law is relevant.

# 16

# *What is Wrong with the Law?*

## Introduction

As with the great religions, there is a lot wrong with the law. The law is formed and shaped by people, with all their failings, their emotions, their selfishness, their rages, their unreason, their ignorance, their prejudices.

Most people complain about the delays and costs involved in the law, especially litigation. They complain of pedantry and obfuscation and incomprehensible documents.

Some laws are quite unbelievably stupid, whole heaps of them. I expect we can all draw up a list of particularly idiotic examples.

Some complain that the criminal law is too protective of the criminal or conversely that criminals are treated too harshly. Others complain that specific areas of law are biased or weighted too far in favour of the poor or the rich, according to your political philosophy. For example, there are complaints that contract law and the law of torts favour big business too much or favour consumers too much, that banking and the law of money favour the well off or that they favour poor debtors, that bankruptcy law favours creditors or it favours debtors, that the law of corporations is too soft on management or else it is too tough on management, that the laws on sex and the family are too liberal or not liberal enough—one could go on. These approaches often hinge upon whether the commentator is left wing or right wing—terms which mean little nowadays.

A particular law will never please everybody. All one can say is that overall the peoples of the world have probably complained less about the law than they have about religion. For example, the law rarely gives rise to atrocities or to ritual killings.

Nevertheless there is much to criticise. I do not set out to write polemics on particular areas of law but rather to select some key generic areas which in my view exhibit general defects in our legal regimes or which are symbolic. The selection is not exhaustive but we have to get on.

The objective of correcting deficiencies in the law is to enhance our opportunities for survival since the moral code is the basis for a peaceful and industrious society.

I discuss six weaknesses in the legal regime:

1. Non-observance of the rule of law.
2. The unfree state.

3.  The heretical cult of abusive litigation.
4.  Excessive size of the law.
5.  Inadequate harmonisation of the law.
6.  Abuse of money and financial oppression.

# Non-Observance of the Rule of Law

In far too many sovereign states the observance of the rule of law is deficient. The rulers are corrupt and despotic, the judiciary accept bribes, there is little due process in the courts, the government expropriates without compensation, arrests are arbitrary and detention without trial is normal, the police are gangsters and personal security is low. In these states any kind of progress is impossible.

At the sovereign level, it is plain that the rule of law is often not observed between states, particularly in relation to unlawful seizures of territory and compliance with the rules of war and other conflicts, such as the treatment of prisoners and non-combatants.

In both these cases, it is not that the law is defective (although sometimes it is)—it is that the basic principles of law are not observed.

# The Unfree State

Many people complain about the bureaucracy, the red tape, the hassle of modern law and regulation.

They have no idea how pervasive has been the intrusion into our societies of the law, how we have become hemmed in, fettered, manacled, by legal control, how creeping the process has been, how the monster of law has crept stealthily through the undergrowth. The law is in part a system of restriction in the interests of survival. But the rationale of survival has been drowned by waves of special pleading as though the legal wand had some magical properties. Even the priests, with their fussy rules about ritual, never approached the triviality of much modern law. The main culprit is regulatory law. We live in regulated states of our own making.

In some countries, the blue sky is blotted out by the bars and chains of regulation. A cowering and frightened populace uses regulation to snap at each other. A frightened government uses regulation to snap at its cowering populace. A frightened government and the cowering populace use regulation to snap at foreigners.

The main reason that excessive law is detrimental to survival is that freedom is crucial for invention, creativity and imagination. It is crucial for enterprise and prosperity. Out-of-date religions are dramatic proof of the claustrophobic effect that the fog of irrelevant rules can have on innovation, the smothering of invention. If the law walks the same old path, then our hopes and aspirations on this planet are brought into question by mistakes we made once and did not need to make again.

The law creates risk. This is because the violation of the law results in some sanction, either a criminal sanction or a civil sanction in the form of damages or some other remedy. But one of the basic objectives of the law is to reduce risk and thereby improve the chances of survival. This collision of objectives is at the heart of the study of legal risk. It is at the heart of the study of the law, whether we should be free or not free. The justification for the restrictions of law is that they liberate us from a worse existence without the restriction.

A situation where the law becomes an enemy, not an ally, is unjustifiable. The law is our servant, not our master.

For anyone trying to set up a new business or to run a business, there are regulations of the utmost detail blocking the way—forms you have to fill in, permissions you have to get, and rules you have to comply with. Everywhere there are regulations about taxation, about health and safety, building regulations, about data protection, about transportation, about employees, about antitrust and competition, about trades and professions, about the environment, about real estate development and zoning, about sanctions and embargoes, about money-laundering, about consumer credit, about food and drugs, about immigration, about corporate governance and listing, about financial reporting and disclosure, about landlord and tenant.

In emerging countries in particular there are regulations about foreign direct investment, about exchange controls, about subsidies and trade restrictions, and about the alien ownership of land. These are largely protectionist measures which are unsympathetic to the idea of a free and open economy.

In advanced societies there are probably about 50 or more regulatory regimes, each with its own big book and each with its own sub-specialities and sub-sub-specialities.

Although regulatory law has historical antecedents, it is almost entirely a 20th-century invention. The concept of extreme state interference through regulation paralleled political philosophies in the early-20th century favouring absolutism. People thought that the state would rescue us from all problems. The conflict between legal freedom and legal despotism has not yet been resolved.

For every restriction there must be a good reason to limit our freedom. The limitation must be matched by a compensating liberation. Most of the regulatory regimes we have are necessary and useful in the core concept. For example, it is necessary in a market economy to have laws ensuring competition between corporations and ensuring that they do not engage in restrictive practices or do not achieve a monopoly position. We have to have building regulations, regulation on pharmaceuticals, on health and safety, on land development and against pollution. But some of the regimes pose rule of law problems for the reasons given below. Some have elements which are disproportionate or nannying or over-prescriptive. Probably the worst regulatory regime is financial regulation—the regulation of banks and other financial firms which seems in some countries to reflect attitudes to money and finance which hark back to the 13th century and medieval fulminations against usury by priests and imams alike.

At the international level, some of the most undesirable sets of regulations are economic and protectionist, especially those designed to shut out foreign direct investment or which impose exchange controls or which grant unwarranted subsidies. Sometimes ordinary areas of regulation, such as transportation or employment, are used to achieve a nationalistic and protectionist object.

**Why regulation is different from the ordinary law** Regulatory law differs from ordinary law (such as contract law or corporations law) for three main reasons:

1. A governmental regulator which is an agent or arm of government is at the same time the legislator in the sense that it makes rules, the executive in the sense that it monitors compliance with the rules, and a judicial tribunal to punish offences. In other words, many regulatory bodies are an affront to basic constitutional notions of the separation of powers and involve a concentration of power in a single governmental body.

2. The law is criminalised in the sense that people can be disqualified from holding office in the case of violations and offending firms can be faced with substantial fines. The offending firm can be ruined or broken up. Notwithstanding the criminal nature of the sanctions, the subjects of the law often do not have the basic protections of the criminal law, for example, the right to silence, proof beyond reasonable doubt, a right to trial by an independent tribunal, not a regulator which is both judge and prosecutor, open justice instead of secret settlements where nobody can tell whether the rule of law was observed or what the law is, proportionate penalty, restraint from threatening behaviour which smacks of extortion, proof of dishonest intent not just negligence or some vague offence of lack of supervision without proof of complicity, and other rule of law principles. Regulation sidesteps due process by re-labelling the enforcement remedies as administrative penalties but criminal they are beyond doubt.

3. The rules are usually extremely detailed, prescriptive, intricate and subject to rapid change. By virtue of the legislative power of many regulators, with or without central government control, they tend to use their rule-making powers to the full, so that many regulatory codes are enormous in size and disproportionate. Regulators have a mania for rule-making, even more prescriptive than Calvin's Geneva.

4. The rules are sometimes extraterritorial so that they apply to everybody everywhere on the basis of some very flimsy contacts with the regulating jurisdiction. Accordingly one state imposes its regulation and criminal penalties on residents of another state whose citizens are not represented in the legislature of the regulating state.

We must have regulation in most of the fields mentioned apart from protectionism. In most countries the regulatory regimes are administered fairly most of the time. But the lesson of the above disadvantages is that regulation should be applied with caution and restraint. Very often it is not. Regulatory authorities should recognise that the rule of law applies to them as much as to governments.

# The Heretical Cult of Abusive Litigation

All religions have their heretics. So does the secular religion of law.

A good example of heresy is vexatious litigation. The commencement of litigation is generally a sign that all else has failed and the costly jousting must commence. The uncertainties of litigation, plus the stress and costs involved, make litigation extremely unattractive for most people. The costs of a major piece of litigation involving corporations can be enormous, in excess of $250 million in some cases. Some lawyers are particularly bad at fomenting litigation. The aim should be to discourage litigation and lawyers should do whatever they can to achieve an out-of-court solution. Nevertheless litigation is ultimately essential and due process needs to be accessible on reasonably equal terms to the entire population.

Litigation is intended to replace the resolution of disputes by warfare, by force of arms and violence. Disagreements are determined by peaceful means before a court and the parties have to abide by the result. The courts are the ultimate deciders, the most crucial institution at the apex of the law. If the court system is abused, this strikes at the heart of the rule of law. That is why I choose this topic. It is symbolic of the law generally and the role the law plays in the integrity of our societies. It is symbolic of the duties under which lawyers have to put the client before their own interest and have to promote the rule of law necessary for our survival.

One of the most striking examples of litigation heresy is the activities of a few of the US lawyers who specialise in acting for plaintiffs—usually small claimants—or rather a minority of these lawyers. These specialist lawyers are called the 'plaintiff bar'.

In many US states, the litigation rules are abusively favourable to plaintiffs. These rules include:

— Huge punitive damages for civil claims. Punishment is for the criminal law, subject to rule of law criminal protections of the accused not the civil law. The civil law sanctions are compensation, not a trebling of compensation. Criminal protections are sidestepped.

— Jury trials for civil trials—some US juries might tend to favour the small against the big so that justice is not equal.

— No award of litigation costs against a losing plaintiff and contingent legal fees dependent on success. Hence a plaintiff can sue without any risk of having to pay the costs of the other side or his or her own costs if the plaintiff loses. Those who are attacked by litigation have to pay their own costs even if they win.

— Class actions. The essence of the class action by a representative claimant is numerosity of claimants and common issues. All members of the class are bound by judgment or court approved settlement, whether they have heard of the action or not. This is good for the lawyers because it increases the size of the cake from which they can take a big cut.

— An apparently unrestrained ability for plaintiffs to make any allegations that they like of fraud and dishonesty against a defendant in the hope that the defendant will be pressured into giving up and settling the case out of court. The effect can sometimes be of abusive defamation and the menacing of defendants prior to trial under the cloak of judicial immunity. The hope of some of these lawyers seems to be that, if they make sufficiently abusive allegations, however unfounded, which are lavishly reported in the media, they will be able to extort a settlement out of a firm just in order to get rid of the costs and harassment of litigation.

— An exorbitantly wide disclosure of documents worldwide, so that a plaintiff can conduct a fishing expedition to see if there is anything which looks bad and which might influence a jury, such as a silly email by an employee. Excessive disclosure can involve millions of documents, huge costs and time, and amount to disproportionate pressure under judicial authority.

In the United States the combination of the plaintiff-orientated litigation rules leads to settlements favourable mainly to the lawyers—typically 33 per cent of the award, a few million—while each claimant receives only a tiny amount.

The United States is not the only country to have a litigation system which is abused.

The aim was to bring the court to the people but the system was then manipulated to enrich lawyers. It is contrary to the rule of law and it is oppressive for plaintiffs to be able to make abusive and unsubstantiated allegations of criminality to threaten a defendant. It would be perfectly possible to adapt the system so that it still protects the weak and the poor.

The cost to society of these activities includes an increase in insurance premiums paid by the general population, absurd and expensive contortions by the people generally and their companies to exclude liability, and an atmosphere of fear.

The conduct of those who habitually overreach in litigation is rendered even more egregious when they claim that they are doing this in the cause of morality, justice and the small litigant. Lawyers are guardians of the legal order.

Even the luxurious medieval clergy did not take as big a cut as those more aggressive members of the plaintiff bar do under the banner of morality and charity. They bring the magnificent US legal system and lawyers worldwide into disrepute. As Geoffrey Chaucer remarked in the 14th century, 'If gold rusts, what will iron do?'

The lawyers concerned are not doing anything unlawful or improper under their bar rules. They are doing their best for their clients. Yet, they taint the legal profession. If lawyers are to lead on the ethical rules for society, they can't behave like this.

The result is the same whenever people use the law to abuse the law—when they use the law unjustly to threaten others or frighten them or torment them or to shut them up.

# Excessive Size of the Law

The excessive volume of the law is a major defect. The volume of law is now out of control internationally and is unmanageable. The reasons include globalisation which puts all jurisdictions in touch with each other, the massive increase in the intensity and the amount of regulation, and the volatility of the law.

There are grounds for believing that the situation could get worse, much worse. Those who propose laws are evidently not good at simple arithmetic and are not knowledgeable about how to count.

Few people probably realise how dramatic the growth in size and complexity of the law has been if we stand back with a big historical view. This disproportionate increase in size and complexity of the legal regime makes the law inaccessible and therefore directly offends the rule of law. Naturally in every complex field, people have to consult advisers. But if the law is even beyond their capacity, then the rule of law is threatened.

**A metric for measuring the size of law** One possible metric which could be used for measuring the size of a legal regime is how many pages of concentrated law a single individual could actually learn in one year.

This metric is what I call a 'uni-year' which is based on the amount which in my experience a student taking four courses at postgraduate level, typically an LLM, would learn in a year for the examinations at the end of the year in the four subjects. I base my measures on the amount of notes which I gave to students in courses I taught.

As a rough estimate and rule of thumb, I calculated that the most fanatical student, a student who never went out, who never went to the bar, who never said hello, who hardly ever left his or her room and who worked all the time, would learn 1000 pages of concentrated notes for the examination. By 1000 pages, I mean not the pages which the student would actually read for the exam—which would be much more in terms of articles in law journals, judicial cases, textbooks and the like—but the amount of concentrated learning notes necessary to achieve a top mark in an examination at first class standard.

The upper limit was 1000 pages of notes—about 250 pages of concentrated notes for each topic. In practice most students actually learnt very much less than this, probably less than 100 pages of synthesised swotting notes in some cases.

If we apply this metric of a uni-year—the amount a very diligent individual could learn in one year of work—we can apply this to the size and dimensions of a particular statute or area of law in concentrated form.

For example the Dodd–Frank Act of 2010 of the United States, which reformed financial and related regulation as a result of the financial crisis of 2008, runs to about 1000 pages. However as the statute is only an enabling statute to be implemented by regulations, one has to count the volume of the regulations themselves. It has been estimated that these are likely to run from somewhere between 20,000 and 50,000 pages including commentary and explanation. If, just for the sake of the argument, we say that the total amount of US financial regulation, including the Dodd–Frank Act and all the legislation previously passed, amounts to 100,000 pages, then it follows that this would be 100 uni-years. In other words it would take a particularly dedicated individual 100 years—a century—to learn the financial regulatory regime in the United States. Whether it is a century or just ten years, it is over the top.

And this is only one country and one segment of one area of law—a sliver of a particle of a morsel.

In the case of Dodd-Frank, people were indignant about what happened. So they got round a table and, full of rage, shouted out their demands for vengeance, this clause, that clause. The statute book expresses the rationality of the people, their civilisation. The statute book is not the place to rant and rave. The statute book is a holy thing, a sacred place.

This is one reason that the amount of law is disproportionate and that the resulting inaccessibility and incomprehensibility of the law in itself creates legal risks. There is no point in having a law if the people who are subject to the law do not know what it is; and if they cannot conceivably learn it except by a century of effort.

**Soft law** In addition, soft or private laws and rules are everywhere, not just the public laws imposed by governments and courts.

These are the innumerable official codes of conduct which are dreamed up by official associations of regulators, such as codes of corporate governance, codes of good environmental practice, and codes of conduct by journalists and the media. These generally are codes allowing self-regulation on the basis that if soft law doesn't work, then the legislator will have to resort to hard law.

Often this is a sensible compromise and so has resulted in a vast number of rules which are not legally binding but which those addressed are expected to adhere to—Standards of Best Practice. The worst of these are minatory rules written by a person who in a former life would have stood a good chance of promotion in the Inquisition.

Apart from black letter public laws and fuzzy-edged soft laws, there are gargantuan private codes instituted by businesses. Effectively these are contracts. For example, every business above a modest size has a tome prescribing the conduct of employees in minute detail, often running to hundreds of pages.

# Inadequate Harmonisation of Law

In the case of the great religions, there is little prospect of harmonisation or agreement on basic doctrine. They have grown far apart, not in their view of the supernatural or their views about the moral rules of conduct, but in their rituals and their prejudices. There is much commonality but little commonality. Thus in the case of Judaism, Christianity and Islam, they all agree that they are worshipping the same God but after that, they agree on practically nothing. Religions are in the main characterised by sectarianism.

What then is the situation with regard to the law?

One recalls Voltaire's famous quip about pre-Revolutionary France—'When you travel in this kingdom you change legal systems as fast as you change horses'.

It is obvious that there is no common view on the law applying to sex and the family—divorce, adultery, gay rights, abortion and the like—or on inheritance, and there is much discrepancy on such matters as alcohol and drugs.

When it comes to business law, one would expect that as the law becomes larger and more complicated, there would be an attempt to harmonise the law across so many jurisdictions so as to reduce not just costs, but also legal risk, especially in the case of corporate and financial law. The evidence so far shows that this is not happening to a sufficient degree in crucial areas of the law. Rather there is a splintering or fragmentation of the law, like a stone hitting a car windscreen.

This is partly because the law is driven by national legislatures and the desire to protect the local society.

The advantages of harmonisation include the avoidance of legal ambush and surprise leading to a potentially expensive legal risk, the reduction of investigation and transaction costs, and efficiency. Many differences between legal systems are historical, not cultural, ie, they do not reflect differences in the current and national mood or the state of the industrialisation.

Disadvantages of harmonisation include: competition is a spur of our legal systems, leading hopefully to a race to the top to the best models; the jurisdiction has local democratic controls and accountability; there is more freedom to adapt the law and the process is nimbler; and the legal system can reflect the structure of the economy, for example, depth of banking system size and ingenuity of the financial sector, the role of business corporations and the size of equity markets. A jurisdiction may have resources which are far too meagre to develop the legal infrastructure and may have other priorities, for example, getting enough food to stay alive.

The splits in commercial law resulted from the historical triple polarisation of the law in and before the 19th century flowing from the spread of the common law, Napoleonic and Roman-Germanic groups. It also resulted from increasing splits flowing from patchy reactions to the demands of credit economies and the impulse of debtor and creditor politics. In addition, the diversity is driven by national law-making sovereignty. There is internal tiering, as different political views come into conflict, for example, as to whether to protect sophisticated investors or consumers, but leaving a broken middle.

Whether the law needs to reflect cultural differences is highly debatable. Many of these national or ethnic differences seem to be a means of creating identity and are not based on factual differences between human needs. The desire for tailoring is nationalistic and not rational. The fact that most fields of law, outside family and inheritance, do not have to be adapted to local culture is shown dramatically by the voluntary copying from the 19th century onwards of the laws of other countries.

Where market participants are free to choose, they often choose only one or two solutions.

For example, both English and New York law have a dominant position as the governing law of major contracts such as syndicated loan agreements, capital markets bond issues and derivative contracts. These two legal systems have a near monopoly and are effectively like a public utility for the international community, even though they differ somewhat in their detailed attitudes.

As to corporate law, it is thought that about 70 per cent of US listed corporations are formed in Delaware. The US Depository Trust Corporation is the settlement system for virtually all listed equity shares in the United States, among other things. The bank payment messaging system S.W.I.F.T., based in Belgium, is used by virtually all international banks for their payment messages.

The Uniform Customs and Practices for Documentary Credits virtually also has a worldwide monopoly in the field of trade letters of credit whereby effectively banks guarantee that the seller will be paid when the buyer ships the goods to the seller. The UCP is incorporated in nearly all trade letters of credit.

All of these are instances of monopolies chosen by the markets concerned because of the efficiency and fairness of the service. Markets have the freedom to vote with their feet but are not inclined to do so, so long as the service continues to perform.

However in many critical areas of law which lead to legal risk, this freedom to choose is not available, for example, bankruptcy and regulation. In both fields the rules are mandatory and, apart from minor exceptions, you cannot choose your legal regime in the same way that you can choose the governing law of a contract.

Lawyers have a long way to go in standardising documents so as to reduce costs and time. The technology has been there for more than a decade.

## Abuse of Money and Financial Oppression

The hierarchy of legal needs shown in chapter 9 demonstrates that money, banks and corporations feature early on in the ladder or hierarchy of legal needs, only just above basic criminal and constitutional laws protecting the rule of law and protecting the individual from arbitrary and despotic government.

The rule of law is functional justice and is necessary for survival. Morality is not some academic waffle but fundamentally satisfies the desire for just utility. The rule of law and justice are necessities, and not a sentimental ideal unrelated to the pragmatic real world. If wealth increases, if the world becomes even more financialised, the application of the rule of law to money becomes even more important. Money is of enormous importance in people's lives. It is the product of our work. It is a medium of exchange. It connects us to our future. It connects us to other people in other lands so that we can trade with them.

**Inflation** The most common example of financial oppression in relation to money which leads to an injustice is the inflation of money. Inflation has been a favourite tool of despotic governments or of negligent governments from historical times, way before the Romans, and back to the Greeks. Inflation is now much easier because in virtually all countries there is no longer any link between money and some asset such as gold. The link with gold was weakened by the 1930s and was abandoned altogether in the early 1970s when the United States abandoned the right of holders of the US dollar to convert into gold at a fixed price.

John Kenneth Galbraith observed that it was repellent (or some word to that effect) how easy it is to create money. Nowadays central banks do not even have to print it. They can just buy government bonds from banks and pay the price by simply sending an email to the banks advising them that the central bank owes those banks several hundred billion or any figure the central bank cares to name. These banks can then lend out the money and it multiplies.

In very simplistic terms and ignoring multiplier effects, if the central bank and the banking system double the amount of money available, then it will be worth half as much. One of the effects is that debtors only have to pay half as much and creditors only receive half what they are owed. There is therefore a massive redistribution from creditors to debtors and the taking away of the money of creditors, pensioners and savers simply by virtue of the fiat of the central bank.

In most countries, inflation is now recognised as being a corruption and a threat to the rule of law because it functions like an expropriation without compensation. All of the main central banks in charge of the main currencies in the world are subject to an express or implicit duty to control inflation. They can usually do this by virtue of their power to reduce the supply of money and by virtue of other powers, for example, to fix interest rates, or at least short-term interest rates.

**Pricing of money** Central banks also have the power to manipulate the price of money, in other words the interest rates which people pay to borrow money.

They can do this by virtue of their power to create money and to lend it at whatever low price they like to banks with the result that banks can borrow money from the central bank very cheaply, if the central bank so chooses, and the banks can then lend it on at these cheaper rates plus a marginal spread to reflect the risk of the ultimate borrower and to give the banks a profit for their work.

This power to price money is most potent in relation to short-term deposits and borrowing. It is harder for the central bank to do this for longer-term loans, such as medium-term bonds of, say, seven to ten years. Nevertheless it is still possible for central banks to manipulate long-term rates.

The pricing of money at a very low interest rate, or at a negative interest rate after tax and inflation, has a similar effect to inflation. The money which central banks is pricing does not belong to the central banks, even though they create it. The money belongs to depositors with banks, savers. It is their money that is being priced high or low.

The fact that this power to price money can lead to very substantial and unjust losses, so that the rule of law is engaged, is shown by the course of the financial crisis commencing in 2008. Many mainstream economists agree that the 2008 financial crisis was ignited by central bank policy, especially in the United States, in reducing short-term interest rates virtually to zero or negative after tax and inflation from 2001. In other words, the Fed gave money away. It was nice to be able to do this because it meant that homeowners could buy their houses for nothing, that business could borrow money for nothing and therefore compete with Europe, Japan and the emerging countries, and that the United States did not have to pay China for its national debt.

The result of this policy was that the Fed ignited an asset price bubble in the housing sector, which was then fanned by irresponsible lending by banks and irresponsible borrowing by homeowners.

It was as if the central bank forcibly took your car away and sold it at half price. The low pricing of money, that is, the money of the people, was a forcible redistribution and in particular a redistribution otherwise than through the tax system, a redistribution which was opaque to the general public. You can of course justify redistribution. But this ethical question never seriously entered the policy debate. Robin Hood was a very attractive fellow, but he was also a mugger. The result was a catastrophe. This is why the morality of money is functional, why it is about survival.

**Exchange controls** Exchange controls are regulations which typically prohibit residents of a country from holding foreign currency or foreign currency securities, or from paying in foreign currency or borrowing in a foreign currency. Residents must surrender all foreign currency proceeds to the central bank in return for the local currency at a prescribed rate of exchange.

The object is to give the central bank a monopoly of foreign currency and therefore to be able to ration it, control the supply of money, and to control the exchange rate between the local currency and foreign currency.

There are situations where a case can be made for the imposition of exchange controls which are still very common in emerging countries. Such a case might be where the state is insolvent or where there is a run on banks so the exchange control is in effect a bankruptcy moratorium. Exchange controls were ubiquitous in both developed and emerging countries until the 1980s.

Nevertheless exchange controls are a significant intrusion on freedom. If you cannot move your money, you cannot move. You are a slave to the land. If you cannot pay for foreign things without some permission, then this impacts on freedom of trade. Exchange controls strike at the heart of freedom of movement, freedom of trade, freedom of business and freedom of capital.

**Taxation** Taxation is necessary to pay for shared services provided by governments, for example, education, law and order, defence. Much of the tax is now compulsory charity, largely replacing religious tithes and alms giving. It is for the electorate to decide whether taxation should also be an instrument of redistribution from the rich to the poor and the extent of the equalisation. This equalisation is almost always national—the local population does not seek to redistribute to the most poverty stricken peoples elsewhere. Charity is local.

In the late 1970s a British government levied a tax on income at 98 per cent–83 per cent on earned income and another 15 per cent on unearned income, such as interest on a savings deposit at a bank.

Taxation is a coercive taking which we have to have. It becomes oppressive when a small minority bears most of the burden. One of the most persistent complaints of historical rule of law reformers—from Magna Carta to the French Revolution—has been oppressiveness of taxation or its inequality, such as exempting the nobility or the clergy from paying any tax at all. If 1 per cent of the population pay, say, 30 per cent of income tax or 30 per cent of the people pay no income tax at all, then, in the absence of some legitimate justification, the taxation is presumptively oppressive. Quite a few countries have been or are well over these thresholds.

**Financial products** I have already shown that there is likely to be a rapid increase in world GDP, hence a huge increase in the amount of money and near-money in circulation and hence an increasingly fianancialised world. People will hold more of their assets in financial assets, such as bank deposits, bonds and shares. The law should treat these assets as favourably as other assets, such as land or goods. In framing regulatory systems, the right solution for our law is not to go back and repeat the ancient prejudices against interest, insurance and securities exchanges when those institutions first appeared three centuries ago; a return to some distant antique world which no longer exists. The law should not exclude reasonable financial products. The money of the people is their money, the product of their work and effort.

# Conclusion

Lawyers have high fiduciary duties to clients to act solely in their interests with diligence and dedication and to avoid prejudicial conflicts of interest. They also have a general duty to the future to contribute to the making of the fabric of the law in a way which promotes the rule of law and hence survival. This means all lawyers—those on the bench, those in practice, those in universities. They should pay particular attention to why the priests were forced out of influence over the making and administration of the law by the secular authorities.

It may be that our societies will decide that they can do without religion, as many have already done. It is not conceivable that societies can do without law but they can certainly live with bad law—for a time.

Lawyers must explain how morality suffuses all law, from the family to capital markets. They must describe the ethical choices robustly, the choices which count for us. They can no longer cast themselves just as the ministrants of law. Lawyers must be moral leaders.

# 17

# *Scientific Progress and the Law*

## Introduction

Science is necessary to protect us from an apocalypse, to unlock the mysteries of the universe, to unleash our own potential and thereby increase our chances of survival. Without science, without developing our mastery, we are helpless and exposed to whatever fate the universe has in mind for us. Science is a saviour and law is the guardian of science.

The law has been particularly alive to the need to promote science so that on the one hand the law fosters science and on the other hand it regulates science so as to protect us from its dangers. A great many legal regimes are involved, ranging from the control of weaponry, such as nuclear proliferation, through to the regulation of pharmaceuticals and genetics. I do not propose to discuss any of these in detail since this is not a book about the intricacies of the law—this would require many weighty volumes. Virtually every area is extremely controversial and the law is in the eye of the storm.

As Professor Brian Cox points out in his excellent book *Human Universe* (William Collins, 2014), there are (to paraphrase him) many things where you think you are absolutely right and virtually everyone else is a complete idiot. Stem-cell research? Cloning? Genetic manipulation? Climate change? Drones? Robots? Capitalism? Banks? Free markets? He is quite right when he says we have to accept that there are many opinions, but only one human civilisation.

We should stand back and assess what our overall approach should be in the light of history and with regard to the future. We need to take a big view, above the hubbub of contemporary debate.

It would be too sweeping a statement to say that religions now are a serious brake on all scientific progress. In practice the religious have participated more in topics which they regard as affecting the sanctity of life and the family—the 'culture war' topics—while the secular authorities are the driving force in relation to practically everything else.

Much of the general approach which I outline here also applies to financialisation, that is, the very large increase in financial assets held by people in the form of bank deposits, shares and bonds, directly or via their pension funds or other savings. The religious reaction to financialisation has on the whole been unsympathetic but that also is too sweeping.

# The Progress of Progress

Economic historians trace economic history in terms of progress from a pastoral and agricultural economy, through to a manufacturing and industrial economy, through to a services economy. In the modern world in most developed economies, agriculture involves only around 2 per cent of GDP, and manufacturing 25 per cent. The rest is services, such as construction, insurance, banking and retail.

A major cause of the increase in GDP is the advance in science and technology. The attitude which we should adopt to the advance of science and to financialisation can be illustrated by another allegory, again based on a famous painting. This is Botticelli's *The Birth of Venus* painted in 1486 displayed here. It hangs in the Uffizi in Florence.

*The Birth of Venus*

This is one of Botticelli's greatest paintings. He did not try to say too much in the picture and it therefore says a lot.

Like *The Raft of the Medusa*, the main figure is also on the sea and on some sort of raft. In this case the raft is a seashell. Quite a miraculous and magic seashell actually, considering the quite substantial lady it has to carry through the waves. Botticelli was depicting magic, a beautiful illusion.

Botticelli's Venus is a symbol of the purity of some utopian past, a Garden of Eden, a world of simple pleasures, a world of sweetness and light, long before the dull plod of mechanised agriculture, the smoke of industrial factories, long before the fantastic growth of intangible assets in the form of money and banks, companies and securities. This antique world is the world we yearn for.

Yet the past depicted in the picture by Botticelli was a dream, an illusion. It never existed. In fact, in the real past, before our centuries, everywhere in the world life was dirty, dark, diseased and dangerous.

# Life as it once was

Let us contemplate what life was really like for ordinary people four hundred years ago, five hundred years ago, at some point in time before the acceleration of human development from about 1750 in the West and later in many other countries.

Homes were squalid hovels without running water or sanitation. People lived on the mud and hardly ever washed. They stank. Their bodies stank, their clothes stank, the streets stank from sewage. There was no electricity, no light in the dark except guttering tallow lamps, no heating except a sputtering fire emitting fumes and smoke into the hovel. Mothers and children regularly died in childbirth from the filth and contamination. Half your children were taken from you by disease or dirt before they were five. If you contracted cholera or dysentery or smallpox or tuberculosis, that was it. Henry V of England died from dysentery at aged 35. John Keats, a 19th-century romantic poet, died from tuberculosis at the age of 26 in a house at the foot of the Spanish steps in Rome, the loss of an extraordinary genius. The average life expectancy in the world in around 1800 was 28.5 years. In 2001 it was 66.6 years.

If you were sick or wounded, there were no anaesthetics, no antibiotics, and no effective medicine at all. It was only in the 19th century that medicine advanced beyond the most primitive quack guesswork. The job of doctors was to try to make you comfortable while you died. You lay there, panting, fetid and terrified. You knew you had no chance.

Most people were illiterate; they could not read or write, there were no books, no education. If you wanted to travel, there were no planes or trains or cars. You walked or went by cart over roads which were no more than rutted tracks. Any kind of distance travel was impracticable. You were trapped where you were, you were enslaved to your patch of land, you were a feudal serf with no fresh horizons.

If you wanted to talk to someone, there was no post and certainly no phone, let alone a mobile phone, no email. The food you ate was basic, even if you had any. You ate what you grew and, if nothing grew that year because of the weather or plant disease, you starved. You could not pop down to the supermarket and get what you wanted from anywhere in the world you want. Societies were rough and violent. There was no police force and whatever government there might be was likely to be savage and brutal, brigands and predators. The world was full of terrifying demons and evil spirits. Life was grisly, grim and gloomy.

Life is still like this for many people in the world—the bottom billion.

Science and technology have provided an exit from this dismal existence. Money, finance, banks, corporations, and credit involving the sharing of savings have also been a major contributor towards enabling many people to escape the old dark life.

Of course there are some very adverse aspects of modern living. But we cannot and should not insist that people stop migrating to cities or that they stop intellectual enquiry or close down inventions or that they cease to search for prosperity for themselves.

# Fear of Progress

The resistance to progress in the form of science and technology is persistent and indelible among large sections of the population. Science produces fear in many people, a fear of the unknown captured by Mary Shelley's *Frankenstein* in the 19th century. The discovery of atomic structure in the early years of the 20th century by Rutherford and others led to rapid advances in technology and energy capture but it also led to the Manhattan Project in a Chicago squash court and at Los Alamos and to the atomic bomb. Science produces in some people not exhilaration, but a dread, a terror that, if nature is tampered with, the result is a monster.

Science and technology have produced some horrific episodes—the toxicity of DDT spraying, the deformities produced by thalidomide, the industrial accidents—Seveso, Bhopal, Chernobyl. Yet these disasters are an infinitesimal proportion of the medicines produced, the industrial factories in operation, the power stations producing electricity, absolutely tiny. The law governing medicines, factories, power stations and the like is the main instrument of protection against hazard and there is no doubt that it has worked reasonably well in these fields.

# Resistance to Progress in History

History is replete with examples of whole societies turning away from invention and enquiry, shutting themselves away in isolationist exclusion. I can only mention a few epic examples.

In China the isolationist policy of the Ming Dynasty (1348–1644) began in the 1400s with the abrupt termination of the foreign voyages of discovery of Admiral Zheng He and the exclusion of all foreigners and foreign inventions, no doubt mainly to protect the central government but also a rejection of the new and therefore the dangerous. Earlier, the new Ming Emperor Hongwu made it a criminal offence to travel 35 miles beyond your home without permission. He thought that commerce and coinage would be corrosive and damage stable relationships and so he passed laws restricting trade with foreigners and prohibited foreign perfumes. His successors banned silver coins because they thought it would make unnecessary commerce too easy. They were preserving the agricultural world against the unsettling forces of a modern economy which had money, trade and science.

The Chinese did exactly the opposite of what was then happening in Europe where the voyages of discovery and the Renaissance were transforming the continent and where the Europeans embraced the new discoveries, the opportunities for trade, the new resplendent art and architecture, with enthusiasm. At the end of the Opium War in the mid-19th century the British iron ship *Nemesis* sailed to Guangzhou and blasted the opposition to pieces. Despite the obvious threat, the Chinese after that incident were unable to meet the challenge for another 150 years.

From the 1630s Japan adopted a 'closed country' policy for two hundred years until a naval squadron appeared in Edo Harbour unopposed under the US Commander Matthew Perry. The US and European powers subsequently imposed one-sided trading treaties which ended the seclusion policy. That in turn led to the Meiji restoration of 1868 and the rapid industrialisation of Japan.

These episodes were not just inspired by a xenophobic dislike of foreigners. They were also motivated by a fear of progress.

The most horrific expressions of the fear of progress were the Cultural Revolution in China starting in 1966 and the activities of the Pol Pot regime in Cambodia in the 1970s. In both cases teachers, professionals, everybody to do with learning, were forced out into the countryside to rejoin the peasants. In China Mao and his wife unleashed the young Red Guards on these educated deviants with enormous loss of life and innumerable atrocities as these youthful Chinese were incited to express their fury and rage at authority. In Cambodia one and half million people out of a total population of eight million died as a result of the terror tactics of the Pol Pot regime. They were martyrs to reason. The victims were made to understand that the way of the peasant, not the way of the bourgeois scholar, was the true path of socialism.

The West was mercifully free of atrocities of this kind. Yet the West has long had militant movements which protest against the progress of science and against financialisation, work and profit. These movements often express the fears of much larger sections of the population.

In the history of anti-science and technology, one can go back further to the abuse heaped on Galileo and the mockery and derision which greeted Edward Jenner's announcement of a smallpox vaccine in 1798. In a cartoon at the time an inoculated woman is portrayed as simultaneously vomiting and giving birth to cows. People protested against vaccination right through the 19th century, notwithstanding proof of the effectiveness of the vaccine against this terrible scourge.

One recalls the smashing of machinery by the Luddites in the early-19th century. The counter-enlightenment of the English Romantic poets seeking a pastoral purity in the face of the factories, notably William Wordsworth and William Blake, was mild and charming by comparison. In the 1970s and before in the West there arose an academic deconstructionist movement which sought in impenetrable texts to deconstruct everything the Enlightenment stood for. The anti-science protests now come from both the left wing and the right wing. The proponents can be religious or secular. Fundamental Christians and fundamental Muslims often find themselves on the same side. People sometimes seem to base their views on imaginative and stirring movies, admittedly good fiction but not good fact. At its worst, you see in the face of the fanatic a glazed and strident hatred not just of the scientific achievements of humans but of all things human, a mindless motiveless malignity.

The lesson of history is that it is possible to tip whole nations into a violent fearfulness and rejection of the future. The fears might then be expressed in the legal system and hence often have significant adverse implications for our prospects of survival.

**Future directions of science** The question for us is whether we can escape our limitations and see the reality of things. What inventions are we waiting for, what questions need a solution? The answers usually given are in the fields of cosmology, genetics, climate change, nanotechnology, robotics, artificial intelligence via computers, and the mastering of disease, including the common cold. Notwithstanding the advances which have already been made, we are a long, long way from understanding everything, not just ourselves and our consciousness, but also what the universe is, what is behind the universe, what came before the universe.

Some of the questions include whether the search for a grand theory of everything, a single equation, a single force, which explains everything and which combines the four forces of nature, including gravity, will be successful. They include whether we can discover the essence of gravity.

We still have not established the nature of the universe, what lies beyond it and what preceded it, nor have we discovered whether we can make a fuel which will eradicate our need to rely on oil and gas, coal and nuclear power stations, and whether we can safely and fairly manipulate our DNA so as to make humans generally who are immune from disease, who are super-intelligent, super-moral and can live much longer than our restricted span.

Nor have we remotely ascertained whether we can conquer time so we can project ourselves to the furthest reaches of the universe; whether we can unlock the secret nature of time and its function as a dimension.

We have not solved the mystery of whether there is other life elsewhere in the universe. Scientists have estimated that there are between one billion and thirty billion planets in our galaxy and about a hundred billion galaxies in the universe. So there could be more than a billion planets in the universe. Nevertheless for various reasons the start of life on any of these planets by the spontaneous creation of something similar to our DNA appears to be an exceedingly improbable event. Still, we know that it has happened at least once. It has happened here on earth.

Even if there were intelligent life out there on some other planet in another galaxy, it would take millennia for their light signals to reach us. By that time the aliens could have perished. In addition the time gap in which we developed equipment which could receive a signal has been extremely short—less than a century and so the chances of a signal being sent millions of years ago to arrive at exactly the right time here on planet earth are vanishingly small. Any life out there could be just an oozing slime.

And finally, there is the issue of whether we can protect ourselves against some shocking hazard thrown at us by the universe, we know not when or what.

We have a duty to survive long enough to answer questions like these. At the same time, we need our legal systems to ensure that science is liberated where it should be liberated and controlled where it should be controlled.

## Conclusion on Progress

We should enhance our chances of survival by scientific progress, without endangering our chances of survival. Our laws about science play a major role and must strive to attain this balance. We should not in our laws retreat from the future. The law should guarantee science. We have a duty to the future, born of our marvellous ingenuity, our intelligence, our yearning. In that way we aspire to the ideals of Lady Liberty with the flags and the ideals of the Statue of Liberty in New York Harbour. We might then avoid the terrible raft of the Medusa. We might even perhaps achieve Botticelli's vision, the meaning of the allegory of his picture.

# 18

# *A Way of Living*

## Introduction

In this penultimate chapter, there is just one other topic which I ought to cover before I conclude. I introduce this topic for a number of reasons.

The first is that the law generally stops short of intruding on our private moral conduct and our private thoughts. It is right for the reasons that I have given that it should not encroach on our privacy. The law has no business to encourage the thought police or to impose punishments or compensation for minor infractions of politeness or lack of kindness. It would be impractical for the law to require that everybody must be kind to each other. There is therefore a gap between the rule of law and the rule of private virtue.

The second is that if the sanctions of religion no longer have influence on people's private moral conduct, then we have a vacuum unfilled by the sanctions of either law or religion. If people cease to believe in their religions, this is one of the losses they potentially incur. The moulding of conduct is left to social pressures, the desire for reciprocity, our innate sense of fairness and the like.

The third is that there are some areas of desirable conduct which are not covered by either law or religions. For example, neither the law nor religions, generally speaking, require us to be courageous or to work hard.

The fourth is that we only have one life and that life should be as happy and as fulfilling as possible. Neither the law nor the religions (in the main) enjoin happiness as an objective, although to be sure they both aim to create the conditions for happiness.

It follows therefore that there is room for advance beyond the law and beyond religion if we are aiming at the ideal state. There is no question that the law as an instrument to govern our conduct is sufficient for survival if properly framed and administered and that properly framed and administered legal systems would substantially fill the necessary gaps if religions ceased to be a force at all. So what we still have to discuss is what areas remain to be covered if we were being perfectionists about codes to support our existence.

The objectives of a code for a modern way of life is to enable us to survive to perform our moral duties to future generations and to unravel the mysteries which cloud our understanding and at the same time to ensure that people have a good life. The ideal would be to have a happy life which is also fruitful in enhancing the prospects of survival of everyone else now and in the future, that is, a life which combines happiness and contribution, self-pleasure and altruism.

The law provides a framework for our societies in which the twin objectives can be realised. The law establishes the necessary conditions for personal security, freedom from want, prosperity and the upholding of the rule of law which are the fundamental requirements for happiness and invention and for survival. But the law does not provide all the solutions.

The threats to survival which give people nightmares include those we have debated for a long time. Examples are pandemics spreading some terrible plagues to the entire human race, out-of-control climate change incinerating the planet, world wars of horrific destructiveness, dirty bombs, the poisoning of our water or other vicious attacks which freeze us with fear and send us into cowering huddles. Other examples are meteorites smashing into the globe and leading to universal darkness and ice (the asteroid which struck Mexico around 66 million years ago and destroyed nearly all the dinosaurs was probably about 9.5 kilometres in diameter and had the violence of about eight *billion* Hiroshima nuclear bombs), and robots running out of control. Yet others are the lunatic use of nuclear weapons by rogue states sparking a series of obliterating exchanges as thousands of rockets leer out of their silos, the threat of wild terrorists rampaging around the world, or even the collapse of all morality and government.

Some of these are precipitated by ourselves and have to be controlled by our private and collective morality; others are external threats and have to be addressed by our science. Whatever we may think of the relative likelihood of these apocalyptic terrors, the next 50 years could be the most important in the history of the world so far.

Even more terrible still would be the collapse of ourselves into a stupid stupor without energy by reason of some tragedy in us or outside us or created by us. We just die out, remorselessly, inevitably, just vanish, extinct, gone—with nobody anywhere, not in the whole universe, to remember us or discover us, not even our desperate whispers and cries for help, our bodies and minds returned to blind particles of nothing, before we could do anything to save ourselves, everything just meaningless, futile, a void.

I set out below seven propositions which might form the basis of a larger code for a personal way of living. The first two—the weightiest and most essential—deal with honouring the law and aiming at a high level of personal conduct; these are the things which we have been discussing throughout this book. I include them for completeness so that the code is as rounded as I can make it. The other five propositions are ideals above the normal which are hardly covered by either law or religions or, if they are, the coverage is limited. They are utopian objectives.

Propositions in this class are quite unlike rules of law. For one thing, they are voluntary. For another, even if anybody accepts them, they have no sanctions. They are therefore weak and do not have the potency of legal commands. They are mere hopes.

These propositions are not commandments: I am not really interested in that alternative genre of which you can find many modern examples. The propositions are not exhaustive: I don't see how one could be exhaustive. The rules of law and religion already occupy vast libraries, quite apart from works on philosophy or how to live your life. At the same time, they are not just lists of as many virtues as I can think of. Nor do I include obvious things, commonplaces, like keep fit, don't smoke, it's nice to learn to play a musical instrument. They contain some specific proposals which I believe should be considered in framing a more comprehensive code which satisfies the twin objectives of survival and happiness.

The propositions do not apply to everybody and would not suit everybody. For example, the very sick or the very poor have different priorities.

I certainly do not claim to have lived up to these propositions in my own life—I wish I had and I wish I could.

Before I discuss the propositions individually, I list them as follows:

1. Honour and believe in the rule of law.
2. Let your moral life inspire others on your final judgement day.
3. Owe your fealty to all members of the planet, not just your group.
4. Honour and believe in scientific progress.
5. Persevere in illuminating your mind.
6. In matters of sex, follow your best moral conscience.
7. Take delight in your existence.

Each of these will be discussed in turn with a commentary setting out what they mean and why I think they are relevant in the search for survival.

# Proposition 1: Honour and Believe in the Rule of Law

The first proposition is that we should honour and believe in the rule of law. The most fundamental pillar of morality and survival for the planet is the rule of law. Our societies have no future without it. It is perfectly possible to honour both a religious god and the rule of law without any inconsistency.

There are two aspects of the law to be honoured: the written law and the observance of the rule of law. We should respect all proper laws except those which are manifestly and grossly unjust at the most primitive level, not those with which we disagree or disadvantage us. We should observe the most basic laws, for example, not to murder or steal.

Each person has a duty to pay at least some regard in light of the circumstances to the formulation of our laws and to ensure that they exercise their voting and other powers to ensure that the law-makers are true guardians of the spirit of the law and of the rule of law. Each person has this responsibility, should not turn their eyes away and should not support those who violate these canons. Everybody has an obligation to support the basic tenets of the rule of law, not pay or accept bribes, not cheer those who threaten personal security, not support those who carry out arbitrary arrest or ignore due process even in times of great threat and stress, not support politicians who abuse their power, to resist oppression.

This proposition affirms the priority of the fundamental pillar of our societies and, despite all its faults, the most comprehensive code for survival that we have, developed over thousands of years of experience.

## Proposition 2: Let Your Moral Life Inspire Others on Your Final Judgement Day

When we die, people judge us. The test is what people say or think about us when we die. That is when other people assess our lives, good or bad, when all the trivial resentments and rancours are put aside in the face of death, when people judge us. This is equivalent to the final judgement of God on the day of resurrection far in the future. Most of us, including myself, will be a million miles away from these excruciatingly impossible virtues which I set out below. So there is something melancholy and poignant about the fact that we should set ourselves standards which we can never hope to meet.

We would like them to say that we treated others with love, honesty, faithfulness and respect, that we were loyal and trustworthy, that we were forgiving and slow to anger, that we showed loving kindness to others, and that we avoided emotional humiliations or small-scale cruelties or slights which could corrode daily life and cause disproportionate miseries or arouse disproportionate desires for revenge. We would like them to say that we were not deceitful or two-faced, that we were truthful, that we were positive, optimistic and sunny, that we did not burden others with our depressions or anxieties, that we were unselfish, and that we were prepared to listen to others who were suffering. We would like them to say that we lived life with a sense of joy and wonder, that we always sought to learn something new, that we were humorous and laughed a lot, that we were peaceful and restrained, that we were patient, that we did not give way to rages or express needless anger or a desire for revenge, that we bore no grudges and pursued no vendettas, and that we were not violent or dishonest. We would like them to say that we showed courage and fortitude, and that we were brave. We would like them to say that we made a contribution, that we served others, that we were not lazy or idle, that we had self-esteem, that we enhanced the lives of everyone we met. We would like them to say that we were charitable and gave freely to the needy. We would like them to say that we sought to stay alive as long as possible, that we were learning till the end, that we fought for life till the end, that we never gave up.

This proposition deals with aspects of conduct in the realm of private morality. We have these precepts, not to protect our reputation, but in order to guide our private conduct to preserve the future. The proposition contains principles which are central to the private morality of religions but which are not covered by the law. They contain virtues which tend not to be found in either religions or law, for example, courage, fortitude, optimism of spirit. The proposition greatly affects people's daily lives. In addition private morality and private thoughts are the origin of public conduct and morality.

# Proposition 3: Owe Your Fealty to All Members of the Planet, Not Just Your Group

My third proposition is that we should owe our primary fealty and loyalty to members of all human beings on the planet, not just our local or national group. We should consider ourselves one world. In other words we should regard ourselves as human beings, along with the other seven billion human beings, not just members of a group—an ethnic group or a religious group or a nation or a city or a village or a corporation or a family. It is possible that we have parallel allegiance to these groups but our primary emotional allegiance should be to all citizens on earth. We are all on the same side. Tribalism is fine for football, but not for important things.

The variations between ethnic groups are very small in DNA terms but there are very large variations between individuals. The genetic differences between modern humans are trivial. We are all descended from the same root in DNA terms and cultural differences are superficial. In the course of many generations, superficial differences did develop such as height, shape of face, skin colour, and customary courtesies and ceremonial and social behaviour. But we must not allow these factors to obscure the essential unity of human beings. The original Eve of all people on earth today probably lived 150,000 years ago and the original Adam probably between 60,000 and 90,000 years ago.

It is natural for us first to look after the interests of and identify with our family, our town, our country and to promote their interests ahead of the interests of the people on the planet as a whole. This identity confers belongingness, the banishment of corrosive alienation, a fruitful desire to advance the interests of our home group, a healthy competition, a striving for achievement and mastery. I am not suggesting that we surrender these things, but if those interests conflict with the fair and legitimate needs of others on the earth taken as a whole, we should forebear, be tolerant, be patient.

This proposition does not endorse the view that non-violence of all kinds is outlawed in all situations. There are cases where proportionate force is legitimate in self-defence or where survival and stability are seriously threatened.

Nationalism, xenophobia and blind group loyalties present great dangers to survival. The most cursory survey of the history of the 20th century shows how many conflicts have been inflamed by the fires of wounded honour, or tribal or national rivalries, religious sectarianism, arguments about differences which do not merit the savagery and the atrocities which they sparked off.

As the English poet John Donne wrote in 1624: 'Any man's death diminishes me, because I am involved in mankind; and therefore never send to know for whom the bell tolled: it tolls for thee'.

Universal allegiance is a motif which religions seem on the whole to place below adherence to the one true religion. You can nevertheless find genuflections in the direction of the 'one planet' ideal, for example, the Christian admonition to love your enemies. The law at its best acknowledges the principle of non-discrimination on the grounds of race, colour, language, religion, political or other opinions, or national or social origin in human rights codes and has restraints on war. On the other hand it is very easy to find nationalistic laws.

# Proposition 4: Honour and Believe in Scientific Progress

We should honour and believe in scientific progress. Science and technology have power to deliver other progress and to protect future generations, to escape a destiny of doom.

If we are to survive, if we are to understand ourselves, our planet and the universe, our laws should support, not oppose, intellectual achievements in these fields and we should promote our control over our future.

# Proposition 5: Persevere in Illuminating Your Mind

The fifth proposition is to enlighten and illuminate our minds and our intellects and to work with all our might and to persevere in these tasks.

We should not be just onlookers, we should be doers. We should be active in our lives, not passive. We should be constantly improving ourselves and not just idling our time away. We should be the voice, not the echo.

Admonitions to improve oneself have a long history and great potency.

There are several purposes of learning and work. The first is that we will thereby be able to make a contribution to the future of the future. An educated population is more likely to make the right decisions in order to survive. This is particularly so in view of the huge expansion of knowledge when it is desirable for everybody to have some sort of feel for what is going on. An ignorant population is an easily led population, more prone to superstition, intolerance, credulous views, dangerous views.

The second reason is happiness. We are more likely to feel fulfilled if our curiosity is fired and then constantly satisfied. The third is that curiosity, the yearning to explore, the desire to discover are essential impulses which should be cultivated.

This proposition requires self-discipline, industry and persistence, a diversion of effort into long-term gains by willpower. We do not have to have special talent to do anything good. But we have to have endurance. Learning and activity should become a habit.

Some people have jobs which take almost all their time. Their work should also be their play. If they are obsessed with one subject, however minute, which is particularly the case with research scientists, they should develop the learning on that subject obsessively. Everything connects with everything else, even the tiniest sliver of a topic is symbolic, resonant and fills in a chink or a niche in the great wall of knowledge. Those who studied the arts should read science—physics, chemistry, biology, mathematics. Those who studied science should read the arts, the law, economics, history, sociology.

This fifth proposition is a programme that is contrary to the hopes of many thinkers of the last part of the 20th century who looked forward to a life of leisure, allowing people to deliquesce into a torpor. On the other hand, it recognises the Buddhist instructions to develop the mind so that you can achieve nirvana, but a nirvana resulting from intellectual enlightenment and understanding.

Our science, our medicine, our technology, our art—all those achievements have required centuries of painstaking effort. A prodigious amount of littleness is required to push the tide a millimetre up the beach, only often to see it fall back again.

The discovery that our planet was going around the sun and was not the centre of the universe took years and years of meticulous tiny observations by the astronomers of the day, almost a century of effort. Without their detailed work, we would be nowhere with astronomy. We would be impoverished in our anthropological knowledge without the decades of dusty effort by Louis and Mary Leakey in the dry whiteness of the Olduvai Gorge in northern Tanzania where they (strictly the child of a guest visiting them) discovered the footsteps in the soft volcanic lava of a 3.7 million year-old group of three which showed that humans were bipedal by then.

This proposition has a much wider scope than either religions or the law. Religious education focuses in the main on instruction on the tenets of the religion and its liturgies. The law typically requires the education of children and sometimes continuing education in certain jobs. But a wider commitment to perseverance in personal enlightenment is missing in the main ideologies. We should not waste our lives.

# Proposition 6: In Matters of Sex, Follow Your Best Moral Conscience

My sixth proposition is that, when it comes to sex, we should follow our own best moral conscience, that is, that we should do what is reputable and fair. We should be honourable. It is a matter of private conscience, but it is nevertheless infused by morality and the fair treatment of others.

Sex is free but it is not a moral free-for-all. It is a matter of common experience that sex occupies the thoughts of most of the people for a great deal of their time. People have very different ideas about the relation between morality, sex and the family. I do not pronounce on those views, which are often intensely held. Sex is one of the moral issues which most divides cultures.

*The Garden of Earthly Delights*

The picture hangs in the Prado in Madrid, painted around 1500 by Hieronymus Bosch. It is called *The Garden of Earthly Delights*. For students of human nature and morality, this is an astonishing representation. Actually it is a triptych—three pictures, like a cartoon. The left-hand panel is the primitive state, the Garden of Eden. The central panel depicts a world of idyllic pleasure and eroticism. The right-hand panel shows the artist's view of what happens to you if you indulge. The central panel has a boy planting flowers in a girl's bottom; it has two nude figures making love in a bubble as they float around in public. In the right-hand panel a lecherous woman is crucified on a lute and harp. In the centre, a choir singing from a score inscribed on somebody's buttocks, on the right, vomiting and excretion.

To some people, sex is dangerous, repulsive, to be shoved out of sight, out of mind. The teachings of many philosophies and beliefs claim that we attain fulfilment and ecstasy only if we renounce all desire, if we stop desiring, so that we can mitigate our suffering, our pain. This is what the Buddhists advised, what the Greek Stoics advised, what the Christian ascetics advised. To some of them, sex is a matter of guilt, shame and remorse.

To other people, sex is the source of all our inspirations, all our achievements, all our spirituality. It makes us divine. It is the holiest thing we do. Without it, we would sink into a sulky loveless doze, without action and energy and learning. Eroticism, some say, is the source of all ethics, of all good action. Lovemaking, in their view, has a greater purpose. It is our salvation from daily suffering. It makes our lives fully lived. Lovemaking renders us radically free. In this way, we reclaim our immense pleasures and our bodies from the terrible denigration to which they have been subject for centuries. This is the one thing everybody has, rich or poor.

People have their own approach to the above dichotomy. But once a couple have children, a different logic intervenes. The parents should conduct themselves with the interests of their children primarily in mind. Children come before self.

# Proposition 7: Take Delight in Your Existence

My seventh proposition is to enjoy our existence to the full. This is a way of life principle not a moral command as ordinarily understood.

In the first place, the proposition means that we should aim to experience perfect spiritual ecstasy, moments when we feel such delight in existence that we do not care whether we live or die. These moments of extreme visionary exhilaration, outside sex and drugs, are unusual. But they are possible and within our reach. Even if we have only a few such moments in our whole lives, we should be grateful for them. They are the source of inspiration.

In our life, we should savour every moment, feel each sensual and intellectual experience with a sense of delight and optimism.

I am not recommending a life of hedonism. Happy people are tolerant people, more inclined to successful survival, more curious, more fulfilled, less inclined to anger if their minds are at peace.

We should teach ourselves to keep our minds free of dark and vengeful thoughts or rages or corrosive envy. The ancients achieved this by meditation techniques which are not particularly mystical and not particularly complicated. There are many ways of crowding out the brooding, the fears, thoughts which take us over and rend us apart.

We should not allow ourselves to be poisoned by the acid of covetousness and envy at those who have got more or have greater competence than us. If we feel guilt, we should atone for it, feel contrition and remorse, not let it fester—face it and conquer it.

It is right to accumulate material wealth if we can. The work requires grit, creativity, discipline and the ability to shoulder responsibility. Material progress supports health and invention and is a driver of science and prosperity. It underlines the ideology of advancement and it enhances the rule of law.

Delighting in our existence requires effort and it is the effort which reaps the rewards.

We only have one life.

# Conclusion on a Way of Living

My personal list is intended to reflect a philosophy which is sunny and optimistic. It sets high standards, but encourages happiness. In one way or another the list reflects most of the content of religious commandments and codes of morality, other than injunctions to worship a god. It is directed to some of the things needed for survival so that those of us alive now can fulfil our duties to the future. It reflects some of the things which I think are important.

Now that we are almost done, I return to the identity of the terrible charioteer whom I mentioned in the first chapter. You may say that the terrible charioteer is the blind force behind a meaningless universe. We know that we could be smashed by some eyeless rock, drawn to us by some blind force with the doom-laden inevitability of destiny, unseeing, motiveless, merciless. Maybe.

The terrible charioteer is the foul fiend within ourselves, with our savagery and barbarity, our warring aggressiveness, our hatreds and destructiveness, our cruelty, our tribalism and sectarianism, our follies, ignorance, and gullibility, our short-sightedness in seeking present comfort and ignoring the future, our inability to understand the ultimate meaning of our lives.

Yet we are a marvellous creation, maybe the most extraordinary invention of the whole universe. We have intelligence, energy and audacious boldness. We yearn to be good and to discover meaning.

The French physicist Blaise Pascal (1623–62) was a prodigy. At the age of 11 he had secretly worked out for himself the first 23 propositions of Euclid. The universe horrified him:

> When I survey the whole universe in its dumbness and man left to himself with no light, as though lost in this corner of the universe, without knowing who put him there, what he has come to do, what will become of him when he dies, incapable of knowing anything, I am moved to terror.

It is those questions which we have to answer.

# 19

# *A Billion Years from Now*

This is not really a conclusion: it is only a momentary stopping point for now. One can't conclude a subject as central as this, our future—at least, I hope not.

When we watch our clocks ticking by the seconds, we flinch to see how the second hand seems to race round with a manic urgency or the figures flash by, ushering in our future, with such meticulous persistence. Soon, much sooner than we think, it will be 2030, then 2050, then 2100. And then not so soon, it will be 3000, 5000, 7000. Then 1,000,000. So far we have been on the planet in one form or another for much more than a million years so the next million years are shorter than our existence up to the present.

A million will one day become a billion. A billion years from now is just over 14 million lives of 70 years each, laid end to end from now. Many creatures on earth with much shorter lifespans than ourselves have had that number of generations and so the prospect is quite routine.

Where will we be then and what will we be?

Will we with our laws and morality have defeated the blind charioteer, defied the foul fiend? Or will this pitiless shape have engulfed us and we, who were once something, become nothing?

Will we have discovered the real God? Or will we ourselves have become god?